Film Marketing

Finola Kerrigan

Routledge
Taylor & Francis Group

LONDON AND NEW YORK

First published 2010 by Butterworth-Heinemann

Published 2013 by Routledge
2 Park Square, Milton Park, Abingdon, Oxon, OX14 4RN
711 Third Avenue, New York, NY 10017

Routledge is an imprint of the Taylor & Francis Group, an informa business

Notice
No responsibility is assumed by the publisher for any injury and/or damage to persons or property as a matter of products liability, negligence or otherwise, or from any use or operation of any methods, products, instructions or ideas contained in the material herein. Because of rapid advances in the medical sciences, in particular, independent verification of diagnoses and drug dosages should be made

British Library Cataloguing in Publication Data
A catalogue record for this book is available from the British Library

Library of Congress Cataloging-in-Publication Data
A catalog record for this book is available from the Library of Congress

ISBN: 978-0-7506-8683-9

Contents

Acknowledgements

The road to finishing this book feels like a very long one, and many people have helped in getting me here. It is inevitable that some will be inadvertently excluded from this list. During the writing of this book I was unsure of whether I should thank Anna Fabrizio who first persuaded me to write this book for Elsevier and Francesca Ford who followed her for her continued enthusiasm for the project. Having eventually come to the end of the project I am very grateful to both of them for their encouragement. Thanks are also due to Marie Hooper, Amy Laurens and Sarah Long for their patience and cooperation. I am very grateful to Suja Narayana for meticulously proof-reading this manuscript. Particular thanks are due to Sumanta Barua who acted as research assistant in helping to prepare this manuscript. Without Sumanta's tireless efforts, this process would have taken even longer and my lack of attention to detail would have gone unchallenged. Thanks are also due to Huda Abuzeid for her help in trying to secure permissions for this book and to Dirk Vom Lehn for providing me with comments.

Thanks are also due to my parents for many things, not least for taking out cinema advertising for their business when I was a teenager and therefore providing me with free weekly access to the delights of the Gaiety Cinema in Sligo. This started me off as a regular film consumer. Back in the late 1980s and early 1990s Sligo did not benefit from a wealth of international cinema, but I did get access to popular US, UK and Irish films. Thanks to my great friends at University College Galway who queued up to watch the film society films and braved the alleged mice to see great International films in the cinemas of Galway. Particular thanks must go to the Tuesday Night Cinema Group although I have become an unreliable member over the past few months in my final dash to the finish with this book.

I have had the pleasure of working with a number of supportive and inspiring colleagues since I first started to take a serious interest in the film industry and film marketing issues and I would like to extend my thanks to Gisela Gauggel-Robinson, Alvaro Mason, Anne Boillot, and other colleagues who encouraged my work and study of the film industry during and after my time at the MEDIA Programme. My doctoral research was generously funded by the University of Hertfordshire Business School and I am very grateful for the support and friendship that I received from colleagues there. I am grateful to my colleagues at King's College London, past and present for the interesting discussions, feedback on my work and words of encouragement which have created an environment in which I have been able to develop my research.

Over the last decade, I have formally interviewed, informally chatted with and benefitted from the expertise of many film industry professionals. I am very grateful to them all for their time and the insight which they offered me over the course of my study of the film industry. I was particularly fortunate to have the opportunity to participate in the excellent *Strategic Film Marketing Workshop* during my doctoral study which provided me with invaluable insight into film marketing practice. Thanks are due to Paul Nwulu who helped me navigate my way through the Nigerian film industry.

Finally, I would like to thank Susanna Capon for inviting me to teach film marketing on the MA Film and TV Producing at Royal Holloway and Gillian Gordon for allowing me to continue. I have benefitted greatly from this experience and each one of my students on that course has contributed significantly to my thinking around film marketing. To teach such knowledgeable and talented students has been a privilege.

Sections of chapter two have previously been published in Kerrigan, F. 2004. Marketing in the Film Industry in Kerrigan, F., Fraser, P. and Özbilgin, M. (eds.) Arts Marketing, Oxford: Elsevier.

CHAPTER 1

Introduction

As the opening scene for this book on film marketing, this chapter will follow the format of all good opening scenes. In doing so, it will introduce the key characters of this book: marketing and the film industry. In positioning this book, as all good marketers should, in film terms it is a cross-over. Although its core audience is quite niche, i.e. students, researchers and academics with an interest in the marketing elements of film, there is a desire for the book to 'cross-over' into other audience groups, those with an interest in film more broadly and marketers from other sectors who are curious about the world of film marketing. For this reason, this chapter will both introduce the layout as well as introduce the readers to the main characters, marketing and the film industry. As volume after volume has already been written about marketing, what it is, what it is not and what it could or should be, I will not rehearse all of these debates. For that reason, readers may well dispute the presentation of marketing within these pages. My presentation of marketing theory is derived from my study of film marketing and from the elements of marketing and wider management theory that I see as helpful in understanding film marketing processes. Like all areas of marketing, film marketing concerns both the production and the consumption of film and this dual focus is present in this book. In this book, film marketing, or the marketing of film is viewed as primarily concerned with how filmmakers and marketers position the film within the minds of consumers in order to encourage consumption of their film. Scholars of audience reception studies, film studies and related areas have studied film consumption from a number of perspectives and this book will refer to these studies, but does not claim to develop theories of audience reception. Rather, the focus on consumers is concerned with how consumers interpret the marketing messages projected by filmmakers and marketers and how this influences selection and enjoyment of film and on

CONTENTS

recent technological developments which have seen the relationship between filmmakers and consumers of film deepen.

The advantage of writing a book on film marketing is that it is possible to draw very widely on literature which can aid our understanding of film marketing processes without the constraints of submission to a high quality journal. The nature of contemporary academic life, which gives rhetorical credence to the idea of interdisciplinary work, means that academics wishing to publish their work in good quality journals must adhere to the orthodoxy of that journal. This in itself often informs the research design employed by the researcher, the literature they draw on in constructing their analytical and theoretical framework and in contextualising their research results. This results in various silos of 'knowledge' being produced. Studies examining box office data in order to look for success factors, draw on other such studies, studies looking at the impact of award ceremonies look at previous studies about award ceremonies and so on. Consumer researchers may not give great consideration to those looking at the business to business elements of film marketing and film marketing scholars often ignore memoirs of film professionals, film studies scholarship and sociological analyses of film consumption. Similarly, many authors examining 'film marketing' from other disciplines such as film studies or cultural studies do not engage with the marketing literature on this subject. In this way, many isolated pockets of film marketing knowledge co-exist without the benefit of cross-reference.

Although marketing theorists draw heavily upon sociology, psychology and economics and more recently, cultural studies among other disciplines, there is a substantial body of work in the marketing field which must be considered in examining film marketing. Some previous authors have written about film marketing without considering the link between marketing theory and film marketing practices or fully understanding all encompassing nature of the marketing function. Finally, there are many books providing more practical insights into film marketing which are very useful to film marketing practitioners, but discount considerations of the wider macro-environmental issues which impact upon film marketing. For those interested in the 'why' of film marketing as well as the 'how', this book is an attempt to provide such a link and to illustrate the relevance of marketing, specifically arts marketing theories to our understanding of the marketing practices evident in the film industry. While film studies have contributed to our understanding of film marketing, such as Justin Wyatt's (1994) book which introduces and discusses marketing in relation to the high concept film, there is a need to engage more with marketing knowledge in order to move forward our understanding of film marketing practices.

WHAT IS MARKETING?

Marketing as a field of practice and an academic discipline is a contentious area. This is partly due to the perception of marketing as finding ways in which to sell things to people that they do not want or need. Looking to Brown (2006), marketing has been blamed for many social ills such as obesity, consumerism, psychological ills etc. and many critics of marketing and critical marketers have examined the dark side of marketing. In addition to this recognition of 'the dark side' of marketing (Hirschman, 1991), there are various views on the historical development of the marketing function or marketing practice, tensions between those aligning themselves to the marketing management approach, critical marketing, post-modern marketing, relationship marketing, experiential marketing, green marketing, anti-marketing and so on. Rather than discuss these various approaches to marketing, I acknowledge the various scholarly approaches to the study and interpretation of marketing. This chapter and the remainder of the book will introduce some of these theories and approaches that have particular relevance for the study of film marketing. In writing this book, the starting point was film marketing practice and observing these practices prompted me to explore different marketing literatures as well as research from film studies, audience reception studies, cultural studies and other areas of management. Rather than start with generic marketing theories and assess their appropriateness for application to the film industry, I have interpreted film marketing practices through an interpretive lens informed by these various literatures. This book is an attempt to introduce and explore film marketing practices with the aid of existing research as well as to set out future research questions in the area of film marketing.

The starting point for this discussion of marketing theory is exchange theory. Marketing as exchange was written about by Bogozzi (1975) and has provided a useful framework for marketing academics. The marketing management school mainly emanates from US business schools and has viewed marketing as the process of planning and executing the conception, pricing, promotion, and distribution of ideas, goods, and services to create exchanges that satisfy individual and organizational goals (AMA definition cited in Grönroos, 1994: 347). Following this the AMA (American Marketing Association) launched a new definition of marketing at their 2004 Summer Educator's Conference "Marketing is an organizational function and a set of processes for creating, communicating and delivering value to customers and for managing customer relationships in ways that benefit the organization and its stakeholders" (AMA, 2004). This change in definition reflects the movement of marketing academics and practitioners towards a more relational approach to marketing. Such a relational approach has been problematic in its application to film marketing due to the general lack of such a direct relationship between filmmakers and the audience for their film as this relationship is mediated by various intermediaries who have provided access for filmmakers to the limited market. In 2007, the AMA once again revisited their definition of marketing in recognition that marketing was not merely a function, but rather a set of practices which can be undertaken throughout an organisation. The current definition states that "Marketing is the activity, set of institutions, and processes for creating, communicating, delivering, and exchanging offerings that have value for customers, clients, partners, and society at large" (AMA, 2007). What this definition lacks is the role of the consumer in this process. While this definition does include the consumer, the 'exchange' is seen from the perspective of the marketer.

The marketing concept, which has dominated marketing since the 1960s has been defined by Felton (1959: 55) as "a corporate state of mind that insists on the integration and coordination of all the marketing functions which, in turn, are melted with all other corporate functions, for the basic purpose of producing maximum long range corporate profits". Drucker (1954) emphasised the need to place customer satisfaction at the centre of the marketing concept, with profit being achieved as a reward for attaining customer satisfaction and marketing scholars such as Kotler have continued the call for the customer to be at the centre of marketing activities. However, when it comes to the marketing of the arts or within the cultural and creative industries, such notions of putting the customer at the centre becomes contested. As one of the basic elements of the 'Customer as King' philosophical approach to marketing is to find out what the customer wants, there is a clear tension between this approach and the process of product development and marketing in the film industry, in common with other arts sectors. In some ways, the film industry could be viewed as subscribing to the much criticised product approach, where the producers are focused on making the film, without considering the market for the film. Once the film is completed, issues of marketing and consumption of the film are considered. But, this is a rather simplistic analysis of the film marketing process. While consumers are rarely consulted prior to the development of a film script, at various stages in a projects development, market sensing activities are undertaken. Some of these practices are embedded within the practice of film professionals to such an extent that they are not explicit, while others are explicitly undertaken. This book will unpick these practices in order to illustrate that filmmakers and marketers are also subject to some standard marketing practices as well as highlighting the differences apparent when marketing artistic products such as film, rather than more mainstream products or services.

Moving forward from considerations of 'putting the customer first' or 'exchanging' with the consumer, Vargo and Lusch's (2004) paper which proposed a 'New Dominant Logic for Services' and the many papers following this have placed the discussion of the merging of what we formerly considered the goods/service divide. One of the central developments from this body of work is the acceptance of the notion that value can only be created and acknowledged by the consumer in the act of consumption. It is in the act of consumption that value is recognised and embodied. Value can only be evaluated in terms of the consumption experience. In this way, marketing theorists have moved from central ideas of value in exchange to value in use. This book centralises the notion of film having a value in use rather than an abstract value, as film can play a number of roles, but it must be consumed in order for that value to be articulated and made real. Moving on from outmoded ideas of consumers as being 'done to', Vargo and Lusch (2006: 44) reworked their notion of 'co-production' from their earlier (2004) paper. Vargo and Lusch (2006) began to refer to the customer as 'co-creator of value'. This develops their earlier theory of 'co-production' which they acknowledged was more appropriate for a production centred, rather than service centred approach. My study of film marketing began by studying the activities of filmmakers and film marketers which fed into what I classified as film marketing. This involved considerations of how these actors conceived of the consumer and their perceptions of value. Much of the film marketing activities which an organisation engages in presume that there is value in use and market research aims to find out what that value is.

However, much of the rhetoric surrounding the marketing focus and the subsequent marketing orientation which companies adopt as a result of this orientation, focuses on the needs and wants of the customer. As noted above, it is here that arts marketing researchers encounter problems. How do the ideas of customer satisfaction fit compatibly with the creation of artistic works? Are existing theories of marketing sufficiently broad to deal with marketing in the creative industries? In answer to these questions, researchers such as Fillis (2004), O'Reilly (2004) and Rentschler (1999, 2004) have tried to redefine marketing theory in order to provide useful frameworks for the analysis of marketing the arts or creative industries. A problem faced by arts marketing researchers when looking to literatures such as those on market orientation is their lack of transferability to the arts sector. When considering the application of the concept of market orientation to the area of film marketing, we must assess the appropriateness of the seminal articles by Narver and Slater (1990) and Kohli and Jaworsk (1990).

Consumers experience

Narver and Slater (1990) conceive of market orientation as culturally constructed and focused on meeting consumer needs and wants therefore gaining competitive advantage. In contrast, Kohli and Jaworsk (1990) adopted a behavioural approach which concentrated on the process of understanding the consumer's wants and needs through engaging in extensive information collection. The complication when trying to apply this to the film marketing domain is that while it is possible to collect and analyse data on past consumption of consumers, each film is an original, experiential product which may appeal to a consumer against their expectations. This makes it difficult for filmmakers and marketers to adopt a market orientation.

However, it may not be necessary to turn away completely from the marketing concept in order to examine film marketing. If customer satisfaction is seen as the ultimate goal of market orientation (Kotler, 2002), this can be seen as compatible with film marketing aims. It is the process by which this satisfaction is achieved which needs to be reconceptualised following developments in the marketing literature discussed above as well as key theoretical debates in the consumer theory literature which are discussed below. Consumer satisfaction cannot be achieved through asking consumers what they want to watch films about and making them, but can be achieved by making films which are of high technical and/or artistic value and positioning these films appropriately in order to appeal to the target market. If a broad view is taken, we can state that companies or filmmaking collectives can possess a market orientation in the film industry if their focus is upon identifying and targeting an appropriate audience and satisfying the expectations of this audience. As films are made to be watched (consumed), there is a need to focus on the audience. This, however, does not imply a need to 'give them what they want', but rather, that filmmakers and marketers have an understanding of the different film audiences that exist, and how to engage them. This approach emphasises the need to segment the audience for film, to select appropriate segments based on how receptive they will be to the film in question, to target these segments through marketing communications, and to position the film appropriately by setting expectations in relation to its genre, style and so on.

SUPPLY CHAIN MANAGEMENT AND MARKETING

What was clear from this early research was that film marketing begins right from a films conception and continues through to the act of consumption. Kerrigan and Yalkin (2009) found that consumers also extend their consumption experience by posting and reading reviews and going on to watch related films. This need to develop a more holistic notion of film marketing led me to the consideration of the supply chain literature. My early doctoral research confirmed two things: non-Hollywood films suffered from not having vertically integrated supply chains and the marketing process should begin as early as possible in order for it to be effective.

Min (2000) proposed that the marketing concept is compatible with theories of supply chain management as well as that of relationship marketing by linking the marketing concept theoretically to the philosophical origins of relationship marketing and to the underlying philosophy of supply chain management. Min (2000) outlined a clear link between the marketing concept's focus on the customer, coordinated marketing and the profitability aim and the philosophical foundation of relationship marketing. Focusing on coordinated marketing and the customer is equally applicable to analysis of the supply chain literature. This interdependence, which Min identifies between the acceptance of the marketing concept and the practice of supply chain management, has resonance for researching marketing within the film industry. In order to discuss the concept of supply chain management in relation to the film industry, it is first necessary to define these terms.

Mentzer et al. (2000a: 2) define a supply chain as "a set of three or more companies directly linked by one or more of the upstream and downstream flow of products, services, finances, and information from a source to a customer". The three main activities in the film industry are production, distribution and exhibition. For a film to reach the marketplace it must pass through the hands of a production company, a distributor and an exhibitor. There may be one or more production companies involved in a film production, there are generally a number of distributors involved (each with control of various distribution territories) and an even larger number of exhibitors, whether they are individual cinemas or large exhibition companies. Latterly, technological developments have meant that this traditional supply chain has been circumvented by a number of enterprising filmmakers. Just as the YBAs (Young British Artists) circumvented the traditional visual art route to market, these filmmakers are finding an audience outside the formal market structures through developments such as crowd sourcing.

The term supply chain management (SCM) is frequently used but often not sufficiently defined. In acknowledging this confusion in relation to accepted definitions of supply chain management, Mentzer et al. (2000a) attempt to synthesise various existing definitions in order to come up with a definitive definition. Although this is a necessary process, this will only prove profitable if those who have been using the term accept their definition. Wisner and Tan (2000: 1) declare that SCM includes "all value adding activities from the extraction of raw material through the transformation processes and delivery to the end user". This definition is wide enough to be applicable to most industries but, as a consequence of this universality, too general to be useful in the study of a particular relationship or circumstance. Through the use of the term 'raw materials' it is evident that Wisner and Tan see SCM as a concern of the manufacturing industries. However, 'raw materials' in the information age can be extended to include forms of intellectual property and therefore more easily applied to the film industry and other creative industries.

The definition proposed by Mentzer et al. (2000a: 2) defines supply chain management as "the systemic, strategic coordination of the traditional business functions within a particular company and across businesses within the supply chain, for the purposes of improving the long-term performance of the individual companies and the supply chain as a whole". This definition is helpful in terms of the study of the film industry, as it recognises the need to coordinate activities across functions as well as across organisations. What is also welcome in this definition is the recognition for this process of coordination to occur in order to ensure sustainability. In referring back to the discussion of film industry policy developments over the past number of years, this need for sustainability has been recognised by film policy makers at national and supra-national level. Therefore, a discussion of the film industry supply chain, in line with Mentzer et al. (2000a) definition is entirely appropriate.

Mentzer et al. (2000c) also stress that the existence of a supply chain does not infer that supply chain management is being undertaken. In fact, in the case of the film industry, what is problematic is the absence of such management or a coordination that will lead to long-term sustainability. In the case of the vertically integrated Hollywood majors, it can be argued that such SCM does exist, and this explains why they have dominated the film industry since their formation in the 1920s.

The various stages in the film industry supply chain, as well as the activities involved in each of these stages, are illustrated in Figure 1.1. In this figure, the processes are presented as linear, although in fact, some of these stages overlap depending on the nature of the film project, the type of finance and, importantly, the nature (if any) of the supply chain management.

In order to understand the impact of an integrated supply chain on the process of marketing a film, it is important to develop ideas drawn from the supply chain literature such as waste minimisation (in the case of the film industry, this waste is creativity). Building on this, Mentzer et al. (2000b) identify the importance of looking at supply chain relationships, both in the traditional manner of the consideration of operational issues in addition to

Development	Pre Production	Production	Post-Production	Distribution & Advertising	Exhibition
Rights acquisition, script development, financing	cast and crew selection, greenlighting financing,	Above the line, below the line	Editing, Soundtrack	Sales, Distribution, Trailers, Publicity	Theatrical (cinemas) DVD/VCR/ Blu-ray/ TV (free and pay Pay per view Free TV

FIGURE 1.1 *The film industry supply chain (adapted from Kerrigan, 2005).*

considering relationship building as an important function. They focused upon retail supply chains, but their thesis is equally applicable to the film industry. European film production and distribution companies in general conform to the model of 'partnering relationships' where relationships are the result of extensive operational links developed over time.

The above sections emphasise the need for close long-term inter-firm relationships and inter-firm cooperation. These are the two resultant components of supply chain management according to Min (2000: 93). As the film industry is characterised as high risk (Biskind, 1998; Eberts and Illott, 1990; Finney, 1998; Evans, 2003; Phillips, 1991), such close inter-firm relationships and inter-firm cooperation can provide a level of reduced risk. Sheth and Parvatiyar (1995) illustrated how perceived risk is linked to uncertainty. Such uncertainty of outcome is inherent in the film industry and therefore it is natural to seek assurance through established relationships. Such inter-firm relationships are the norm in the European film industry and the nature of the relationships which have formed out of this fragmented structure is documented by Eberts and Illott (1990), Finney (1998) and Kuhn (2003). In these accounts, much emphasis is placed on risk and the need for close relationships to form, where creative and financial risks could be taken due to the high levels of trust in existence in the inter-firm or inter-personal relationships.

DEFINING FILM MARKETING

It is necessary at this stage to define what is meant by film marketing and to show how this book will go beyond some others in illustrating that film marketing is more than marketing communications in the film industry. Film marketing, in line with the marketing management processes in other industries, begins at the new product development stage and continues throughout the formation of the project ideas, through production and into distribution and exhibition. At key stages in the product life cycle, various actors are involved in numerous marketing activities, from marketing an idea or a script to a production company to the final marketing of the film in cinemas, on DVD and through other exhibition outlets such as VOD (video on demand), cable television and terrestrial television. Durie et al. (2000: 5) define film marketing as "any activity that assists a film in reaching its target audience at any time throughout its life." In addition to the managerial functions associated with film marketing, and following Vargo and Lusch (2004, 2006) it is necessary to continue the film marketing journey into the realm of film consumption and out the other side. If film consumption can be seen as a journey, it may be difficult to identify the beginning and the end of such a journey. As Kerrigan and Yalkin (2009) found, film consumption does not end as the credits come up on a film, as consumers may wish to extend their consumption through visiting online review sites, discussing the film with friends or progressing with their film consumption to consumer related films. Consumption of one film may lead a consumer to seek out other films by a particular director or writer, to find out more about the composer of the soundtrack or artists featured on the soundtrack. If a film is a remake, they may be tempted to seek out the original. As discussed by Wohlfeil and Whelan (2008), film consumers may wish to watch other films featuring a favourite actor.

In this way, film consumption may be viewed as a more cyclical activity and film consuming may be inspired by other cultural products such as books, music, television, newspaper articles and so on. This necessitates any study of film marketing to consider both the producer and consumer perspectives and to look at where these intersect. How do consumers create value through their consumption of film and when does this value creation begin and end? I propose that value creation begins at the point where consumers become aware of a film, try to make sense of the messages they are receiving from the filmmakers, film marketers and mediated by the press and other film consumers. The process ends somewhere after consumption when the consumer makes sense of their experience and draws on this experience to consume the film again, to recommend to others or to move on to a related film. It would be misleading to portray this process of value creation as simple and tightly bounded. For example, UK film critic Mark Kermode when reviewing *The Boat that Rocked* (2009), referred to a previous film by the writer/director Richard Curtis, *Love Actually* (2003). Kermode had originally hated the film but when he watched it again, he began to like it. Despite having intensely disliked the film on the first viewing, Kermode was persuaded to revisit the film by his wife and after doing so he revised his opinion, therefore, the process of value creation cannot be seen as being a contract between the film maker/marketer and the consumer, but takes place in what du Gay et al. (2000) call a circuit of cultural consumption.

Academic film marketing literature has been developing in line with the increasing interest in the creative industries and acknowledgement of the economic value of these industries in developed market economies. Following this interest, there is now a significant body of research published in marketing and management journals which considers elements of film marketing. To date, books on film marketing written from a marketing perspective are absent and therefore as noted above, those wishing to engage with film marketing have had to trawl through numerous journals in order to familiarise themselves with the current literature. Although this book is not exhaustive in terms of the literature which is relevant to film marketing, by incorporating film studies, cultural studies, media reception studies, socio-logical and psychological studies alongside core film marketing literature, it attempts to provide a good framework within which to consider the key elements of film marketing. As the approach taken in this book centralises studies of the macro-, meso- and micro-environment and how activities at these three levels impact on and influence film marketing activities, it starts with a broad overview of the film industry before moving on to more specific topics.

OUTLINE OF THE BOOK

The book is structured as follows: the early section of the book examines the historical development of the film industry and focuses primarily on the development of the US film industry as this is the dominant force in the film world. Chapter 2 considers the origins and development of the film industry. This chapter traces the structural development of the film industry, with special emphasis on the integrated Hollywood model. This integrated model is seen as offering the greatest possibility of success for individual films due to the automatic access which filmmakers have to distribution and exhibition once they are aligned with one of the major Hollywood film companies. The current trend in the global entertainment industries is integration. A range of literature is presented which shows the importance of policy and diplomacy in supporting the growth of the US film industry. The chapter traces some key world events which have impacted on the development of national film industries in Europe and moves forward to considerations of the impact of key supra-national policies on the global film industry. In addition to rehearsing established analyses of the dominant position of the US major studios, this chapter also introduces the contrasting examples of the Nigerian, Indian and South Korean film industries in order to illustrate the impact of the wider macro-environment on the development of national film industries. Some key distinctions between the film industry and film marketing practices in Hollywood are contrasted with those in Europe, Nigeria, India and South Korea. The chapter ends by emphasising the power structures which exist within the global film industry.

Chapter 3 examines the development of early film marketing practices. The chapter begins by introducing the key film marketing terms: marketability and playability. This is followed by a brief discussion of the historical development of market research within the film industry. Linking film marketing and development to conventional theories of new product development, the chapter goes on to consider the importance of the development function within film marketing. In doing so, differences in terms of the approaches to development between Hollywood and non-Hollywood filmmakers are discussed. The importance of research in the film marketing process is also considered in Chapter 3 and the various types of research are discussed. This is followed by Chapter 4 which examines the structure of the international film industry. The particular focus of this chapter is on the role of policy in shaping the film market as well as the impact this has on film consumption. In order to understand the current film marketing environment, it is important to examine recent developments in this environment. The supranational environment is introduced and followed by an exploration of European level film policy. This is followed by a relatively detailed analysis of the development of film policy in the UK and an overview of current UK film policy. The impact of cultural and industrial policy on the development and support of the film industries in South Korea and Denmark are then discussed and finally, the case of Nigeria is discussed in order to contrast an industry which has developed in an entirely commercially driven manner with industries where a deliberate policy was established with the intent of supporting and developing filmmakers in these countries.

Following this first section of the book which considers various aspects of the wider macro-environment and how they impact on film marketing and consumption practices, the second part of the book moves to look at specific marketing practices which occur within the film industry. Linking film marketing and the development of a film marketing process to mainstream marketing theory, this chapter begins by proposing a 'film marketing mix' which consists of the core elements which must be considered by filmmakers and definitely by film marketers. These elements can act as signals to the film consumer which can help them to evaluate the film prior to consumption. The first of these elements of the film marketing mix is the star. This chapter develops existing notions of the film star to include the director, director of photography and other key creative personal who may possesses star quality. The next element to be considered is the genre and the associated element of the script, before the age classification and release strategy are discussed. In discussing the film marketing mix, this chapter highlights the need to avoid the painting by numbers approach to filmmaking which some film marketing research may endorse. Although a number of studies have shown the ability to predict box office earnings of films in possession of a particular range of film marketing elements such as an identified cast member, a clearly defined genre and a particular release strategy, each film is an individual creative product and therefore the combination and management of the film marketing mix will depend on the film in question and the target audience for the film.

Chapter 6 introduces the reader to theories related to consumer selection of film. Having considered the various elements of the film marketing mix, this chapter turns to examine how the consumer responds to the presentation of the film marketing mix. The chapter grapples with the idea of quality in film and in doing so, considers the role of critics in influencing and/or predicting the box office return for a film. In addition to considering professional critics as influencers, the chapter discusses literature regarding the role of film fans and word of mouth on film selection and therefore on film performance. Film consumption as an individual and a group practice is considered in this chapter and the methods employed in researching issues of consumer selection are discussed and critiqued. Although this is one of the most researched areas in the film marketing literature, this chapter illustrates the need for more studies with a focus on consumer selection of film to be undertaken. There is a need to question accepted notions of causality and many of the rational choice models which are still applied to the study of consumer selection. There is also a need to understand film consumers in a holistic way. The chapter considers studies which show the variation in film consumers in terms of the role which film plays in their lives and the subsequent differences they display in selecting film to be consumed in various contexts. In addition to examining the processes which lead to film consumption, the chapter also considers what may prevent film consumption.

While the processes of consumer selection of films are worth of study, consumer selection must be considered in relation to the film marketing materials provided as part of a film's marketing campaign. Chapter 7 introduces the reader to the various types of film marketing materials which must be developed during the life cycle of a film. Taking a product life cycle approach, the chapter begins by considering the film marketing materials which must be produced in order to secure funding, either through a sales agent or other financier. Although these materials get little attention outside the 'how to' film marketing literature, they are worthy of attention as a film may never make it into production if these materials are not developed appropriately. Following on from this, the chapter moves on to look at the materials needed for a film festival, and discusses how these differ for films at various stages in the product life cycle. While a film is in production, a unit photographer and unit publicist should be employed in order to create the necessary images and materials which will be required to promote the film from a business to business and a business to consumer perspective. The importance of timing in the compilation of these materials is discussed before moving on to looking at how these elements are used in order to develop the various marketing materials. Finally, the chapter considers the key marketing materials used in positioning a film for a particular, specified audience. Film marketing materials for a number of films are then discussed and the relevance of the 'standardise or adapt' debate is considered. This chapter looks at the process of developing these materials as well as how the materials are received by the intended target audience.

Chapter 8 proceeds to introduce the idea of the film marketing calendar. In this chapter, the relevance of key events such as film festivals and markets is discussed. In addition, following on from Chapter 5, the film release strategy is elaborated upon. There are a number of established practices within the film industry in terms of when and where films are premiered, how festival buzz and awards can be used in terms of the business to business and the business to consumer marketing campaigns and when films are released based on genre and target audience. This chapter examines these industry practices and also looks at instances where they have not been adhered to. Some key film festivals and markets are introduced and discussed in terms of their importance for filmmakers and film marketers. In order to understand the importance of these events, it is also important to understand the role and impact of various film marketing actors. This chapter discusses the role of the sales agent and the distributor in particular and illustrates their importance in moving a film through the film marketing calendar. The relationship between the exhibitor and the distributor is also examined in this chapter. The chapter also examines the literature on the impact of awards on a film's financial performance and in so doing confirms the importance of the Academy Awards for a film in terms of signalling to the audience.

Following consideration of the film marketing calendar in Chapter 8, Chapter 9 moves into different territory by examining the role of film in social and societal marketing. This chapter is concerned with the political nature of film as a form of art and social commentary. Moving away from questions of how to get industry figures and finally consumers to support and then consume a film, Chapter 9 is concerned with the impact of this film consumption. In the early days of the film industry, public figures were suspicious of the possible negative impact which film could have on moral values. Film has also been used as a form of propaganda and a tool for social and political change. This chapter looks at film in terms of these various roles and considers that marketing the film to consumers may just be the start of the marketing process and with many (if not all) films, the consumption of the film may result in forms of social and societal marketing. At the very least, film consumption impacts on how we see the world and various communities within the world. Film either supports established perceptions and norms or challenges then. Following considerations of film as a social or political tool and film as an educator, Chapter 9 continues to explore the blurring of boundaries which has taken place within the media, and within the realm of film in particular. A film marketing continuum which examines the motivations of the film marketer in terms of their perception of consumer demands is proposed in order to represent the various commercial, social and societal roles which film marketing must engage with.

Chapter 10 examines the impact of new technology on film marketing. This chapter begins by examining the interrelationship between developing technologies and film marketing practices from the early years of the film industry before considering recent changes to filmmaking, film marketing and film consumption which have occurred. Developments centred on the digital revolution have resulted in changes to the way in which film is made. Access to cheaper technologies which enabled film production and post-production to be undertaken on much lower budgets and requiring lower levels of technical knowledge than previously needed have had a number of impacts on the industry. Firstly, although the early parts of this book have shown how the film industry is a tightly controlled global industry where a few key organisations control the supply of and access to film, these technological developments, have assisted many filmmakers to produce films outside the normal structures of the industry. While it has been possible for filmmakers to produce low budget film for a number of years, developments in internet distribution and the rise of sites hosting user generated content have opened up the market for these films on a global scale. This previous statement points to the need for consideration of the nature of 'the market' for film in the digital age. Previously the market for film related to those who were willing to pay to see a film at the cinema or at home via renting a film or watching it on television. Now, there are a number of ways in which consumers can access film and notions of how these consumption experiences are funded are changing. Chapter 10 engages with the issues of control of intellectual property in the digital age as well as looking at some new business models which have developed in response to consumers desire to see a film for free. This chapter considers alternatives to the conventional approaches to film marketing practices for filmmakers developing direct relationships with film consumers and in doing so makes predictions about how film marketing will change over the coming decades.

Finally, Chapter 11 reflects on the book as a whole and the current state of knowledge of film marketing. In doing so, this chapter summarises the key issues covered in the book, looks at developments occurring in the film marketing literature which is not included in the earlier chapters and provides suggestions for future research in the area of film marketing. This chapter calls for a greater focus on film marketing studies which embed the study of film marketing within wider understanding of the role of film in society. The need to look at the individual and the group when studying film marketing is proposed as well as a call for integration of studies of the producer and the consumer when looking at film marketing practices and their impact.

This chapter has set the scene for this book and like a consumer who has seen a poster or trailer for a film and then read some reviews, the reader should have some idea of what to expect as they move through this book. In saying that, I hope that like a good filmmaker, I will provide some surprises along the way. This book collects together key literature and concepts which I think will help in understanding what film marketing is, how it is practiced and the impact which film marketing may have on individual consumers and on wider society. In adopting the approach taken, I wish to highlight the need for a focus upon policy in considering film marketing issues as well as the importance of policy in shaping the environment within which film is produced and consumed and to propose an holistic approach to film marketing research and practice.

CHAPTER 2

The Origins and Development of the Film Industry

This chapter will consider the historical development of the film industry from a global perspective. Much of the film marketing literature fails to contextualise the current film market by ignoring the historical development of the film industry. Without setting current practices within their historical context, it is impossible to truly understand why contemporary filmmakers face such problems in accessing the market. This account relies heavily upon the many scholars from film studies and related areas who have traced such developments and highlights the issues seen as most important in developing an understanding of current film marketing practices. In addition to existing literature relating to the history and development of the film industry and marketing within the film industry, a number of biographies and auto-biographies of filmmakers, academic and other accounts of film collectives and formal film companies have been used, in order to understand the structural issues which face those involved as well as to provide insight to the social and political dimension of filmmaking and film marketing. The term 'collective' is introduced here to denote the informal groups of filmmakers who decide to work together on a number of projects without the formation of a formal company.

As the global film industry is dominated by Hollywood, the chapter will present the historical assessment of how the major Hollywood studios came to dominate the global film market. This chapter will also look at some global examples of the film industry and their historical development and examine a variety of literature which will serve as an introduction to the film industry in general and the challenges faced by non-Hollywood film producers in their quest for market share. The causes of some of those obstacles are explored in terms of historical and structural reasons which underlie the domination of the worldwide box office by the Hollywood film studios. As acknowledged by

CONTENTS

Kindem (2000: 2) "many countries' domestic movie markets have been greatly impacted if not dominated by Hollywood movies since at least 1917" which necessitates any examination of the film industry to engage with an analysis of the role of the Hollywood majors in that industry.

The chapter starts by outlining the nature of Hollywood's domination of the worldwide film markets and then investigates the reasons why. Early technical and industrial developments are outlined and analysed, followed by an examination of the early European film industry, the birth of today's majors and introductions to the development and structures of Bollywood, Nollywood and the Korean film industries in order to illustrate the influence of structural considerations in shaping national film industries and film-makers' engagement with the global industry.

HOLLYWOOD'S DOMINATION OF THE GLOBAL BOX OFFICE

The film industry is just over one hundred years old, and, for the majority of its existence, has been dominated by the Hollywood majors. Despite sporadic success for non-Hollywood films both within their home countries as well as overseas, US films tend to dominate the international box office. In order to understand the magnitude of this domination, we can examine the current domination of the box office by Hollywood films.

According to the European Audiovisual Observatory (EAO), cinema attendance across the 27 member states of the European Union has decreased slightly (by 1.3%) from 2006 to 2007, while the share of box office revenues has increased from around 25% in 2003–2005 to over 28% in 2006–2007. These global figures mask some stark differences between territories. For example, cinema attendance figures were up by 34% in Lithuania while Slovakia showed an 18% decrease in attendance (http://www.obs.coe.int/about/oea/pr/mif2008_cinema.html, accessed 14/10/2008). While these figures are encouraging, it is worth noting that 19 of the top 20 films by box office revenue for 2007 were US films or US/European co-productions. This shows that US, or to be more specific, Hollywood films are dominating the box offices across the European Union. Europe remains united in its appetite for US films while, in general, not accepting non-national European films. Reasons for this apparent rejection of European films and other world cinema in favour of Hollywood films will be discussed later in this chapter.

This pattern of box office domination is evident in the majority of film markets. However, there are some exceptions. India has a thriving film industry, both Bollywood films, the Hindi blockbusters coming out of the Mumbai film studios, and regional films made in regional languages domi-nate the Indian box office leaving less room for Hollywood films. A similar picture existed in South Korea during the 1990s and early twenty-first century, but the end of the 40% film quota in Korea may be linked to the lower numbers of Korean films being produced and released in this market during 2008. Another exception to the Hollywood domination rule is Nigeria where Hollywood films have little impact on local film consumption. This leads us to consider the difficultly in representing a true picture of film consumption due to the limited information that is available to film marketing researchers. It would be necessary to aggregate cinema box office, TV viewing, DVD/VHS/VCD/Blu-ray sales and internet download figures in order to produce a clear picture of film consumption. It is not possible to access this range of data and therefore, cinema box office figures are generally used in order to assess the performance of films nationally and interna-tionally. The US centric approach to studying the film industry is com-pounded by the difficulty of accessing accurate box office and production data for the Indian and Nigerian film industries.

With significant improvements in home cinema technologies and the simultaneous increase in the cost of cinema attendance and decrease in the cost of such home cinema technologies, it is accurate to assume a shift to film consumption in the home, rather than at the cinema. This shift can be used to explain the relative decrease in cinema attendance which has occurred across many developed film markets over the last decade. However, there are still significant returns at the cinema box office which indicates that consumers are not fully abstaining from film consumption in cinemas. Although acknowledging the shortcomings of using box office returns as accurate measures of film industry revenue, the cinema box office is still seen as an accurate indicator of overall earnings in most markets where a devel-oped film exhibition network exists.

While European and other filmmakers struggle to compete with Holly-wood in terms of big budget films, a number of low budget (certainly in Hollywood terms) European films have done well at the box office and there is a belief among many independent filmmakers, confirmed by the PACT/MMC report (1994), that independent distribution companies can recoup a greater profit for films than the marketing machine of the majors. In recognition of the strength of independent distributors in maximising return on investment for smaller European films, Stephen Woolley a successful independent producer said "...when you are making something as big as *Interview (with a Vampire) (1994)*, there is an appropriate marketing machine waiting for it. The Warner Brothers' machine would have been useless for *The Crying Game (1992)*; it wouldn't have known what to do with such a specialised movie" (Woolley quoted in Finney, 1998: 292).

Apart from shortcomings in data available to gain a clear picture of film revenues, due to the nature of filmmaking, it is very difficult to attribute nationality or even regionality to a film and various formulae are used in identifying what constitutes a film from a particular country. Generally these classifications are drawn up nationally and may differ from country to country. For details of the criteria for gaining a certificate of nationality for a film, readers should consult national film bodies such as the UK Film Council, Korean Film Council, Screen Australia, Centre National de la Cinématographie in France and the Danish Film Institute.

Another issue worth discussing here is the poor overall performance of non-English language films outside their country of origin or linguistic area. In this respect, the UK and Ireland should have an advantage over other European Union member states in terms of the ability of their films to travel. In fact, their performance outside their country of origin is not hugely out of line with that of their non-English speaking counterparts. This is also the case for films from Australia, New Zealand and Canada which indicates an additional problem. It is not just language which seems to stop films from travelling; films may also have appeal only in the country of origin due to their subject matter. But, fundamentally, there are additional problems related to how these films are marketed and structural problems within the market which prevent them from travelling.

HISTORICAL DEVELOPMENT OF THE FILM INDUSTRY

In line with the view of marketing outlined in Chapter 1 it is only possible to engage with marketing issues by understanding the wider environmental context in which marketing takes place. Although the importance that marketing plays in ensuring a film's box office success is often referred to, understanding of the process is not well understood and very little academic attention has been given to studying the marketing of films from a holistic perspective. Bourdieu (1977) emphasises the need to understand the historical formation of the field in order to fully understand the current processes and how they have been formed. It is in situating the current process of film marketing within this historical and wider industrial context that this book pushes forward current understanding of the nature and practice of film marketing. The following sections begin to address the existing shortcomings by outlining the rise of the film industry and developments which contributed to Hollywood's dominance in the industry.

In this section, examples will be drawn mainly from the US and European industries, although later in the chapter, other film industries are discussed.

The usual starting point for academics discussing any area of the arts is the debate regarding the commercial versus the artistic nature of the arts, in this case, film (Kerrigan et al., 2004). Is the commercial only achievable by the sacrifice of the artistic? One of the foremost debates that prevail in the study of the film industry is concerned with whether it can, in fact, be viewed as an industry at all. Kerrigan and Culkin (1999) separate the notions of industry and art form, differentiating between 'the film industry' and 'cinema'. The former, by virtue of its phrasing, implies that the film industry can be seen in purely industrial terms, while the latter intimates that film is, in essence, an art form and therefore the rules of industry cannot be strictly applied to it. Common historical discourse on the matter divides filmmakers into two camps. The US (i.e. Hollywood) is seen as approaching filmmaking from an industrial angle, while Europeans believe film to be the preserve of artists where industrial models could not be applied without sacrificing the necessary artistic values of true filmmaking. Puttnam (1997: 114) sums up this difference using the words of a 1926 cinema critic,

> Film is not merchandise...Indeed, precisely because film is not merchandise we can compete with America... In the cinema, Geist (spirit) can balance the monetary supremacy of the competition.

Buscombe (1977) discredits those theories that suggest such a separation between art and industry can exist in relation to film. Instead, he points out that both elements are evident, to greater and lesser degrees, in each and every film that is produced. In order for a film to be realised, it is necessary to secure a budget, irrespective of size. This debases the proclamations of those who support the theory that filmmaking is merely an art form, as commerce does enter the equation to some extent, despite the regard or lack of regard which the filmmaker attributes to it. The reverse is also true. In following the procedures necessitated by film production (creation of a storyline and script, shooting the scenes, the verbal and visual processes inherent in a film's genesis) there is an intrinsic artistic quality in all filmmaking. Various memoirs (Eberts and Illott, 1990; Evans, 2003; Kuhn, 2003; Phillips, 1991) of feature filmmakers document the artistic processes undertaken in making a variety of films from those viewed as 'artistic' to more commercial block-busters like *Jaws* (1975).

The failure to recognise this duality has resulted, according to Buscombe (1977), in the concentration of studies upon the artistic aspects of film, to the detriment of an examination of the underlying industrial mechanisms which produce such art. While this imbalance has been addressed by the rise in academic interest in the commercial side of filmmaking (Elberse, 1999; Eliashberg and Shugun, 1997; Litman, 1983, 1998), this failure to attach equal importance to these two elements which constitute the film industry, culture and economics, can be viewed as partially responsible for the failure of non-Hollywood industries to sustain their film industries.

The current domination of the international box office is not surprising if one examines the structures which are in place in America in terms of production and distribution and the historical context in which this is founded. This is reinforced by an examination of the motivation behind filmmaking in the US as opposed to Europe. As discussed above, the former views the film industry as just that, an industry, while the latter has traditionally placed cultural consideration over commercial gain. This spirit of cultural protection is evidenced by the words of Jean-Luc Goddard: "Films are made for one or maybe two people" (Puttnam, 1997: 291). In the United States the 'Movie Business' was always viewed as a business that had to make a profit in order to survive. After Thomas Edison's development of the Kinetoscope, those who took advantage of his advancements were able to conduct thriving businesses, initially in the 'nickelodeons'[1] and subsequently in movie theatres (Balio, 1985; Gomery, 1991; Thompson and Bordwell, 2003). In fact, Edison's influence in creating the structured industry that exists today cannot be underestimated.

Edison, technical developments and their effect on the infant industry

By August 1897 Edison had secured three motion picture patents. On achieving this position, Edison's organisation began to defend itself by issuing lawsuits against its competitors and, in certain circumstances, against its own associates (Robinson, 1996: 101). In 1889, Edison invented the motion picture camera (Huettig, 1944). He did not recognise the potential of his invention and failed to take out patents on his inventions outside the United States. While Edison dominated the market for equipment and films in the United States, his lack of international foresight resulted in his inventions being used in England and France free from the threat of litigation (Huettig, 1944).

The exhibitors, being at the coalface of interaction with the consumers, were the first to recognise the significant demand that the general public had for this new form of entertainment. In so doing, they communicated

---

[1] The nickelodeons were entertainment halls where people could insert a nickel into a viewing machine in order to view images.

the need for an increase in both product and projection equipment. Edison's policy was to rent or sell projection equipment to the exhibitors and, in addition, to supply them with product, which was sold by the foot, therefore diminishing any interest in the content of the film. In order to safeguard their productions' position, they refused to rent or sell any cameras. In retaliation, inventors patented their own cameras, which were all based to a greater or lesser extent on Edison's invention (Balio, 1985; Litman, 1998; Thompson and Bordwell, 2003). In this way, the early industry progressed in line with technical developments. The lucrative nature of the industry was recognised by early entrepreneurs who were determined to take advantage of potential earnings through this infant industry.

The formation of the Trust

Edison's main competitors, Lubin, Selig, Vitagraph and Essanay, were finding it very hard to compete by the turn of the century. This was due to the endless threat of litigation posed by Edison's control of the patents to the majority of equipment which was used in the production and exhibition of motion pictures. The United Film Services Protection Association was formed in November 1907 in order to protect collective patent rights but was replaced in February 1908 by the Film Service Association. This organisation united Edison, Pathé, Vitagraph, Selig, Lubin, Kalem, Essanay and Georges Méliès. The only major company that refused to join the Film Services Association was the American Mutoscope and Biograph Company. They objected to Edison's elevated position within the organisation and so chose to remain outside. Upon acquiring the patent for the 'Latham Loop', they re-entered negotiations and agreed to join the Motion Picture Patents Company (MPPC), the name adopted by the Film Services Association from 1 January 1909 (Robinson, 1996).

'The Trust' was the common name given to The Motion Picture Patents Company (MPPC), which began to operate on the first of January 1909. The formation of the Trust arose as a result of the litigation frenzy which had become a central element of the motion picture industry from the latter part of the 1890s until 1907. Its activity was restricting the other participants in the Motion Picture Industry. They granted licenses in return for royalty payments. In a further move to protect their domination of the market, they signed an agreement with Eastman, prohibiting Eastman from supplying other producers with its film. In this way, they sought to control all aspects of the industry and to therefore prevent entry by non-members. However, the mistake that the Trust members made was in excluding prospective new members from joining, excepting Kinemacolor, which joined in 1913 (for a detailed discussion of the Trust see Anderson, 1985; Bowser, 1990; Brownlow, 1979; Robinson, 1996).

Aims of the Trust and economic background

The formation of the Trust was in line with the economics of the time. Jefferson's model for an American future based on small, independent, mainly agricultural enterprises was being usurped by the Hamiltonianism that was greatly in vogue by the late nineteenth century. Hamiltonianism embraced finance capitalism and industrialism as opposed to the cottage industry approach taken by Jefferson (Dyer McCann, 1987). The political economy is an essential influencer of industrial formation and still influences the operation of contemporary film industries.

One of the main aims of the Trust was to harmonise the activities within the film industry. They wished to gain exclusive control over production and distribution channels in the industry. They did so by renting prints to the exchanges for a fixed fee each week and had taken control of the vast majority of exchanges (the agencies who then rented the films to exhibitors) forbidding them from sourcing product from the independents. The exchanges in turn rented these prints out to the nickelodeons. Such levels of standardisation were not adopted by the last link in the distribution chain, with the exchanges charging the nickelodeons varied fees in accordance with the quality of, or demand for the prints being hired.

This grouping can be identified as the first monopoly to exist in the film industry and is characterised by Anderson (1985) as the definitive force in terms of safeguarding the developing US film industry against European competition. Anderson characterises the developments made by the Trust as overwhelmingly positive for the film industry. By this, Anderson means the US, or more specifically, the Hollywood majors. During that period, such co-operation to protect patent rights and, in effect, the creation of a monopoly, was commonplace in all of the main utilities and in manufacturing. In parallel with many fledgling industries, there was a developed spy system in place by this stage (Dyer McCann, 1987). Robinson (1996: 102) highlights the aggressive nature of the Trust members in enforcing its provisos and the penalising measures of license cancellation as a response to non-compliance with the dictates of the Trust.

The opposition and their dependence on Europe

The prohibition on new members led to the opposition forming a coalition of its own (Robinson, 1996: 104). Dyer McCann (1987) credits John J. Murdock with the creation and strengthening of the independent sector during the

Trust. Murdock saw the opportunity of sourcing films in Europe and exploited this. When it was obvious that these European films were not enough to satisfy the US audiences, he encouraged Americans to commence the manufacture of films under his protection. Due to the restrictions on accessing film because of Eastman's allegiance to the Trust, the Alliance (the name applied to the independents when they united to resist the activities of the Trust) turned to France to source their film. Their successful import of raw Lumière film stock from France forced the Trust to seek further restrictive measures. The tactic that the Trust employed was to introduce Eastman's non-flammable film into common usage and to endeavour to get the French nitrate-based film banned for safety reasons.

The growth of the independents

As referred to earlier, the foundation and evident determination of the Alliance inspired the creation of many small independents. The independent sector soon became organised and market leaders emerged. The most noteworthy of these independents is Carl Laemmle who was instrumental in bringing down the Trust. Laemmle, one of the original Trust licensees, abandoned it after a membership that only lasted three months. His reason for withdrawing from the Trust agreement was that the MPPC had not lived up to its promises to Trust licensees. Laemmle quoted in Robinson (1996: 104) despaired that the MPPC had promised to protect the "little fellow in the small town" but had not lived up to this promise. Not only did Laemmle end his association with the Trust but also his dissatisfaction with their actions inspired his subsequent anti-Trust campaign. He enlisted the assistance of an advertising agent, Robert Cochrane, and proceeded to launch a series of cartoons in the trade press which were pointedly aimed at the Trust. One year after the foundation of the MPPC, in retaliation to the establishment of the General Film Company by Trust members, Laemmle launched a new cartoon character, General Filmco.

The General Film Company was established in order to deal with all of the licensed exchanges and was legally independent from the MPPC. This autonomy was compromised by the fact that it was run entirely by members of the MPPC. The General Film Company proceeded to take over all of the licensed film exchanges with the exception of William Fox's Greater New York Film Company. Fox had refused to agree with the General Film Company over pricing details, so the GFC retaliated by cancelling his license and refusing to deliver on contracted shipments. Fox issued a lawsuit against this action, which was instrumental in the demise of the Trust. In competition with this, the independents established the Sales Company, which centralised control over the independent film exchanges. When they were investigated for violation of the Sherman Antitrust Act, this caused internal difficulties, resulting in the division of the members into three distinct groups. These groups released their films through Universal, Mutual and other disparate companies.

In recognising that the public wanted a more sophisticated product in advance of the Trust members, the independents endeavoured to create features of higher quality than had previously been in existence (Balio, 1976: 107). Zukor (1954: 40–49) was one of the first to believe in the American audiences' capacity for longer features. Zukor bought the distribution rights for the French production *Les Amours de la Reine Élisabeth*, but felt that in order to achieve success with features, it was necessary to produce them in the US. For this he needed the permission of the Trust. He approached Jeremiah J. Kennedy, the head of the Trust, who dismissed his idea of feature production saying "The time is not ripe for feature pictures, if it ever will be" (quoted in Zukor, 1954: 49).

The rising importance of market awareness

In failing to recognise the public's receptiveness to feature films at that time, the Trust left the independents with no option but to vertically integrate in order to fulfil this identified niche. Kerrigan (2005) has shown how modern supply chain theory places great emphasis upon the role of the Trust in maximising the positive effect of an integrated supply chain and found that the existence of the Trust can enable those involved in the various integrated operational processes to share a common creative vision and produce a product (film) with a coherent identity and message. This framework is useful in retrospect in order to illustrate how the vertically integrated model ensured the independents' success. The Trust was not willing to enter into such voluntary integration and to engage in the exchange of information that underpinned it.

Zukor (1954) recognised the importance of audience research in enabling the film industry to provide the consumer with the films they wished to see. As discussed in Chapter 3, his audience research took a very crude form, but it can be seen as beginning of a trend in film market research (which remains part of the majors' ethos today) of applying market research to the film industry. The independents' acknowledgement of the importance of data flows between the various individuals involved in the supply chain has ensured their market success and is reflected in the information exchange which exists in the successful, vertically integrated film companies and in well-established filmmaking collectives.

In addition, the independents saw the attraction of introducing a star system while the Trust members felt that such a move would merely cost them more in actors' fees without creating the revenue necessary to stabilise profits. As Litman (1998) points out, Zukor understood that he could charge higher rental fees for films featuring stars such as Mary Pickford, Douglas Fairbanks and Gloria Swanson. When the adoption of stars of the stage by the film industry was proven to be profitable, even the Trust members could not ignore it. As Balio (1976: 106) said "The star craze hit the industry like a storm and forced even the conservative members of the Trust to change with the times". According to Scott (2005: 24), it is this increased concentration upon market awareness that contributed to the 'independents' in their development of Hollywood as the centre of filmmaking.

The Trust and anti-Trust

By 1912 the evidence of unfair practice was stacking up against the Trust. This culminated in the government's decision to bring anti-Trust proceedings against the Motion Picture Patents Company under the Sherman Antitrust Act. They issued proceedings on the 15th of August 1912 and due to the extensive evidence that had to be presented, the decision was not arrived at until October 1915. The court ruled that,

> The agreements and acts of the defendants in the present case went far beyond what was necessary to protect the use of the patents or the monopoly which went with them, and that the end result...was the restraint of trade condemned by the law (Robinson, 1996: 106).

In January 1916, the Motion Picture Patents Company was prohibited from retaining their present organisation by decree. Their subsequent appeal was dismissed in 1918 and this ended the matter. Nevertheless, as Robinson (1996) observes, this lawsuit was not the single influencing factor in the fate of the Trust. Robinson cites five factors that contributed to the demise of the Trust – the strength of the independents in their organised opposition, the financial drain ensued by constant litigation, the failure of the Trust to look to Wall Street for finance, the inflexible nature of the organisation and finally, the loss of the European markets which resulted from World War I (WWI).

Despite the relatively short-term impact of the Trust on the US industry, in the long run it can be argued that it was instrumental in the creation of a cohesive, structured and competitive international industry which remains today (Anderson, 1985). This is in part due to the US success in implementing Hamiltonian strategies coupled with the creation of a united opposition who would go on to form the studio system, which dominates the worldwide film industry today.

World War I

The United States' limited involvement in World War I had a major impact on the development of its film industry (Ellis, 1995; Trumpbour, 2002). The four main film producing countries, namely, France, Germany, Italy and Great Britain were disadvantaged by their involvement in the War from the outset. This had the combined negative effect of restricting raw materials needed for film production and curtailing film distribution for the European film companies, as photographic film and high explosives require many of the same materials. Thompson and Bordwell (2003: 56) support this by saying that "without the War, Hollywood might not have gained a pre-eminent global position". Due to the expansion in the market for US films, budgets could also afford to rise as they were based, according to Thompson and Bordwell, on potential earnings. This was an additional factor which ensured continuing US domination of global and certainly European markets. In saying this, Thompson and Bordwell recognised the foothold which US films had in the English speaking world and Germany prior to World War I.

While the international markets for films were hugely disrupted as a result of World War I, there was still a market demand for films during this period. This resulted in a rise in domestic production of films in Sweden, Russia and Germany, which prior to this period were relatively low producers of films. Conversely, the industries in France, Italy and Denmark reduced in capacity during the War, due to their inability to trade in the international market (Thompson and Bordwell, 2003).

Puttnam (1997) also accords great significance to the impact that the War had upon the simultaneous fortification of the American film industry and the decimation of the European industry. According to Puttnam (1997), the initial aim of the American independents was to develop their domestic market share due to a reduction in European competition. It was only after this that they looked to Europe for greater development possibilities. The US was now in a position of natural advantage as they had a large receptive audience for their films, combined with a stimulated wartime economy, talented filmmakers and an acute business sense. Balio (1976: 388) describes the effect of the war as such that,

> American distributors were able to gain control of the foreign field without competition. And by the time capital was once more available for production abroad, American films had obtained almost complete control of world markets.

Product differentiation

Betts (1973: 46) argues that, in the case of the UK market, quality of the films being produced was also a factor in explaining the dominance that America secured over domestic films at this time. Betts identifies the years between 1914 and 1927 as the crucial time in America's domination of the British film market and offers an explanation for their success, saying that the American films were simply better than those from the UK. Film quality has always been a contentious subject, with British films, filmmakers and public funders being repeatedly admonished by film critics and commentators for producing films with either limited appeal or low quality. Barr (1996) acknowledges the poor reputation which British cinema held historically and tries to refute this impression. This returns us to the debate regarding the classification of film as art or commerce. Hollywood has the resources needed to make high budget films with very high production values and their dominance in the market for these films is unquestionable. But, the strength of European films often lies in the story they tell and the stylistic nature of their direction. This is the case for films which broke through both in Europe and the US over the past number of years such as *Trainspotting* (1996), *The Full Monty* (1997), *All About My Mother* (1999), *Billy Elliot* (2000), *Amelie* (2001), *Slumdog Millionaire* (2008) and so on.

The opinion that British films were of low quality was challenged in relation to film production in Britain during World War II. MacNab (1993: 35) draws on various sources who proposed that British film during this period was of high artistic quality, although the scale of production was drastically reduced. In doing so, MacNab (1993) quotes Manvell who attributes this high level of quality to the fact that British filmmakers possessed "an individuality of style contrasting strongly with the rubber-stamp Hollywood entertainment" (Roger Manvell, quoted in MacNab, 1993: 35). This is still posited as one of the differences between European films and those produced by Hollywood. European films are often viewed as more creative, artistic or individual than their Hollywood counterparts, although this is not always the case.

One European company which was early in recognising the US domination of the film industry and the importance of appealing to the sizeable American audience was Pathé. French film companies were successful in capturing a substantial part of the global film market between 1896 and 1910, culminating in 1910 when Pathé opened their first US film studio in Bounds Brook, New Jersey (Spehr, quoted in Dyer McCann, 1987: 39). Pathé Frères recognised that the tastes of American audiences were different from those in Europe and began making films specifically for the American audience in order to successfully compete. This proved very successful, until Pathé sold his production company and moved fully into distribution. This went against the trend of vertical integration which he is credited with starting, and resulted in his business ultimately failing.

While the US companies were vertically integrating in order to reduce costs, Pathé and Gaumont (Pathé's main domestic rival) were reducing their risk by concentrating on the revenue earning activities of distribution rather than the high risk, expensive activity of film production. This left a gap in the market which the US companies could exploit by providing these distributors with their films.

Gomery (1991) highlights the independent sector's introduction of product differentiation in opposition to the Trust. These independents later became the Hollywood majors which we know today. By emphasising popular stories and developing films as star vehicles, films no longer were sold by the foot and became valued on the basis of the popularity of these stories and the stars of the films. It was also during this period, according to Gomery, that widespread marketing came into play in terms of communicating with the film going audience. Such marketing was used in building the profile of the stars of these films, who were obliged to enter into contractual relationships with these independent film companies in order to star in their films.

The birth of Hollywood

The Trust has been viewed as one of the contributing factors in the move from New York to California which began early in the 1900s. The increasingly difficult operating environment created by the official, and more so by the unofficial activities of the Trust, had created an unwelcoming location for independents wishing to continue activity in the film industry. As Scott (2005) acknowledges, the shift of film industry activities from the East to West Coast of the US is well researched by film historians. Scott (2005: 13) accepts that one of the reasons for this move was related to the climate and landscape of Southern California, which were suited to year round film production. The need for constant sunshine, which had driven filmmakers, independents and the Trust members alike to destinations from Jacksonville Florida to Cuba, was also instrumental in inspiring this move to Southern California. Southern California offered a combination of easily accessible and varied locations, good weather and a haven for non-Trust producers "who wanted to skip across the Mexican border at a moment's notice" (Zukor, 1954: 37) to avoid litigation by the Trust. But, at the same time, Scott (2005) is dubious of the explanation proposed by Litman (1998) who points to the proximity of the Mexican border as an incentive for the independents as they could flee to Mexico if their defiance of the Trust was discovered.

Another incentive proposed in explanations of this move was the lower wage bill resulting from a move to Los Angeles, "the country's principal non-unionized city" (Puttnam, 1997: 77). A third factor in this relocation was the ease with which the independents and the studios could find premises, for a fraction of the rent that they were paying in New York and New Jersey (Robinson, 1996: 104). Scott (2005) casts doubt on the belief that those who relocated to Southern California were doing so to escape the stranglehold of the Trust, as he notes that some of the firms to locate in this region during the period from 1909 to 1912 were in fact members of the Trust, although their headquarters were still located in New York or New Jersey. Rather Scott (2005: 19) believes that the location of many film companies' activities in Los Angeles up to 1912 was arbitrary. However, in saying this, Scott (2005) draws on theories of industrial agglomeration in order to explain the development of Hollywood as the centre of the film industry and why it has retained this dominance. Scott (2005) proposes a theoretical framework within which to place the analysis of the development of Hollywood as the centre of film activity. Scott's investigation is focused not on how and why the companies that became the Hollywood majors were located there at that time, but why they have remained there ever since.

At this time, another important development was occurring in the American film industry. The Edison litigation combined with the mushrooming of nickelodeons combined to create a shortage of films (products) for film exhibitors in the US. This, in addition to the superior quality of the European productions, inspired the exhibitors to look to Europe in order to source product. George Klein secured distribution rights for the majority of European films shown in the US, but many of the Europeans also set up their own branches in the US at this time. By 1907, Robinson (1996: 133–137) estimates that two-thirds of the films released in the United States were European. This period has resonance today as the film industry moves towards digital exhibition of films. This digital era is seen as both a threat and an opportunity for filmmakers seeking a marketplace.

United States conquers Europe

The US filmmakers began to recognise the importance of the European market during WWI, and developed this market in the early 1920s. German and Soviet films were receiving great critical admiration in this period while in the US the concentration was upon industrial issues. It was in the 1920s that the US began its domination of the box office, which it retains to this day. Ellis (1995) highlights the new forms of economic development and cultural products that began to emerge between the end of World War I and the stock market crash in 1929.

This was a period of expansion for business in the US, which began to export its industrial products throughout the world. There was widespread interest in the arts as a form of cultural expression in the US at the time, which was echoed in American writing in the aftermath of WWII. As Ellis points out, the film industry most closely connected art and commerce and played a central part in the quest for cultural conquest.

This shows that the importance of film as a form of cultural expression was recognised in the early stages of the industry. The 1920s seemed to signal the beginning of the industry that remains today. In this period, the relatively new production studios saw the need to expand further in order to survive in the competitive market. The recognition of the need to expand into distribution and exhibition resulted in a greater demand for capital.

The majors are born

Three companies had firmly established themselves in the area of exhibition by the middle of the 1920s. Paramount gained most control during this period. Between 1919, when it floated a $10 million issue of preferred stock, and 1921, Paramount had succeeded in building up an empire which had the foremost production, distribution and exhibition capacity in the US, as well as being in control of the vast proportion of the acting talent of the period. Paramount faced competition from First National, which had been formed by a group of exhibitors who identified the need to become stakeholders in film production in order to ensure supply of product. The final grouping that was in competition with Paramount was Loews.

By the middle of the decade, practically all of the majors and first run theatres in North America were being run by one of these three groupings. Huettig (1944) discusses the motivation behind the expansion and integration strategy of these groupings and also highlights their belief in the power of advertising during their expansion period. Ellis (1995) noted that Universal and Fox also had some theatres but that these did not pose a threat to the domination of the sector by the big three. In this way, the majors controlled the market, independent producers could not access the theatres and independent exhibitors could not gain access to product in order to exhibit. This was especially the case in the New York area where this activity was centred. Ellis (1995) estimates that approximately four to five hundred feature films were produced annually in the latter part of the 1920s. In order for the programmes to change weekly in the theatres, each of the majors had annual release figures of 52 films. Distribution was handled regionally by the six hundred exchanges, which were situated in forty-six of the leading American cities. Average attendance for each of the twenty thousand or so theatres in the US was approximately four thousand a week.

The newly formed majors had recognised the need to vertically integrate in the areas of distribution and exhibition, in order to allow their films access to the market, and in all aspects of film production: script development, acting, physical production, editing and so on (Scott, 2005). From the late 1920s until the late 1940s, with the introduction of sound, increased unionisation and so on, Hollywood enjoyed what Scott (2005: 32) refers to as its golden age when it operated as a "mature oligopoly".

Spiralling costs

During this period, expenditure on films increased, as did that on creating and building lavish theatres for exhibition. Ellis (1995) depicts this time as one of extravagant spending on salaries for directors, writers and especially stars. However, despite spiralling budgets, the staples of the studios' production were the 'B-movies'. As the cost involved in production rose, the importance of the production supervisor usurped the director. Not only was this person involved in the financial side of production, but also in an increasing way in the creative aspects. With the advent of sound in the latter part of the 1920s, this control became more manifest due to the increased cost incurred by the use of sound. At this stage in the US industry, the business element of filmmaking took priority over the artistic.

The big budget feature

The increase in budget size had begun in the mid-teens with Griffith's 1915 production *Birth of a Nation*. Following this, Americans began to produce the first big budget features, which have become synonymous with today's Hollywood. Griffith has been hailed as the American filmmaker who brought the film form prominence in separating it from theatre. The sheer size and elaborate nature of this film earmarked it as the model for the big budget Hollywood films that have succeeded it. *The Birth of a Nation* (1915) cost five times more than Griffith's *Judith of Bethulia* (1914) which had up until then been the most expensive film to be produced in the US.

In addition, *The Birth of a Nation* (1915) also heralded in a new era for the consumption of film. Balio (1985) recalls how the economic potential of film was confirmed when this film was released at Liberty Theatre in New York and played there for forty-four weeks. This run, according to Balio (1985: 113), was to a large extent due to the "exhibition format, consisting of reserved seats, scheduled performances, orchestral accompaniment, souvenir programs, costuming of ushers, intermissions and the like" which increased the level of luxury experienced by film goers at that time. This analysis indicates the importance of marketing from the early days in presenting a film in a sympathetic manner rather than relying on the quality of the film alone to satisfy the cinemagoers.

Such a sizeable investment was rewarded by exceptional box office success. The film was a current day marketers' dream. This big budget film, based on a bestselling book and subsequent play about the American Civil War combined with the controversial treatment of African Americans, was ensured success at that time. Ellis (1995: 29) sums up the significance of *Birth of a Nation* (1915) by saying that it was "More than merely a motion picture, it was a cultural phenomenon that everyone felt obliged to witness". This is the ultimate marketing aim and reflects how so called 'event' films are marketed. In differentiating one film from the others, the aim can often be to convince the public that not seeing the film will exclude them from public debate.

The difficulty in calculating box office receipts for *Birth of a Nation* (1915) is caused by the organisation of American distribution at the time. Theatrical distribution was arranged on a state by state basis, which precluded the possibility of collecting accurate data relating to nationwide receipts for *Birth of a Nation* (1915). Although rarely getting theatrical release outside film societies today, *Variety* estimated that it grossed approximately $50 million (Ellis, 1995: 29). While *Birth of a Nation* (1915) was an undoubted commercial and creative success, the first such epic film in the history of the cinema, it was also controversial as the book it was based upon was *The Clansman*, by Thomas Dixon, a well-known racist author. Despite Griffith's watering down of the racist elements of the book in his adaptation, according to Thompson and Bordwell (2003), the film fell foul of the National Association for the Advancement of Colored People (NAACP). Such a reaction strengthened the view held by early social commentators that film played a role in influencing social perceptions and behaviours. This role of film will be explored later in this book when we consider the interplay between social marketing and film.

Griffith followed *Birth of a Nation* (1915) with *Intolerance* (1916), which comprised of four shorter films set in various time periods but with an underlying common theme. This four-hour successor to *Birth of a Nation* (1915), which cost $1.9 million to make and ran to approximately four hours, was critically acclaimed. Despite the positive reaction from the critics, the audience did not mirror this, confusion and frustration with its length causing a predominantly negative response to *Intolerance* (1916). This, combined with the failure of the theme to inspire audience sympathy, resulted in the film's unmitigated failure at the box office. The lack of a clear link between critical acclaim and box office success and cinemagoers' reluctance to engage in innovative forms of film is still a challenge to contemporary filmmakers.

WHY DOES AMERICAN STILL DOMINATE?

The above sections traced the development of the Hollywood industry and the problems posed by this increasing domination for the European film industry since the early twentieth century. Despite early beliefs that this domination could be redressed, the European and Hollywood Film Industries are in constant battle. Similarly, despite strong domestic performance by Indian, Nigerian and to a lesser degree, Korean film, American film still dominates the global box office. While the number of films produced respectively in India, Nigeria and Europe is greater than in the US, numbers of films produced does not correlate to the level of international exposure or revenue earned. The reasons behind this disparity have long been the source of investigation and many explanations have been proposed.

The commercial element

European filmmakers are at last acknowledging that they must make money to survive in all sectors, and that while there is a place for artistic and sensitive films which do not achieve major box office success, these must be subsidised by blockbusters. The recent success of non-Hollywood films like *Slumdog Millionaire* (2008), *Amalie* (2001) and *City of God* (2003) is testament to the fact that a filmmaker can retain his/her creative integrity while achieving commercial success, one, therefore, does not exclude the other. What cannot be overlooked is the marketing and positioning of such films.

The problem facing many film industries is a combination of lack of business acumen, reluctance of many to watch non-Hollywood, non-national films and structural shortcomings (Kerrigan and Özbilgin, 2003). Many of the basic structures in place outside the Hollywood, Bollywood and Nollywood industries are disjointed and fail to provide the level of support and market information and access necessary in order for films to perform well commercially. It is interesting to note that the vertical integration, which is now an integral part of the Hollywood film industry, was a European invention. As discussed above, Charles Pathé saw the immense potential of the American market and sought to exploit it. His visionary tactics form the basis of the film industry in the United States today. Pathé introduced vertical integration, perceiving that the real money to be made emanated from the distribution of films rather than from their manufacture.

This difference in the approach of the Hollywood film industry and European filmmakers can perhaps be summed up by Zukor (quoted in MacNab, 1993) when he said that British filmmakers had not studied the American film market in terms of what American audiences wanted. Zukor attributed the success of Hollywood films to such a focus on the audience which existed in Hollywood but is not replicated internationally. Although Zukor believed that the success of Hollywood films was due to their superiority, this superiority seemed to lie with Hollywood filmmakers' desire to be market-focused. This remains as true today as it was in the 1940s when Zukor made this statement, but it does not necessarily mean that non-Hollywood filmmakers need to 'give them what they want' in order to achieve a certain level of success.

A lack of commercial incentive does not seem apparent in the Bollywood and Nigerian film industries. Bollywood films are predominantly made by film dynasties located in Mumbai and mostly follow a tried and tested formula. Indian cinema has long been popular outside the subcontinent with large audiences in the Middle East and Africa and latterly with the Diaspora in the UK and USA. Such success has seen an increase in the numbers of Indian films exhibited in UK and US cinema chains. Although these films perform well, they are marketed predominantly to the Indian community and little evidence of cross-over to the mainstream is apparent. Nigerian cinema is also governed by commercial motivations. Nollywood works on a high volume model of film production where many new titles are released each week and distributed through established retail outlets to the population and to the Diaspora internationally. While there are cinemas in Nigeria, these mainly show US films and are out of reach of the majority of the population due to ticket prices. Similarly to Indian cinema, Nigerian films are popular with the Nigerian Diaspora in the UK and USA. But, unlike Indian films, they do not enjoy theatrical distribution, and rely on similar methods of distribution as in their home market, distribution through retail outlets for home viewing.

Marketing and distribution

It is undisputed that the Hollywood industry has more star appeal with more internationally recognisable stars than any other film industries. In addition, as outlined above, the majors control the worldwide distribution networks and have a prevailing foothold in the exhibition sector. Through maintenance of this control, they retain their domination of the worldwide film industry. The distribution sector is undoubtedly the most instrumental element in a film reaching its audience. Irrespective of the talent of the writer, director, technical staff and stars involved, if a film fails to secure a distribution deal with one of the majors or a respected independent distributor, it will not be widely exhibited and will certainly not recoup its production budget. A good marketing campaign, which is coherently planned with the production team and distributor from the earliest possible stage, is essential in order to secure good box office receipts. Durie (1993: 13) stresses, the goal of film marketing as the maximisation of the audience for a film resulting in expanding its earning potential.

As mentioned above, Nigerian film is distributed directly to consumers through retail outlets and Indian films have large local and national audiences with many of these films travelling outside the home market. South Korean film has performed well in the domestic (and neighbouring) marketplace(s) due to various industrial measures which saw both an increase in venture capital funding for films and support for film exhibition in the form of a quota. However, for most filmmakers, when access to the integrated supply chains of the US majors is denied, the need for marketing techniques to be employed is increased. It is through the clever use of marketing that smaller films can try to find their audience. This need was recognised in 2000, when an international symposium was held in Zurich in order to outline the specific problems small European countries face in the area of film marketing (Joeckel, 2003). Film producers from across Europe concerned with the importance of marketing attended this symposium. Indeed, over the last number of years there has been an increase in public support for film marketing initiatives, like the Lithuanian Institute for Art's summer school for young filmmakers which focused upon marketing, the Danish Film Institute's programmes which focus on marketing techniques for film producers and the Power to the Pixel project in the UK which has a focus on marketing through harnessing new technology.

Suspicion of distributors

Another problem for filmmakers when looking for distribution for their film lies in the suspicion which still surrounds distributors. Rhetoric surrounding the industry abounds with rumours that directors or writers are asked to change certain aspects of their project in order to fulfil market demands as determined by the distributor, or by one of the major studios offering European directors production finance. For example, Kirk Jones, the writer/director of *Waking Ned* (1998) sought production finance from one of the

US majors, but turned down the offer as it would have meant compromising on casting to a greater extent than he felt desirable (Jones, 1998). Another example is the Neil Jordan film, *We're No Angels* (1989), where Jordan felt that the final film had been edited to such an extent that it no longer remained the film that he shot (Jordan, 1997). There are also accounts of the lengths that filmmakers have gone to in order to avoid distributors editing a film or making alterations prior to release (Phillips, 1991). However, such stories have so far been restricted to the US majors and not independent distributors (Biskind, 2003).

As will be illustrated later in this book, recruited audience screenings (RAS) are primarily used in order to ascertain if a film has connected sufficiently with the original target audience and whether cross-over potential exists.

Structural considerations

This chapter has looked in detail at the formation of the Hollywood film industry up until the mid-1940s when the Hollywood majors operated as a mature oligopoly. At this stage, according to the analysis of Christopherson and Storper (1986), Storper (1989), Storper and Christopherson (1987), this strongly and vertically integrated oligopoly was forced to restructure as the Paramount Anti-Trust case of 1948 found that the fully vertically integrated structure of the majors was unfairly restricting competition in the post war film industry. This was coupled with the arrival of television in the 1950s which also impacted negatively upon the film industry. As a result of the Paramount case, the majors were forced to sell off their cinema chains, as it was agreed that ownership of production and distribution as well as exhibition resulted in an anti-competitive market for film. Christopherson and Storper (1986) argued that this resulted in a disintegration of the majors at this time and a focus on flexible specialisation where smaller independent firms were involved in various filmmaking activities, and the majors' role was restricted to acting as the coordinators of these networks. Scott (2005) depicts this period as one of instability where the industry restructured itself in the face of these pressures. It can be argued that we are currently in another period of restructuring where many micro-filmmakers are harnessing opportunities provided by new technology in order to access the market.

There has been some disagreement with regard to the degree of control exerted by the majors over the film production process since the 1950s. Critics of the views of Christopherson and Storper such as Aksoy and Robbins (1992), Blair and Rainnie (2000) and Wasko (1994) have stressed that despite the more disintegrated structure which existed during this period, the majors still exerted economic control over the film production process. Blair and Kerrigan (2002) have emphasised the cyclical nature of film production and consumption throughout the film industry's existence, and in doing so, acknowledged that these cycles took place under the control of the majors, despite the periods of integration and fragmentation which occurred. The current phase of restructuring has yet to settle into established patterns, but it would appear that there is still a place for the established film distribution and exhibition network, but this will exist alongside a radical new wave of filmmakers who are developing direct relationships with their audiences in niche areas.

Lack of a strong international film lobby

Another important and often overlooked explanation of the domination of the global film industry by Hollywood is the existence of a strong film industry lobby working on behalf of Hollywood in opposition to the lack of such a lobby in Europe. The origins of the Hollywood film lobby are laid out in detail by Ulff-Møller (2001). The strength and importance of the film industry were recognised by the US government from the early days of trade in film and they used their diplomatic networks in order to promote their films around the world. Puttnam (1997) has documented how this strong film lobby, now presided over by Jack Valenti of the Motion Picture Association of America (MPAA), mobilised itself during the Uruguay Round of the GATT negotiations which took place between September 1986 and December 1993. This will be explored in Chapter 5. It is clear from Puttnam's account that the European industry could not safeguard itself without forming a collective which would take on the role of lobbying GATT and safeguarding Europe's protection of its film industry during this period.

Although the Europeans succeeded in maintaining levels of public support for the film industry at the end of the Uruguay Round, this was done so with the assurance that they would start to liberalise the industry. The strength of the US political lobby is also apparent when observing the negotiations currently occurring between South Korea and the US. The US has insisted that South Korea should lower its current quota on the percentage of indigenous films which are shown at South Korean cinemas from 40% to 20% in order to increase other trade with the US. Since South Korea introduced their quota system, their industry has seen success both at home and in foreign markets such as Japan, Hong Kong and to a lesser extent, in Europe.

This chapter has sought to examine the key drivers behind the dominant position that Hollywood holds over the global box office. Historically, the structural problems, which are seen to hinder the non-Hollywood film industry, emanate from the organisation of the industry itself combined with reluctance on the part of some filmmakers to adopt industrial and marketing tactics readily embraced by Hollywood. Whilst acceptable growth could have been achieved in its domestic market, the US majors felt little need to dilute their effort and develop a foothold in Europe. However, as the home market became saturated and demand for US product in Europe rose, the majors found it relatively easy to mobilise their marketing machine and take a significant share of the European distribution and exhibition market.

The majors' domination of the distribution sector continues to cause problems for non-Hollywood filmmakers. The additional problems which non-English speaking countries have in relation to language and culture are merely asides to the question of industrial organisation and market awareness. It is upon these areas that national policy makers are concentrating their efforts to increase the commercial success of the global film industry and loosen the stronghold that America currently has over this market.

This abridged historical account is necessary in order to acknowledge the role played by policy in shaping the existing film industry and also in identifying early recognition of the tools used in order to differentiate films within the market. In piecing together this account, a number of documentary sources were used, from social history, film history, political science, economics and sociology to biography and journalistic sources.

As shown above, non-Hollywood filmmakers are still struggling with the imbalance that exists in the film industry. The might, experience and structure of the Hollywood majors are difficult to compete with. This chapter has outlined the macro-level issues which impact upon the market, namely, the overarching structures of the film industries concerned, primarily that of Hollywood and non-Hollywood cinema, the role which public policy has played in shaping and sustaining these structures and the current issues facing European filmmakers at a macro-level. In doing so, emphasis has been placed upon the impact of the field (Bourdieu, 1977) upon the macro- and meso-level activities of film marketing. Only by understanding the external pressures and the power structure of the industry it is possible to fully understand the constraints under which film marketers in Europe operate. In recognising these constraints, this thesis pushes forward existing explanations of the performance of films in the market and contributes constructively to the development of a holistic view of the film marketing process. While, as shown above, there are still areas for disagreement between the historical accounts of the development of the Hollywood industry, what is unanimously accepted is the power which the Hollywood majors continue to exert over the worldwide film industry. It is within the context of this domination that my analysis of film marketing is set.

CHAPTER 3

Development and Market Research in the Film Industry

Two terms used in film marketing are 'marketability' and 'playability'. These form important questions which must be asked about a film in order to position it within the marketplace. If a film is marketable, this means that the film sounds appealing and will be relatively easy to market. This could be due to the wide appeal of the story, the calibre of the cast, director or other key personnel or the genre. Other reasons that a film may be marketable may be due to its being an adaptation of a successful book, such as *Bridget Jones Diary* (2001) or *High Fidelity* (2000) or the recent wave of films based on successful computer games such as the *Pokemon* (1998) or *Resident Evil* (2002) films or graphic novels such as *Ironman* (2008), *Hellboy* (2004) and *Watchmen* (2009). For these films, there are obvious unique selling propositions which can be highlighted in the marketing campaign in order to attract large audiences. Playability relates to how the film will be received by those watching it. This is a combination of how the film meets expectations set by the name and other cues communicated through the marketing campaign as well as the story, acting, directing, cinematography and so on. Ideally, a film would be both marketable and playable, but in reality, many marketable films, such as *The Avengers* (1998), do not play well and more commonly, and more problematic, many playable films are not very marketable, for example *Año uña* (2007), a Mexican film which is both artistically innovative and well made, and also very funny. This film plays extremely well but what makes it interesting – the fact that it consists entirely of still photographs which originally formed part of a documentary photography project – also makes it difficult to 'sell'. This chapter investigates the role of market research in the film marketing process. In doing so, the concepts of marketability and playability will be returned to in order to

CONTENTS

assess the role of research in segmenting, targeting and positioning a film within the marketplace.

Market research plays an important part in any industry and the role of research in developing and positioning new products, entering new markets and understanding the competition is recognised. However, in the film industry, structural issues have prevented many organisations from engaging in meaningful market research activities. There has also been reluctance on the part of some filmmakers to consider the market for their film and therefore, market research was not seen as a necessary activity. This chapter will trace the origins and development of market research in the film industry and show how such research originated from concerns regarding the social and psychological impact of film. Following this, the chapter will discuss the types of research that are undertaken in the film industry and where they are used within the industry. Following on from this, the chapter will highlight some innovative practices undertaken by filmmakers who are challenging existing industrial models through building fan communities and gaining insight into these communities through innovative methods.

EARLY FORMS OF MARKET RESEARCH

Although the early movie moguls in the US were established businessmen, the impact of marketing was not immediately apparent. Early signs of the importance which market research had gained in Hollywood were evident by the late 1920s when a crude form of market research had begun to take place (Zukor, 1954). Box office success factors had been identified and studios incorporated these observations into their production strategy; Albert Sindlinger began to plant ushers in the cinema toilets where they would discuss a film with audience members who had just exited a performance (Jowett, 1985).

Initial audience research was socially motivated with psychologists and sociologists recognising that film could be an effective research tool. The films themselves were not being investigated, they were merely used to draw in members of the public in order to collect data (Jones and Conrad, 1930). Attempts to ascertain consumer demand only really came about with the recognition that using film as an efficient method of social research necessitated the identification of the interests and preferences of the audience. Small-scale studies of audience preferences began with simple observations of content in the early cinema forms. This proved sufficiently popular to support the foundation of the Hollywood film industry that flourishes today (Jowett, 1985).

In the 1930s, industry professionals began to be more scientific in their data collection and analysis of their customer base. This was a response to the depression combined with the restrictions of the self-censorship, known as 'the Code' instigated by the industry in the face of criticism on the grounds of the negative moral impact of films. Immediately after World War II, Chambers (1947) identified the need for Hollywood to introduce sustained research into film production and audience composition in order to retain its lead in the world markets. He stressed the adoption of a global strategy to establish a sufficient understanding of the overseas markets in order to compete successfully (Chambers, 1947).

The 1930s also heralded the introduction of the 'sneak preview' as a means of determining success and failure factors of a newly produced film. These early Recruited Audience Screenings (RAS) did not have the advantage of today's more sophisticated testing systems. Their biggest impediment to accuracy was the lack of discrimination employed in audience selection. Those currently running RAS are careful to attract clearly defined audience segments in order to determine accurately a film's potential impact on the target group. They also endeavour to ensure that each participant returns a fully completed questionnaire; there was a tendency towards self-selection in the early years, whereby only those who enjoyed the film completed the questionnaire.

In addition to investigating audience tastes while at the cinema, early research also began to consider the motivation behind cinemagoing as a pastime. Through his work, which drew upon the methods employed in other communications research, Paul Lazersfeld highlighted a trend of equivalent consumption of "mediums of mass entertainment" (Lazersfeld, 1947, p. 164). For example, frequent cinema visitors were also heavy readers of magazines and regular listeners to the radio (Lazersfeld, 1947). Film audiences may still be seen as the most prolific consumers of other media as the London Film Festival organisers claim that the audience for the festival are very heavy consumers of other cultural forms.

Whilst Lazersfeld's study attempted to explain the psychological motivation underlying why individuals go to the cinema, he was unable to identify any decisive factors. However, in using a demographic analysis of film audiences that drew upon research into audiences for radio, Lazersfeld did conclude that age was a significant determinant when examining audience profiles and in the older segments of the population, educational level was important.

These early forms of market research concerned with evaluating the impact of cinema on the population, understanding the motivation to attend the cinema as well as indicating the factors which result in enjoyment of particular films based on demographic or psychographic considerations continue to date. While impact studies are located primarily within the remit of cultural studies, psychology and sociology, the latter two types of research are undertaken by those investigating the film industry from a marketing perspective. The following section will outline the current situation with regard to the film industry's use of market research, before identifying the marketing tools identified in the literature as impacting on the selection of films by audiences. Adapting Borden's (1964) marketing mix philosophy, these marketing tools when combined, constitute the substantial value-adding activity that new product development in the film industry demands and is reflected in the marketing processes undertaken at the various stages of a film's life cycle.

PERCEPTION OF MARKET RESEARCH IN THE FILM INDUSTRY

Certain European filmmakers are scathing of the practice of audience research as carried out by the majors in the US, but lack of direction or knowledge of the appeal of a project from the early stages is likely to restrict the effectiveness of the marketing campaign. All too often, such research is left until the latter stages of production when it is ineffectual. Puttnam articulates the European situation by claiming that many filmmakers in Europe still find the concept of audience research distasteful (Puttnam, in Ilott, 1996).

While market research is widely used in the US film industry, its introduction into the European industries has met with some resistance, particularly in continental Europe. Recruited Audience Screenings (RAS) are events where a film is shown to an audience consisting of members of the target audience with the purpose of testing various aspects of the film to see if it does in fact appeal to this group. Resistance to such research is gradually being overcome. An example of this is the interest shown by the Danish Film Institute in introducing a system of RAS to the industry though at the time they were hampered by the fact that there was no specialist film research company in the country. The situation is different in the UK, where a number of companies specialise in RAS. Unsurprisingly, with US films accounting for the majority of box office revenue in the UK, their client lists are mainly composed of US companies operating within the UK.

Research processes in film marketing

Research of various sorts is drawn upon throughout the film making and marketing process. Reflecting on the structural issues highlighted in the first two chapters, those benefiting from horizontal integration across the supply chain benefit both from access to the marketplace as well as access to valuable market information which can be drawn upon in planning, budgeting and constructing the appropriate marketing strategy for each film. Distribution companies compile data on the performance of their films throughout various markets and across time. This can be combined with external databases on film performance. This data can be used in order to predict new projects' financial performance and this information fed into the development stage. The budget can then be set according to the projected earnings of the film.

New product development and film marketing

In common with other industries, successful innovation and the creation of a continuous stream of new products are essential for the survival of companies in the film industry. Although in many industries, the term new product development (NPD) is commonly used, this is not the case in the film industry. Despite the lack of common terminology between film and other industries, the generic NPD processes are in existence in the film industry and these processes are examined in the following section. According to Zacharia (2001: 134) new product development is defined as "the process of conceiving and creating a new product and the outcomes of that process". This is essentially what filmmaking is concerned with and film marketing has the dual function of informing and being informed by this process. Various categorisations of NPD have been produced by researchers such as Hall (1991) and Meyers and Tucker (1989). Nevertheless, while these categories have some resonance for the film industry NPD process, it is more useful to adapt these in order to provide functional categories for film. Using Hall's (1991) framework, which proposes five categories, Table 3.1 shows how this can be adapted in order to apply to the film industry.

Table 3.1 NPD Categories in Film Based on Hall's (1991) Categories

	Hall's (1991) NPD Categories	NPD in Film Categories
1	The break-through product	Art house film which crosses over to mainstream
2	'It's new for us' product	Copycat films
3	The new, improved, next generation product	An innovation on a tried and tested genre
4	The line extension product	Adaptation from popular novel, graphic novel, computer game, or other pre-existing cultural product
5	The three Rs (repackaged, repositioned, recycled)	Blockbuster/franchise film

The ultimate aim for an independent film producer and therefore the concern of the film marketer involved in such films is to find an art house film which will 'cross over' from its generally small, niche audience, to the mainstream. Recent examples of this type of NPD are the British film *Slumdog Millionaire* (2008), the French film *Amelie* (2001) and the US film *Sideways* (2004). All of these films were thought to have a small but appreciative audience and initial marketing targeted this audience, yet the stories and quality of these films saw their appeal broaden out to mainstream audiences.

The second NPD category presented above relates to films hoping to benefit from the previous success of films of a similar kind. These films generally have easily identifiable genres, examples include the number of British gangster films released in the years following the success of *Lock, Stock and Two Smoking Barrels* (1998). This is a dangerous tactic since tastes change and audience can tire of the same genre offered to them repeatedly.

The third NPD category in Table 3.1 is the variation on a tried and trusted genre, examples would be comedies, action films, science fiction films which utilise the main elements of these films but update the setting and context of the film. This is a film which, while unique in its story, can be seen as one of a number of related films.

The fourth category is the line extension where films are adapted from popular books, graphic novels or other forms of cultural product. Recent examples of this type of NPD are *The Lord of the Rings* (2001) and *Harry Potter* (2001) franchises, the highly successful film *Mamma Mia* (2008), which was based on a musical incorporating the music of 1970s Swedish pop group Abba and the recent spate of films based on characters from graphic novels. This type of film promises a certain level of financial security as it has a definite and generally captive audience.

Finally, category five is the blockbuster/franchise film. While not all blockbuster films are franchises, the success enjoyed by blockbusters can lead to sequels in an attempt to repeat the financial success of the film. These films are generally highly promoted, have widespread appeal and do not cause offence. Blockbusters are most commonly to be found in the action or comedy genres. Due to the high budgets involved, this type of film is normally produced by the American majors and seldom attempted by independent companies such as those in existence in Europe. However, British film production company Working Title, is responsible for a franchise of sorts with their series of romantic comedies following on from the surprise success of *Four Weddings and a Funeral* (1994). While these films are unlike the bond franchise in that they feature different characters and are not a continuation of a story in any way, they do have largely the same creative team and some of the same actors involved and a common genre, romantic comedy. Examples of the Working Title romantic comedy franchise films are *Notting Hill* (1999), *About a Boy* (2002) and *Love Actually* (2003).

The nature of the supply chain and supply chain management also dictates the manner in which NPD is undertaken. Due to the fragmented nature of the film industry in Europe, the NPD process undertaken is generally of a sequential nature as described by Zacharia (2001: 137–138). In sequential product development (SPD) the functional areas involved in the NPD process work independently and in a prescribed order. The problem with SPD can be that there are no early warning systems in place. It is often precisely for this reason that non-Hollywood films fail in the market. If initial development activities take place without consulting distribution, sales or marketing personnel, little market or customer intelligence is considered at that stage.

In a vertically integrated company or where a functioning, integrated supply chain is in existence, flexible NPD is possible. The benefit of flexible NPD, according to Iansiti and MacCormack (1997) is that changes can be made to all NPD processes at any stage in its development. The benefits of flexible NPD in the film industry can be seen by in the success of the Hollywood majors where such changes are possible. However, it would be overly simplistic to infer that the integrated supply chain necessarily allows flexibility and the independent film cannot have such flexibility. For example, accounts of film making under the Hollywood studio system often highlight the lack of flexibility allowed to the film maker due to the heavy emphasis on costs and projections in this system. Conversely, a benefit of independence is the ability to adapt and change a film which it is being made, in line with the needs of that film. For example, in a British Film Institute screening of *Slumdog Millionaire*, in January 2009, director, Danny Boyle recounted the decision to have much of the dialogue in this film be in Hindi as the children cast were not proficient in English and the film would be much more authentic if they spoke in Hindi. But, although *Slumdog Millionaire* is considered an independent film, it was partly financed through a distribution deal with Warner Brothers and Fox Searchlight. Having assured the distributors that the film would be in English, Boyle had to convince them to allow him to shoot some of it in Hindi once filming had begun.

DEVELOPMENT – PROJECT BASED VERSUS THE SLATE APPROACH

The development stage is one of the most important and often neglected aspects of the production process. Historically, this has been due to the fragmented structure of the industry (Kerrigan and Culkin, 1999). As the producers do not earn any revenue during the development stage, the emphasis has been upon pushing films through to production, rather than developing them fully or deciding that they are not marketable and abandoning the project in development stage (Finney, 1996; Dale, 1997). Tim Bevan and Eric Fellner, Working Title producers, have indicated that one of the benefits of being part of an integrated supply chain is being able to commit resources to fully developing their projects (Higgins, 2005). Due to the integrated structure within which they operate, finance is available for development:

> Before Polygram started backing us, we were both independent producers to whom the end is getting a film financed, not made. So now, we spend far more time on the content of a movie and as things have progressed we've got a slate (Tim Bevan, Working Title).

Traditionally, public funding for films focused on production finance, but during the 1990s there was a move throughout Europe to finance development and distribution activities. This was a very welcome development. Information garnered from independent film makers and distributors prior to the publication of this book indicated that currently, development funding from distributors is very difficult to access as distributors have become more risk averse, preferring to invest in films once they have been completed. Exceptions to this are where a distributor has developed a relationship with a producer over time and through this process builds up trust and willingness to finance development costs.

The term 'slate' of films, refers to a situation where one company has a number of films in various stages of pre-production, production and post production simultaneously. This process is conducive to a thorough development process more in line with the practice in the US. Under this system, each successful film provides the finance for the films to follow in the development process. Being able to have a slate of films in development allows filmmakers to proceed with those securing production funding and be able to write off those that do not. Having films in various stages of development also allows the filmmakers to transfer learning from one project to another.

Types of research undertaken in film marketing

Marich (2005) indicates seven types of research undertaken during the film marketing process. These are concept testing, positioning studies, focus group tests, test screenings, tracking surveys, advertising testing and exit surveys. For a full discussion of these types of research see Marich (2005, pp. 32–52). As Marich points out, concept testing occurs prior to greenlighting a project and therefore is undertaken by those developing the film. The majority of research which feeds into the marketing process is considered the responsibility of the film's distributor and therefore takes place once the film is in production or after completion.

Concept testing

Formal concept testing is uncommon for most films and mainly found among the Hollywood studios. However, in line with new product development processes in other industries, a form of concept testing is always an element of the development process. Although such testing may take place within the inner circle of those involved in developing and producing the film, this can count as an early form of research. An example can be seen in the case of the Working Title film *Elizabeth* (1998). According to Debra Hayward (Kerrigan, 2005), co-producer of *Elizabeth*, the concept for this film came about during a staff meeting where they raised the idea of making a film about a monarch and came up with Elizabeth. At this stage, a concept must be tested in terms of its possible marketability and commercial potential in order to inform the budget. Although this film could be seen as a costume or historical drama, this is generally an unpopular and hence, not a high performing commercial genre and therefore, the producers were determined to highlight the plot rather than make a traditional 'frock flick'. In focusing on the plot, the producers positioned the film as a thriller and made the decision to avoid cast and crew traditionally associated with historical dramas. In taking this example, we can see that concept testing is an essential part of the development process and can be seen as carrying through to the production phase as it can inform decisions such as script development and casting. Marich (2005) also includes title testing in this phase of testing, however, as can be seen from the trade press, a number of projects do not formalise their titles at such an early stage, preferring to use working titles for films until they have finalised the title later in the production process.

Positioning studies

The next phase of research which Marich (2005: 33) refers to are positioning studies, which analyse the various elements, or 'marketing assets' of the film. Based on the data collated by the Distribution Company and data which is commercially available, the distribution team can analyse the potential financial performance of the film based on its genre, cast. Going one step further, Marich (2005) claims that studios also isolate elements of the film such as a particular character and test these with audiences. They use the results of such tests in order to develop early marketing strategies. Such practices are not common outside the Hollywood studio system.

Both concept testing and positioning studies in their most basic forms can be seen as key elements of the development process. In their advanced forms, such processes can be viewed as detracting from the creative process of film making as they involve taking elements of a film in isolation from the complete project. Testing the attractiveness of a single character without situating this character in the narrative of the film or testing a concept without considering the creative context of the film may not be helpful.

Business to business testing

Again, as in other industries, business to business testing occurs within the film industry. However, unlike in many other industries, such 'testing' also functions as a marketing tool for the filmmakers in a business to business context. Preview screenings for film distributors can take place either in private screening rooms at any time or as part of a film market or festival. Private screenings may present unfinished films which are still seeking further investment in production whereas festival and market screenings almost always take place once a film has finished post production and are used in order to secure additional distribution deals. Such screenings are often organised by international Sales Agents who can use their networks and established relationships in order to attract distributors to these screenings. A more detailed discussion of film festivals and markets is included in Chapter 7.

Business to consumer testing

This is the main focus of the tests that are used by film marketers and among these, the recruited audience screening is the most common and valuable research tool. Recruited audience screenings (RAS) are also known as preview screenings and test screenings. However, I would like to distinguish RAS from preview screenings as this term is more commonly used to describe publicity screenings rather than elements of research. The term preview screening is more commonly applied to screenings of the completed film prior to general release. These screenings can be organised for film critics and industry insiders or for 'avids', the term applied to film marketing mavens or opinion leaders (Kerrigan, 2004).

What is a recruited audience screening?

Recruited audience screenings are one of the main elements of research undertaken in order to gauge the reaction of film consumers to a particular film. Such screenings are run by the distributors, and usually employ specialist research companies to organise the screenings, collect and analyse the data. While there are stories which circulate regarding drastic changes which have been made to films; endings changes, characters removed and so on, the main purpose of such screenings is to assist in marketing the film to the correct audience. In addition, if a film is too long, the RAS may also be used in order to identify scenes which could be edited out of the film while retaining the central meaning or plot. An example of such editing occurred when *Notting Hill* (1999) was tested with UK audiences. The original cut was so funny that the audience were missing chunks of dialogue as they were laughing so much during the screenings. The film was then re-edited in order to reduce the number of jokes to allow the audience to engage with the story more (Kerrigan, 2005).

Primarily, RAS are run in order to test if the predicted audience is the correct target audience and if they do, in fact, like the film. In order to test this, RAS usually focus on recruiting this audience for the screenings. Recruitment can occur in person or through the use of existing panels of possible audience members. In person recruitment often takes place in crowded shopping areas, close to cinemas and other leisure venues. Recruiters approach people who look like they fit the demographic and psychographic profiles of the target audience. Demographics refer to descriptive characteristics such as age, gender, income, level of education and occupation, while psychographics combine these with behavioural descriptors.

Respondents are generally asked a series of screening questions starting with an invitation to attend a free film screening. Some researchers explain at this stage that this is a test screening and that their views will be used by the film makers. In other cases, recruits are merely offered the opportunity to attend a free film prior to general release. In order to qualify, recruits are asked about their general film consumption habits in order to understand if they fit the core segment which the film marketers have identified for the film. They answer questions about the frequency of cinema going, types of films watched and liked and usually they are asked which of a number of specific films they have seen and liked. Once they meet the criteria set by the research company (in consultation with the distribution company), respondents are either given tickets for the screening or their name and address is taken and added to the list. It is normal practice to over-recruit as in order to get usable findings from the research, it is important to have a full cinema. Respondents are told that admission is on a first come, first serve basis and therefore, it is hoped that if some do not gain admission, then they will not create a fuss. In some cases, RAS recruits are told what the film is and to others they are just given some generic details regarding the type of film to expect. It is usual that each recruit can bring a friend to the screening.

On arrival at the RAS, which usually takes place in a commercial cinema venue in order to retain the authenticity of the process, the recruits are given a questionnaire (either before or after the screening) which contains a number of standard questions about the recruit and then about the film which they will watch. The demographic information allows the research company to segment the audience for the film into the various audience groups commonly used by distributors. Basic demographics are commonly employed such as age and gender. Some data on their film consumption can also be collected in order to contextualise their response in light of the sorts of films which they like. Once the cinema is full and the recruits are told that this film is not on general release and elements of the film may be changed before release, they are asked to complete the questionnaire prior to leaving the cinema. The film is then screened. It is usual that members of the production and/or distribution company attend these screenings in order to assess the audience response to the film and in addition, a small number (usually 10–15) or the recruits are asked to remain after the screening to take part in a focus group. This allows the research team to explore their responses in more detail than is possible through the questionnaire. Table 3.2 provides an example of the structure of a RAS questionnaire.

Up to the point of the RAS, only those involved in the production or distribution of the film have offered their views on the potential appeal of the film. The RAS allows these views to be tested in order to inform the marketing campaign. One example of where the RAS results challenged the assumptions of the film distributors was in the UK RAS for David Lynch's *The Straight Story* (1999). David Lynch films have a very loyal fan base and are known for his trademark style, unconventional characters and challenging narrative style. Films such as *Eraserhead* (1977), *The Elephant Man* (1980), *Blue Velvet* (1986) and *Lost Highway* (1997) established his cult following who welcomed his quirky take on life. *The Straight Story* (1999) was a departure from his signature style as it was a slow, contemplative film documenting the true story of a man in his seventies as he travels across Iowa and Wisconsin on his lawnmower in order to see his brother. The film is slow and sentimental and therefore thought to appeal to women more than men. It was also thought that the hardcore David Lynch fans would not respond to the film. For this reason, a test screening was undertaken in London in order to understand who the core audience was. The results were surprising as the film did in fact appeal to the traditional David Lynch fan base and also was more appealing to men than women. This was important information which

Table 3.2	Recruited Audience Screening Questionnaire

Example of RAS Questionnaire

1. How would you rate the film?
2. Would you recommend the film to your friends?
3. Would you recommend the film be seen at the cinema opening weekend/at the cinema sometime/rent on DVD/see it on pay TV/wait to see on free TV?
4. What did you like best about the film?
5. What (if anything) did you dislike about the film?
6. Which was your favourite character?
7. How did you rate the following characters? (Followed by list)
8. What was your favourite scene?
9. Which of the following words would you use to describe the film? (Followed by a list)
10. How would you rate the following elements? (Followed by a list including relevant elements such as music, pace, humour, story, setting, ending)
11. Do you think that this film will appeal more to women/men or both women and men?
12. Which age group do you think that this film will appeal to most?
13. Does this film remind you of any other films? If so, please state the name of the other film.
14. Are you male or female?
15. What age are you?
16. What is your level of education? (Followed by categories)
17. How often do you go to the cinema? (Followed by categories)

could then inform the positioning of the film through paid for advertising and public relation activities.

Marich (2005) highlights the fears of film marketers regarding the impact of RAS on word of mouth. If a film does not test well, changes can be made either in terms of adjusting perceptions of who the core audience is, editing the film to exclude scenes that do not work or irritate audiences or adding the final film soundtrack (which is often done after the research process is completed due to licensing deals and so on). These changes may see a more playable film being released than the one which was tested but negative word of mouth generated during the RAS period may have a negative impact on the box office performance of the film. Marich (2005) also highlights the role played by the internet in increasing this possible negative impact as RAS recruits post reviews of the tested film on film review websites.

The results of the RAS can be used in order to understand both the playability of the film among the target audience as well as the marketability of key cast members, genre and so on. This can inform the marketing materials such as the poster and trailer design as well as the placement of paid for advertising and promotion in appropriate media.

Testing of marketing materials

In addition to testing the film in terms of its playability, the marketing materials can also be tested prior to release. Posters, trailers, postcards and print ads can all be tested in focus groups in order to test the understanding of the target audience. In order for the marketing materials to communicate effectively with the target audience, there need to be shared cultural codes (Bourdieu, 1984). Chapter 7 will deal with this in more detail.

The above sections outline the development of market research practices in the film industry and link this to generic notions of new product development. These are the established methods of researching the film audience from a practical perspective. However, a new generation of film makers are embracing social media as a method of researching their audience. In this way, filmmakers are moving closer to consumer researchers such as Brown et al. (2003), Kozinets (1999, 2002) in using the internet and social media to understand fan communities. A good example of this is the maverick film-maker M dot Strange, director of *We Are the Strange* (2007) as is discussed in more detail in Chapter 10. This California based film maker makes his film by harnessing his online fan community in a number of ways. Fans were recruited as extras in his film and rather than being seen as possible consumers, were viewed as collaborators in the film making and marketing process. The advantage which has had in engaging with his fan base directly lies in the authenticity of as a part of the online social media community. By offering his fans' outtakes of his film and encouraging them to make their own music videos and fan artwork and displaying these on his site, he is able to essentially collect data about their wider cultural tastes which can be used in developing more sophisticated methods of communicating with his fans as well as getting an understanding of the geographical locations of his fans. By having a presence on his own personal channel, as well as popular social media sites such as YouTube, facebook and mySpace, he has been able to earn revenue through selling DVDs of his film. This type of audience research, which follows a netnographic approach, is suitable for a new type of film maker who engages in DIY (Do It Yourself) filmmaking and marketing. While mainstream outlets such as theatrical distribution through cinemas and conventional retail outlets for film are not accessible for many film makers, a new generation of film makers are finding ways to build up international audiences for their films. By belonging to their target audience, such filmmakers can develop innovative methods of researching this audience, while at the same time, harnessing them in order to bring their films to a wider marketplace.

This chapter has outlined the development of market research in the film industry and linked this to a broader discussion of the (new product) development process in film. As discussed above, a number of established practices have been developed within the film industry, including the recruited audience screening and testing of artwork. In addition to these established (and expensive) methods, it is also possible to use social media in order to gain a better understanding of potential and actual audiences. Through using social media, there is the dual benefit of collecting valuable information about the target audience but also the opportunity for fans to collaborate with the filmmakers and film marketers in developing the audience for such a film. This process will be discussed in more detail in Chapter 6 in considering consumer selection of films. Although the use of market research in the film industry is seen as contentious, this chapter has illustrated the need to understand the target audience and who they will respond to the film and to the marketing mix elements as expressed through marketing communication materials in order to plan an effective marketing communications campaign. As marketing practices within the film industry develop, the nature and design of marketing research will also evolve. While the field of human computer interaction has made some headway into understanding how and why consumers consume film through the range of media devices now on the market, there is a need to do further research regarding what types of audiovisual products are being consumed on the various types of media devices which are now available.

CHAPTER 4

Structural Considerations and Film Marketing

This chapter will look at the formation and existing structure of the global film industry and the role played by policy in shaping and regulating this environment. In doing so, the global nature of the film industry will be clarified. Film is viewed as both an economic commodity and a cultural good (Moran, 1996: 1) and for this reason, the formation and operationalisation of public policy which supports the film industry is problematic and under constant scrutiny. During a speech made at the opening of the 2004 European Film Awards in Barcelona, German film producer Wim Wenders referred to the European Film Industry as a work in progress, likening it to the Gaudi designed Sagrada la Familia. This chapter examines the historical role played by policy, at national, regional and supra-national levels in creating the film industry which exists today. In addition, the role of public policy in supporting the formation and development of an industrial environment within which film marketing can have maximum positive impact for non-Hollywood films will be assessed.

The initial focus of the chapter examines the need to engage with the film industry on a policy level. This is followed by a discussion of the evolution of public policy in the film industry and the impact which this has had upon the formation of the film industry in the present day. Following this is an analysis of supra-national, national and regional policies, both those relating to film specifically, in addition to policies which impact on filmmaking but have general industrial application. This macro-level analysis of film policy is followed by a discussion of film policy within some key film industries. From this comes an examination of the impact which these policies have had upon the structure of the film industry supply chain and the nature of marketing in the film industry.

CONTENTS

57

IS THERE A NEED FOR POLICY INTERVENTION IN THE FILM INDUSTRY?

In 1923 Will H. Hays, then head of the newly formed MPPDA (Motion Picture Producers and Distributors of America – now knows as the MPAA, Motion Pictures Association of America), in a speech concerned with the aims of the US film industry delivered in London stated: "We are going to sell America to the world with American motion pictures" (quoted in Trumpbour, 2002: 17). Since Hays made this declaration, we have seen the success of his aim in that Hollywood films control the global box office, as discussed in Chapter 2, and also such films have often been identified as the medium through which globalisation (in its interpretation as the communication of American ideals and consumerism throughout the world) has travelled (Trumpbour, 2002: 8).

During the numerous crises that have occurred in the European or British film industries, various solutions have been suggested. Many attempts have been made at solving the problem of Hollywood's domination of the global film markets, but to date, none have succeeded. In the UK, J. Arthur Rank proposed some solutions to the stranglehold which Hollywood has over the British film industry. These suggestions, according to Mullally (1946), were based upon the desire to mimic the Hollywood approach by using American stars and directors, producing large budget epics and tailoring British films in order to appeal to the US market. This suggestion has been repeated numerous times and the opposing argument has also been posed. Kuhn (2003) once again called for the need to form a European studio which could compete with the US majors. However, this approach may not be the most sensible for European filmmakers. However, Kuhn's plans can be criticised as being very much based around the US model. In this chapter, I argue that film policy must be in line with national and regional culture and the wider socio-cultural environment within which filmmakers work.

As it stressed throughout this book, little has changed in the overall ecology of the film industry since the early years. Many small European filmmakers ignore the US market in their projected earnings. In 1926, J.D. Williams, then managing director of British National Pictures Ltd., warned producers that ignoring the US market would result in restricting their market to forty percent of the total world market and urged them to compete with the US in terms of quality and variety (quoted in Higson and Maltby, 1999). In his communication, Williams stressed that European films' competitive advantage was their quality over those produced in the US where quantity was resulting in their domination of the market. This is often the argument posed in the current day; Europeans make artistic, quality films, while Hollywood makes bland, low quality films. In reality, as discussed by Blair and Kerrigan (2002) and Biskind (1998), the Hollywood studios respond to the cyclical nature of the market and have backed a variety of film styles in response to market demand.

It has become so difficult for European, particularly non-English language films to penetrate the US market that European producers are often turning to co-production partners in other European countries in order to access finance and tax breaks as well as an additional market. Julie Baines, a successful British producer, has spoken about how she looked for European co-producers in order to access additional public funding and tax breaks, as well as to secure additional markets for the films that she was making (Baines, 2004).

While it is undisputed that the Hollywood majors' control of the film industry is a result of their size and power in the market, Mullally (1946) stressed the problem which ensues from full integration of the film industry supply chain. As the exhibition sector is the most profitable element of the supply chain, if this supply chain is fully integrated, this will reduce the desire of the exhibitors to take risks on challenging films due to a possible reduction in their profit. If it is accepted that film is a cultural product and an important means through which diversity and national identity is expressed and communicated, then the exhibition sector should be encouraged towards supporting this diversity, rather than moving towards a monopolistic, market-driven approach. For this reason, there is a need for policy intervention at the levels of distribution and exhibition as well as production, in order to ensure that the commercial drivers of exhibitors do not diminish the diversity of the films which are available to cinemagoers. This problem of the commercial considerations of the cinema owners versus the need for access to diverse films which governments must safeguard is discussed in Kerrigan and Özbilgin (2002, 2004).

It is interesting that the MPAA, representing the major Hollywood studios object to government support for film in smaller film markets. This is despite the fact that the US gained such power over the global market precisely through the development of trade policies which supported their film industry. Higson and Maltby (1999), Trumpbour (2002) and Ulff-Møller (2001) have provided extensive evidence of the use of international diplomacy by the US in securing their dominant market position over Europe. Ulff-Møller (2001) also supports the view that the US identified the commercial potential of film much earlier than the Europeans. In Europe, there was greater fear of the possible negative impact which film could have upon society and a number of legal restrictions were placed on film exhibition in Europe prior to the 1960s. While the US was using its extensive diplomatic network in order to support the expansion of US films during the 1920s and 1930s, various European countries responded by instituting various restrictive measures on film imports. It is obvious from the list provided by Thompson that the domination of European markets by the US was of concern even at that early stage in the development of the film industry.

THE SUPRA-NATIONAL POLICY ENVIRONMENT

Chapter 2 traced the development of the early film industry in the US and in Europe. The role of industrial policy and state intervention is apparent. Despite Hollywood's reliance on early protectionism for its development, Hollywood, under the auspices of the Motion Picture Association of America (MPAA), is opposed to forms of industrial protection and state intervention in the global film industry. The film industry has been governed by trade rules since the establishment of the General Agreement on Tariffs and Trade (GATT) in 1947. From its inception, GATT acknowledged the special characteristics of the industry and subsequently awarded it special protective measures in recognition of the difficulties faced by the industry in the aftermath of WWII. During the Uruguay Round (1986–1994) of the GATT negotiations, there was much controversy over whether or not the European film industries should be forced to liberalise (Chantan, 1994; Clark, 1996).

Although on the surface the debate focused on the media of film and television, the outcome of these discussions had much deeper ramifications for a range of allied industries. The debate arose out of the American desire to change the methods of regulation relating to intellectual property, in order to safeguard the interests of corporate bodies dealing with the information society as well as the entertainment industry (Chantan, 1994). The importance of these negotiations was due to the expansion of the audiovisual industries predicted for the future.

Primarily due to the organisation of the French and the role played by David Puttnam, a 'cultural exception' was granted to European Community filmmakers. The Marrakesh Final Act was signed in 1994 and through signing this, the Europeans legally committed to begin liberalising before the Millennium Round of the World Trade Organisation (WTO) (Miller, 1996). Talks on liberalisation were due to take place from the 31 January 2000. However, due to disruptions during the Millennium Round, there has been little advancement on this position since the end of the Uruguay Round. In an interview conducted with a European Commission official involved in the liberalisation talks, it was noted that, as the future nature of the film industry would be determined by technological developments, it was difficult to predict what the nature of these developments would be. This situation is similar to the early years of the film industry as outlined in Chapter 2, when industrial developments were technologically driven.

This benefit of hindsight has instilled a note of caution into the European Commission negotiators when moving forward legislation on this matter. It is interesting that the US has called for the audiovisual market to be liberalised and subsidies for filmmaking curbed, when such protectionist measures were responsible for the growth and development of the modern Hollywood (Ulff-Møller, 2001). Following on from the Marrakesh agreement, the WTO was established in 1995 in order to progress the decisions taken during the Uruguay Round and enshrined in the Marrakesh agreement. The WTO recognised the move from focusing on trade of physical goods, to acknowledging the area of trade in intellectual property by establishing three councils: The Council for Trade in Goods (Goods Council), The Council for Trade in Services (GATS) and the Council for Trade related Aspects of Intellectual Property Rights (TRIPS). Castells (1996) recognised this change in direction and attributed it to the influence of the US government. This movement challenges the desire to protect the cultural industries in the face of increasing focus on the creation of an international trade environment which reduces barriers to trade. Harbord (2002) characterises this move as a triumph for Multi-National Corporations (MNCs), and overwhelmingly, for the US in terms of global trade.

PAN-EUROPEAN POLICY

On a pan-European level, there are two main bodies that produce and control audiovisual policy, the European Commission and the Council of Europe. The following sections will trace the development of audiovisual policy in both of these institutions and evaluate their current activities. European filmmakers and policy makers have been defending their right to protect their film industries and to develop policy in support of these industries in light of criticism from the MPAA over what they see as protectionism.

THE EUROPEAN COMMISSION

The European Commission has recognised the need to develop policy in support of the film industry from both an industrial and a cultural perspective. The need to protect the cultural industries was enshrined in Article 128 of the Treaty of European Union which came into force in 1993. The European Commission is active in support for the film industry in three main areas, continually assessing the legal case for state support for the film industry in line with competition legislation, protection of film heritage, in terms of archiving European films across the member states and promoting the European film industry. This section will focus on developments regarding the promotion of the European film industry. Article 128 was followed by the establishment of the Mésures pour Encourager le Development de L'Industrie Audiovisuelle (MEDIA Programme) in 1987. The first stage of the programme, MEDIA I ran a pilot scheme from 1987 to 1990, and in 1990 it became a full Community programme. MEDIA, in its first form, was heavily criticised for being too fragmented and having too low a budget (Finney, 1996; Dale, 1997). This programme was replaced by MEDIA II, which ran from 1995 to 2000. This programme moved away from financing many diverse activities towards a concentration upon training, development and distribution. While the majority of its budget was invested in distribution activities, as lack of access to distribution was seen as the greatest obstacle for European filmmakers, the need to provide development funding was also acknowledged, as European member states' public support for film focused upon production. Finally, MEDIA II invested in training initiatives across Europe aimed at all areas of the film industry from scriptwriting, through initiatives like Moondance and Arista, to production and financial considerations, through the support of the initiatives such as the Media Business School and Strategics, a programme dedicated to training film professionals in film marketing.

MEDIA II was recognised as being more commercially orientated than its predecessor and aimed at developing a more sustainable film industry across the member states (Jäckel, 2003). This programme required film companies to develop relationships with co-producers in other member states and to develop business plans with an emphasis on developing a slate of films rather than one film at a time. Jäckel (2003) summarised the achievements of MEDIA II as increasing the number of films which travelled outside national borders from 246 in 1996 to 456 in 1999; supporting 145 training initiatives which involved having partnerships with more than 400 institutions throughout the member states. Criticisms of the programme were that it no longer financially supported production, that it benefited larger companies rather than individuals (Jäckel, 2003), and that it was slow in responding to applications, according to one of the programme co-ordinators (interviewee).

MEDIA Plus came into force in 2001 with an increased budget of €400 million over five years. MEDIA Plus moved from supporting the development of single projects to supporting single projects in addition to assisting companies with established track records that wanted to develop a slate of projects. In addition it continued to support distribution and training activities, as well as promotion and the provision of funding for 'pilot projects', from the multimedia industries like prototypes for video games. One of the problems in developing the MEDIA Programme which was encountered while I worked there and echoed by the Commission official whom I interviewed later, was the difficulty in predicting changes in technology and how such changes will impact upon the nature of the film and other audiovisual industries.

MEDIA 2007 which is currently running (2007–2013) has an increased budget of €755 million to cover training, project development, distribution and promotion of films around Europe. On January 9th 2009, the European Commission announced a new programme, MEDIA MUNDUS which will run from 2011 to 2013 and will provide support for European filmmakers working with filmmakers from what are termed 'third countries', i.e. countries outside the remit of the MEDIA Programme (http://ec.europa.eu/information_society/media/docs/mundus/mm_09_en.pdf).

In addition to the MEDIA Programme, which focuses entirely upon the film and related audiovisual media, the European Commission has various other programmes which provide financial and structural support for the film industry. Framework Five, Six and Seven, and the European Structural Fund contribute more financially to the film industry than MEDIA. These programmes have wider aims and as they are not directly concerned with the development of policy which supports the film industry, they will not be analysed in detail here. Suffice to say that each of these programmes is charged with developing the member states in general through various infrastructural measures, the effects of which are inevitably shared by those in the audiovisual sector. Another area of public policy which impacts upon the film and other audiovisual industries is the European Commission's Competition Directorate. It is here that proposed mergers and acquisitions are considered and judgements made regarding the impact they will have upon competition in the marketplace. A number of cases have come before the Competition Directorate regarding companies involved in the film industry.

Despite the work undertaken by the European Commission, Europe's film industry is always overshadowed by Hollywood. This domination has not escaped the attention of the Commission who examined the business practices of the Hollywood majors in Europe upon receiving complaints about anti-competitive practices in the distribution and exhibition sectors, but due to lack of evidence, no charges were brought against the majors. Nonetheless this, anecdotal evidence such as that expressed by Eberts and

Illott (1990), Kuhn (2003) and a number of those interviewed for various film marketing projects over the last ten years, supports the view that practices such as block booking and negotiation over release dates are widespread. The activities of the European Commission in developing policy which supports the European film industry are supplemented at a European level by the activities of the Council of Europe through its programme, Eurimages, which is discussed in the following section.

EURIMAGES

Eurimages (http://www.coe.int/t/dg4/eurimages/default_en.asp/) a French initiative, was established by the Council of Europe in 1988 (Jäckel, 2003) with the intention of consolidating public funding from the twelve founding members in order to develop co-production and distribution of films from these member states. There are now 33 members, with Lithuania the last to join in May 2007. Eurimages is financed by annual subscriptions from member states in addition to various legacies and private sources of funding that the programme has received. Wayne (2002) asserts that approximately fifty percent of Eurimages funding comes from the private sector. Member states should contribute an amount which is calculated based on GDP and the population size (Wayne, 2002). Eurimages is administered from Strasbourg, where the Council of Europe is based. Jäckel (2003) asserts that Eurimages has a greater "cultural" remit than the European Commission programmes, which have more commercially focused aims. In supporting this claim, Jäckel (2003: 76) draws upon the words of Eurimages Executive Secretary, Ryclef Rienstra, in describing the main aim of the fund as "not to get its money back but to support an activity which is both industrial and cultural, and which asserts Europe's identity".

Unlike MEDIA, Eurimages provides production finance, but like the MEDIA Programme, it is criticised for providing contributions which are too low to make a substantial difference to European producers (Jäckel, 2003). As the programme's intention is to develop a European film industry, it aims at developing networks of filmmakers from different member states (Wayne, 2002). Initially, productions were required to have three partners for feature films and two partners for documentaries in order to qualify for funding; and production companies from non-member states were allowed to apply, but their contribution was restricted to 30% of the budget (Jäckel, 2003). The support is provided in the form of what Finney (1996) classified as "soft loans". These loans are repayable, but are interest free (hence the classification as soft loans). The loans are repayable only after the film makes a profit.

The UK joined Eurimages in 1993 but left again in 1996. Both Wayne (2002) and Jäckel (2003) stress that the mood among producers in the UK at the time was in favour of remaining as members. This illustrates how the film industry operates in a wider political context which needs to be recognised. The UK's decision to leave the programme seems strange when it is acknowledged that UK filmmakers increasingly became involved in co-productions during their membership of Eurimages. Thirty four percent of all films produced in the UK in 1995 had secured some funding from Eurimages (Wayne, 2002). Both Wayne (2002) and Jäckel (2003) show how the British film industry was a net beneficiary of the scheme during its short membership and that the sudden decision to leave Eurimages was poorly received by British filmmakers.

DEVELOPMENT OF FILM POLICY IN THE UK

Film policy in the UK has been much debated and arose largely in order to safeguard the indigenous industry from the power of Hollywood. However, early attempts at doing so did not have the intended result. As documented by Mullally (1946: 10) and Petrie (1991), the first Cinematograph Films Act was adopted in 1927 reserved an annually increasing share of exhibition time for British films and obliged renters of imported films to acquire a proportion of British films, known as "the renter's quota". According to Mullally, this did result in an increase in production of British films, but these films were not of a high quality due to the pressure applied by the Americans to produce cheap films in order to fulfil their quota obligations. This period of producing "quota quickies" remained from 1927 until 1933 when United Artists began to look for higher quality films which they could import to the US in the face of market pressure from the MPAA.

Historically, access to distribution has been one of the principle problems faced by European filmmakers. There have been various attempts to overcome this structural impediment, some of which are documented in the preceding sections. In the case of the British industry specifically, the need to improve access to film distribution inspired the 1927 Film Act. This resulted in the first of a number of attempts to create a vertically integrated film consortium, where production would be financed through the profits from distribution. This early attempt failed according to Petrie (1991) due to its partnership with the US studios that safeguarded their interests at the expense of the British film industry.

This left the way open for J. Arthur Rank, head of the Rank Organisation, to establish his vertically integrated film organisation during the 1930s and 1940s. Rank's investment in the various filmmaking activities from production (including studio facilities ownership) to distribution and exhibition are well documented (Petrie, 1991; Mullally, 1946; MacNab, 1993). Mullally's depiction of Rank himself and the Rank organisation are overwhelmingly negative, focusing on Rank's promotion of religious causes through his media empire and the monopolistic presence the Rank organisation occupied in the British film industry during this period. MacNab (1993), on the other hand, focuses on the positive side of the Rank empire, affording J. Arthur Rank the title of possible saviour of the British Film Industry during this period in saying that Rank succeeded in bringing the disparate elements of British film culture together.

> *In his bid to set the industry on its feet, he intervened on every level. He pioneered technical research and developed equipment. He invested in 'B' pictures. He started up a 'charm school' to generate stars. He financed the making of children's films, newsreels, cartoons and educational shorts as well as features. He even bought a meteorological company so that his units on location would know when it was going to rain. For a brief moment in the mid-1940s, it seemed as if he had managed to introduce a measure of harmonious sanity to the schizophrenic organism which the British film industry has traditionally been (MacNab, 1993: x–xi).*

Nevertheless, both positive and negative accounts of Rank highlight that while Rank's stated purpose in forming his film empire was to regain market share for British filmmakers in the American market, he had little actual success in doing so (MacNab, 1993; Mullally, 1946). Britain's economy was weak in the aftermath of World War II and the main focus of Attlee's post-war Government was upon providing the basics, such as food and shelter, for the British people. In 1947 the British government, in an attempt to vastly increase exports and reduce imports, used increased import taxes on American films as one of a number of such measures. Hollywood responded to this ad-valorem duty whereby 75% of an American film's box office earnings would go to the British Exchequer, by claiming it was illegal (MacNab, 1993: 173). This action, known as the Dalton Duty (after then Chancellor of the Exchequer, Hugh Dalton) is in keeping with what Ulff-Møller (2001) referred to as the diplomatic wars, which existed between European and American governments over the film industry.

The British rationale for imposing these measures was so that they could afford to keep purchasing goods from the US. However, this tax was seen as contravening the spirit of the British Loan Agreement, a programme of loans established to allow British firms to borrow funds from the US in order to support the reconstruction of the post-war economy, and in breach of the British/American reciprocal trade agreement. The Hollywood studios refused to export any more films to Britain until the tax was lifted. Rank played an important role in the ensuing negotiations due to his professional relationship with the American majors. They needed access to his exhibition circuits in the UK, while he needed their distribution networks in the US. While Hollywood films monopolised British screens, British films were seen in the US as foreign films despite their shared language according to MacNab (1993: 178). This relegated them, irrespective of subject matter, to the art house or specialist category, which did not hold much negotiation power on the distribution circuits. Art house is a heavily debated term, but in general, it is applied to films which are considered artistic as opposed to purely commercial.

The boom in film production which occurred in the mid-1930s was seen as the beginning of Britain's road back to prominence in the global film market. At that time there were three main groupings which controlled the structure of the British film industry. One of these grouping was American controlled and consisted of the companies associated with the MPAA. The next was the Anglo-American grouping, United Artists, which had acquired a number of financial interests in British companies in order to secure access to films for their US market and was closely tied to the British Odeon group. And, finally, two independent film industry empires, Associated British Pictures and Gaumont-British (Mullally, 1946: 11) were in existence at that time.

By 1941, the Rank Organisation had gained control of the UK film industry through a series of expansion programmes. As a result of this, Rank now had controlling interests in film studios, production companies, distribution companies and in exhibition circuits (Petrie, 1991). In addition to this, as noted by Petrie (1991) and Mullally (1946), Rank had very highly developed relationships with US film companies such as Fox, United Artists and Universal. The power which Rank was now able to exert over the film industry, in addition to its strong links to US companies are cited by Petrie (1991) as contributing to the production of the Palache Report in 1944, "Tendencies to Monopoly in the Cinematograph Industry". This report led to calls for greater state intervention in the film industry, but was not acted upon by the government at that time.

When the Dalton duty was removed, American films flooded the British market again. Once more, the British film industry was calling out for the need for public intervention. Finally, the government responded with the establishment of the National Film Finance Corporation (NFFC) in 1949

(Petrie, 1991: 56). The NFFC acted as a film financer, providing repayable loans which would partially finance film production. It was established in order to complement existing sources of finance, rather than as a film production subsidy. Despite some successful films, such as *The Third Man* (1946), *Saturday Night and Sunday Morning* (1960) and *Gregory's Girl* (1981), benefiting from this source of finance, the fund lost a lot of money. Petrie (1991) attributes this to their provision of 'end money', which was used in order to finish off a film, and was repaid once the earlier production finance had been recouped.

The second state intervention in the UK at that time was the Eady Levy. This scheme was based on similar schemes in France and Italy where exhibitors paid a proportion (levy) of each ticket price into a fund established for the benefit of British film producers. In return, entertainment duty would be decreased for those agreeing to pay this levy. In 1957, this was changed from a voluntary scheme to a statutory arrangement. Petrie (1991) cites the liberal use of this production finance in explaining why it was not as successful as the similar French or Italian schemes. Like many public policy initiatives which have been established across Europe since then, it was used as a source of production finance by American companies who established production interests in the UK in order to access the fund.

As cinema audiences declined in the UK with the rise in popularity of television, there was a resultant rationalisation in cinema exhibition, with only those with sufficient resources surviving. Many independent exhibitors went out of business during this period, resulting in a consolidation of the American control of the British film industry. This was recognised by Dickinson and Street (1985: 238) when they defined the film industry in the UK during the 1960s as "Anglo-American" rather than British. This resulted in the vulnerability of British filmmakers and, in the 1970s, when US audiences began to embrace the New Hollywood films such as *Easy Rider* (1969) and *The Graduate* (1967) (Biskind, 1998), the US majors withdrew from production in the UK.

The British film industry was in crisis in the early 1970s, but the Conservative Government responded by reducing financial support for the film industry. When the Labour Party regained power in 1974, despite commissioning the Terry Committee to evaluate the film industry, they did not introduce any new support systems at this stage. Public policy in the UK film industry continued in this manner until the Conservative Government introduced Capital Allowances in 1979, which allowed film companies to treat films as plant and machinery for depreciation purposes. This allowed film investors to write off their film investments in the first year. This *n. 際頂回祖 ·*

scheme developed until the Government decision to phase it out between 1984 and 1986. A similar sale and leaseback scheme has since been reintroduced by the Labour Government and has benefited film investors since the late 1990s. In 1985, the Conservative Government also abolished the Eady Levy and the NFFC and replaced this with the British Screen Finance Consortium.

THE CURRENT POLICY ENVIRONMENT IN THE UK FILM INDUSTRY

A unified and strategic approach to policy making in the UK film industry is a very recent development. The British Film Council was established in November 1999 in order to develop the film industry and film culture in the UK. The formation of the Film Council was the result of the amalgamation of all of the disparate film bodies in the UK into one strategic body. This development was a welcome change as the previous structure of the UK policy making system was not capable of providing a strong enough response to competition from the US. The two objectives of the Film Council reflect the council's desire to unify the industry around long term and pluralist objectives: 'Developing a sustainable UK film industry' and 'Developing film culture in the UK by improving access to, and education about, the moving image' (Film Council, 2000).

British Film Council. late 1990s

The Film Council promotes a desirable policy discourse, which uses key terms of social responsibility such as 'sustainability' and 'widened access'. The Council propagates sustainability for local producers through restructuring the industry and offers support in the form of financial subsidies based on thematic priorities. It also promotes widened access to non-mainstream and national productions and a commitment to increasing diverse audience participation in cinema going. It is too early to appraise the effectiveness of these policies, bearing in mind that the period from production to consumption is on average between two and eight years for films. Despite this, critics of public subsidy such as Alexander Walker, former film reviewer for the London *Evening Standard* unjustifiably attack these policy initiatives, claiming that they reinforce the production of inferior quality films rather than support the development of a sustainable indigenous industry.

The British Film Institute (BFI) has also been realigned to fit in with these new objectives of the British Film Council, its parent organisation. The BFI is now responsible for increasing public appreciation of film, which can be achieved through improving public access to cinema, film heritage and educational provision.

BFI.

BFI in ARE
exhibition

The Film Council recognised a number of weaknesses in the British film industry in relation to the exhibition sector, both in terms of industry provision and audience tastes. British films are not given priority by distributors and perhaps in response to this, demand for and take up of Hollywood films is greater than for UK films. They also identified the failure of the industry to reflect British society as a whole, both in social and cultural terms. In line with other European film councils (or equivalents) the Film Council is committed to increasing audience access to films from other European countries in exchange for British films achieving greater audience exposure across Europe. In order to realise this commitment, they will need to seek ways to make British film more appealing for the European audience. Since its formation, the UK Film Council has overseen a number of projects aimed at increasing access for British and other European filmmakers to audiences (schemes like BFI @ UCI and the digital screen network), to increase diversity on screen and behind the camera, to tackle piracy and to fund film production, distribution and exhibition. In addition, the Film Council has committed itself to ensuring that British film receives appropriate exposure. As a non-commercial body, the Film Council can concentrate on widening access to non-mainstream film, unlike commercial organisations. In trying to achieve its aims, the Film Council recognises the need to work with the private sector in order to encourage a change in terms of film distribution and consumption provision within the UK. In working with organisations like Arts Alliance who were put in place to oversee the Digital Screen Network, the Film Council is actively seeking to influence commercial policy of film exhibitors. In addition, the UK Film Council recognises the need to develop policy aimed at widening access to films for audiences and have a number of programmes which have this aim. In particular, the Digital Screen Network and the Prints and Advertising Funds are designed in order to increase access to non-mainstream film across the UK. To date, these schemes have had some success, with audience attendance for foreign language films increasing over the last number of years.

The European Union has implemented anti-trust laws and a competition policy in order to curb state intervention and to promote a 'free enterprise' system. The practices of the 'major' distributors were investigated by the Mergers and Monopolies Commission (MMC) in 1998 and the European Commission's Competition Directorate in 1999. However, it was found that the 'majors' were not engaging in anti-competitive practices. Despite this, due to their size and strength it is extremely difficult for independent distributors to exist in a market which is dominated by the majors. Nevertheless, PACT/MMC (1994) found that films distributed by independent companies recouped a greater percentage of their budget than those distributed by the majors in the UK. The domination of the market by the 'majors' constitutes a grey area between ethical and legal legitimacy, although legal objections can be avoided in the present climate of deregulation, the ethical stance of the majors bodes ill in terms of widening access and removing barriers to entry for small independent companies.

The national and institutional policies in the UK rely on self-regulation of the film industry, rather than recourse to legislation. Stiles (1997: 47) explained the reasons why self-regulation is seen as appropriate by the British government. Firstly, legislation, with its reactive stance, does not necessarily guarantee better behaviour; secondly, particularly in the creative industries, a legalistic approach may hinder innovation and creativity, and lastly, change induced by self-regulation is more effective and immediate than change proposed by legislation. However, it should be noted that self-regulation would be a sound alternative to legislation if the film business were to observe these self-imposed controls. Frequent breaches of established codes of conduct may ultimately require legislative controls. However, as far as the film industry is concerned, self-regulation is currently promoted as a viable method for promoting inclusive marketing practices. Schaefer and Kerrigan (2008) have examined the implications of such disintegrated and self-regulated control within the film industry and noted that there may be a need for increased intervention in order to safeguard non-commercial considerations.

The following sections will look at the film industries in South Korea, Denmark and Nigeria as they offer insight into how policy influences film-making and marketing practices. In the case of South Korea, the combination of liberalisation of the economic environment with increasing focus on the film industry resulted in the industry developing in a particular way. The Danish film industry has also benefitted from policy aimed specifically at developing the market for and competitiveness of Danish films. Finally, the Nigerian case offers a counterpoint to these industries as the industry there has developed without any state intervention. Through considering the impact of these various environments on the films produced and the consumption of films, we may understand how mimicking Hollywood is not the answer to the development of competitive, creative film industries in other countries.

DEVELOPMENTS IN THE SOUTH KOREAN FILM INDUSTRY

While the majority of national film markets are dominated by US films, South Korea provided an encouraging case study for smaller film industries during the 1990s and early years of the twenty first century; 1954 to the end of the 1960s has been depicted as a 'golden age' for South Korean cinema (http://koreanfilm.org/history.html), as cinema admissions increased in line with the number of domestic films produced. Yim (2002) identifies concerns regarding national identity as central to South Korean cultural policy. As Yim (2002) points out, this is in common with the majority of cultural policy systems which clearly link cultural policy with issues of identity. In contrast, the 1970s was seen as a period where censorship inhibited quality and quantity of films produced and cinema audiences declined. Park (2002) in an in-depth discussion of the development and impact of censorship between 1987 and 1992 names this censorship as the most significant impediment to the development of Korean films. This censorship began to relax in the early 1980s and the 1980s also saw significant changes to the industrial environment within which film was produced. Jin (2006) characterises the industrial changes of the 1980s as almost detrimental to the film industry as the previous authoritarian policy was replaced with more neo-liberal policies encouraging inward investment and liberalisation of the market. The picture is quite mixed as some of the relaxation in the regulatory environment provided advantages for local filmmakers, while others threatened them by opening up the market for US imports.

In 1983, Korean films held 51% of market share (Kim, 2004: 212) in the domestic marketplace. In 1984 regulations which had been in place restricting film production to a number of large companies were relaxed, allowing independent domestic film producers to enter the market. In 1987, import restrictions were lifted which opened the door to inward investment and allowed Hollywood studios to set up in South Korea (Kim, 2004). Park (2002) characterised this move as a 'side effect' of trade negotiations between South Korea and the US. Following this, the numbers of domestic films released in comparison to imports significantly declined and this decline was accompanied by a reduction in box office earnings for the domestic films in the face of international competition. The main support mechanism which remained in place during this time was the film quota which required Korean films to be shown for 146 days per year in Korean cinemas (Berry, 2003). Berry refers to the struggle which South Korean filmmakers engaged in during 1998 and 1999 when the quota system was threatened during talks prior to South Korea's admission to the WTO. South Korea is very dependent on trade with the US. In 2005, it was estimated that the US was the third largest export market for South Korean goods following China and Japan (Manyin and Cooper, 2006).

While the cultural significance of the film industry allowed for an exception to be made at this stage, the US continued to exert pressure on the government of South Korea and eventually succeeded in gaining concessions in this area. In January 2006, the screen quota was halved (Manyin, 2006). Manyin and Cooper (2006) refer to disagreements over liberalisation of the markets for beef, automobiles, pharmaceuticals and film as impediments to moving forward on a free trade agreement between the two countries. This is reminiscent of negotiations during the Uruguay Round of the GATT negotiations where European countries finally achieved a cultural exception for audiovisual products.

During the period immediately following the liberalisation of the film industry, the number of films produced in South Korea increased dramatically, as did the number of imported films shown in South Korea. Park (2007) states that non-domestic films were no longer viewed as a scarce resource during this period, and therefore consumers could be more discriminating about imported as well as domestic films. Park also describes the conditions which lead to the rise of what is now known as the Korean New Wave (or Korean Wave). Firstly, as noted above, prior to this phase of liberalisation, the number of film production companies allowed was strictly controlled by the government, censorship was a dominant force and therefore, filmmakers learning their craft during this period were influenced by this institutional environment. According to Park (2007), filmmakers coming into the industry in the latter part of the 1980s until the mid-1990s did not come from this system. Many of them had developed their work through making 16-mm film and had not worked in the established state controlled film companies. Paquet (2005) also refers to the transition to commercially driven filmmaking which occurred in the early 1990s following the liberalisation of the film market. This period is characterised as one in which South Korean films dominated the home market and performed well in many international markets. Alongside the success of South Korean film, music and television programmes found very eager export market, particularly in neighbouring countries such as Hong Kong, China and Japan (Shim, 2006). Shim (2006) draws our attention to specific economic factors which may have also contributed to the success of South Korean audiovisual products during the late 1990s. This coincided with the Asian financial crisis and Shim (2006) points out that Korean television drama, which became popular in this period, was much more affordable for neighbouring countries than other international audiovisual products. This financial consideration may have impacted on developing audience tastes for South Korean audiovisual products.

There are possibly two significant triggers which signal the beginning of the popularity of domestic films in the South Korean market. Shim (2006) characterises the domestic market as drawing its last breaths in the early

1990s, prior to the release of *Sopyonje* (1993). Shim (2006) surmises that domestic audiences responded to the subject matter; the film was about an itinerant Korean family who performed a traditional form of music 'pansori' which, according to Shim was neglected in the rush to Americanisation which was overtaking the country. Shim draws parallels between this dying and neglected art form and the Korean film industry at that time. Around this time, the government began to recognise the film industry as worthy of investment, not just from a cultural perspective, but also in terms of its commercial potential. With government encouragement, large South Korean companies (*chaebŏl*) such as Daewoo and Samsung entered into the film industry and provided their experience of operating in a competitive global environment (Paquet, 2005). *Marriage Story* (1992) was the first film to be part financed by the chaebŏl, as 25% of the budget came from Samsung (Paquet, 2005). It is not surprising to see this development as makers of hardware such as VCRs can be seen to have a vested interest in the development of the film market. The more popular watching films becomes, the more people are likely to purchase high quality hardware on which to watch these films. This move can be seen as similar to that of Phillips when they entered the film market and is similar to the development of the video film movement in Nigeria in the 1990s. Following their initial entry into the film industry, the chaebŏl engaged in vertical integration, similar to that which occurred in the US in the early film years. When the Asian financial crisis threatened the stability of the *chaebŏl*, venture capitalists entered the film market, which by this time was seen as a secure and profitable venue for investment (Paquet, 2005).

For many, the release of action/thriller *Shiri* in 1999 heralded the start of what Shin and Stringer (2007) refer to as the debate around the Korean blockbuster and the interplay between the indigenous film industry and Hollywood. The film is significant for a number of reasons. Firstly, admissions for this film soared in comparison to any other recent domestic film. Secondly, this film became what Shin and Stringer (2007) refer to as a cultural phenomenon. It was a key taking point in the domestic market and related products such as the first shown in the film and the album which featured the theme tune of the film sold in unprecedented quantities. However, Shin and Stinger (2007) evaluate the significance of *Shiri* (1999) in terms of both the centrality of the themes of the film to social and political life in Korean at that time as well as the signalling of an appropriate type of Korean blockbuster which incorporated relevant themes within a well-executed plot and high quality audiovisual product. For Shin and Stinger (2007), *Shiri* (1999) can be seen as an attempt to 'out Hollywood Hollywood', or to convince local audiences of the superiority of domestic films.

In providing many of the elements associated with Hollywood thrillers to the domestic audience, but setting this within a specifically Korean storyline (the conflict within North and South Korea), this point is reinforced.

Following this period, Korean New Wave films achieved a golden period of success in both domestic and international markets. Such films were both commercially and critically acclaimed. But, while this success was welcomed, the turn towards the commercial has been criticised by some who call for a more artistic approach to filmmaking in Korea. Shim (2006) refers to the slogan 'learning from Hollywood' in characterising the approach to the development of the film industry in South Korea. However, in line with other commentators, what seems to have worked for South Korean filmmakers is their ability to apply the industrial lessons of Hollywood to locally inspired scenarios. The filmmaking processes which developed under the control of the chaebŏl privileged clearly identifiable genres and star driven films, much like their Hollywood counterparts (Paquet, 2005) and a similar pattern of imitation of successful films which took place in the UK film industry (as discussed above) was evident in the South Korean industry at this time. Paquet (2005) stresses that although the large chaebŏl who had entered the market motivated by increasing the market for related hardware had moved out of the film industry by the end of the 1990s many of the practices which they developed remained within the industry.

This marked a new phase of activity within the industry as the focus shifted from developing large, vertically integrated companies, to investing in film finance alone. The venture capitalists that entered the industry during this period were interested in relatively fast returns on investment and controlling production costs. The combination of the business know how, a new breed of MBA students entering the film industry coupled with the rise of a number of film school trained creative personal saw the industry flourish since the mid-1990s (Shim, 2006). In this period of government support, strong private sector investment in film and a surge of creative talent, the Korean New Wave films outperformed other non-Hollywood/Bollywood films. However, recent years, notably since the reduction of the screen quota, have seen this success wane a little and there are questions being raised regarding the sustainability of the level of success of South Korean films, both at home and in the international marketplace.

THE DANISH FILM INDUSTRY

While the global film industry is dominated by US films, considerations of the structural dimension of the film industry must also include analysis of much smaller filmmaking countries. Mathieu and Malou Strandvad (2008) studied the Danish film industry in their attempt to provide a ten parameter typology within which to compare film production systems. The Danish film industry is worthy of study for a number of reasons. Denmark is a small country which is linguistically isolated. Lorenzen (2008) found that film industries with sizable home markets, such as India and China, had a better chance of success than smaller countries. Denmark has a population of around five and a half million which results in a very small domestic market. Despite this, according to Bakker (2003) the activities of the Danish Nordisk company resulted in a flourishing film industry at the turn of the twentieth century. According to the Danish Ministry of Culture prior to the 1960s, Denmark had a very successful, privately funded film industry. Much of the funding for film came from a cinema levy which was established in 1938 and abolished in 1972. These funds were directed back into the production of films seen to have 'cultural value' (http://www.kum.dk/sw3076.asp). The Danish Film Museum, founded in 1941 was established in order to preserve cinema in Denmark.

The establishment of the Danish Film Institute (DFI) in 1972, following the Film Act of that year saw an increase in the level of state involvement (control) of the film industry. Prior to this, support had been provided for the Danish Film Museum (since 1950) and for the National Film Board of Denmark (established in 1938) which supported the production and distribution of educational films (http://www.kum.dk/sw3076.asp). Through a series of subsidies and support mechanisms, there was a transition from largely privately funded film to the majority of films receiving support from the DFI. In 1997, the National Film Board of Denmark, Danish film Institute and Danish Film Museum were merged into one organisation which continued life as the Danish Film Institute.

The Danish film industry can be characterised as a tightly knit network of film professionals. Most Danish filmmakers have graduated from National Film School of Denmark in Copenhagen. Mathieu and Strandvad (2008) characterize the Danish film industry as operating within an institutional framework clearly understood by the actors which make up the industry and stress the high context nature of interactions within the Danish film industry.

Similarly to other European film support programmes since the 1990s, the DFI provides support for development, production and distribution of Danish films, within the Danish market and internationally. Since 2008, the DFI has begun funding computer game development in recognition of the continuing convergence occurring in the media sectors (http://www.dfi.dk/english/about/aboutdfi.htm).

Mathieu and Strandvad (2008) identify the period from the late 1980s onwards as one of significant recognition for the Danish film industry. In 1987 and 1988, Danish films won Academy Awards for Best Foreign Film with *Babette's Feast* (1987) and *Pelle the Conqueror* (1988), respectively. Following this period of critical acclaim, the Dogma 95 movement brought Danish filmmakers to further prominence. The Dogma movement was governed by the 'vow of chastity' which listed the ten rules of filmmaking. The ten rules can be found at http://www.martweiss.com/film/dogma95-thevow.shtml in the declaration made by Lars Von Trier and Thomas Vinterberg. This declaration indicated the determination of the Dogma filmmakers to engage in a form of extreme realist film which has gained a following internationally as well as within the original group of Dogma 95 filmmakers. Alvarez et al. (2005) note that Von Trier established his production company *Zentropa* in 1992 with producer Peter Aalbaek Jensen in order to provide an alternative to the Danish film establishment. Interestingly, since its creation, *Zentropa* can be viewed as part of the distinctive Danish film establishment, with creative personnel moving between the DFI and *Zentropa* and *Zentropa* receiving substantial financial support from the DFI. Alvarez et al.'s description of *Zentropa's* internship scheme, which lasts three years and sees interns move from positions in reception to production positions over the course of the three years can be seen as adding to the tightly knit nature of filmmaking in Denmark. Interns at *Zentropa* must leave following the completion of their three-year period although they may return at a later date (Alvarez et al., 2005).

In the 1990s, the Danish Film Institute introduced a series of measures to support marketing related activities to support Danish film promotion (Kerrigan, 2005). These measures include the development of a recruited audience screening programme where all films supported by the DFI would benefit from RAS testing, which up to that point had only been available to those films picked up for the international market by the US majors. Film marketing expert John Durie consulted to the DFI in developing this scheme. In addition to this, the DFI began to actively promote Danish films in the international marketplace and to develop mechanisms to ensure their domestic success. One of the stipulations for receiving production and distribution support from the DFI is that release dates in the domestic market do not clash with those of other similar domestic films.

Although Danish films have not been receiving so much critical acclaim in recent years, according to the Danish Film Institute (2008), Danish films still account for over 25% of the total box office receipts in Denmark. Danish films were second only to French in terms of performance of European films in the domestic marketplace between 1999 and 2007. Finally, Danish films have accounted for 8 of the top 20 performing films each year between 2005 and 2007.

THE NIGERIAN FILM INDUSTRY

In stark contrast to the highly regulated, government supported Danish film industry is the Nigerian industry, known as *Nollywood*. Similarly to the incorrect categorising of all Indian cinema as *Bollywood*, *Nollywood* cannot be used to describe all film emanating from Nigeria. Again, similarly to the *masala* films of *Bollywood*, *Nollywood* films are associated with common genres, concerns with religion, witchcraft and the contrast between country life and the city. Okome (2007a) traces the history of filmmaking in Nigeria, where the established Yoruba film industry could not survive the economic situation of the 1980s. This builds on Haynes and Okome's (1998) earlier paper which lists a number of problems which faced Nigerian filmmakers at the end of the 1980s. As film stock was imported, Nigerian filmmakers could no longer afford to pay for it due to the devaluation of the Nigerian currency. In addition, there were safety concerns due to civil unrest and the cinemas which were in existence were falling into disrepair (Ebewo, 2007). During this period, the style of filmmaking now known as 'video film' came into being.

In contrast to Francophone cinema in Africa, filmmaking in Nigeria is a commercially motivated endeavour. Low cost filmmaking and distribution due to filming on video (and latterly a slow move to digital filming) has meant that Nigerian video filmmakers can keep costs low and look forward to earning a profit from their films. Barnard and Tuomi (2008) highlight the commercial might of the Nigerian video film industry. Although they acknowledge the difficulty in obtaining accurate figures regarding the value of the industry, Barnard and Tuomi estimate the industry to be worth between $200 million and $300 million in sales per year. Okome (2007a) indicates another distinctive feature of the Nigerian video film industry, its internal focus. While the developments in the Korean and Danish industries referred to earlier in this chapter indicate a clear desire to compete in the international marketplace, Nigerian video filmmakers are catering to a home market of over 100 million people. Similarly to the Indian film market, this enormous domestic market is supplemented by a very substantial Diaspora, particularly in countries such as the UK and USA as well as neighbouring countries. Nigerian filmmakers are concerned with telling local stories, within a local context. Barnard and Tuomi (2008) propose that Nigerian audiences have been able to develop their own film culture due to the failure of Hollywood to infiltrate the Nigerian market. They compare the Nigerian and South African film industries in terms of their exposure to Hollywood films, and in doing so they challenge the applicability of the theory of economic upgrading to the film industry. They conclude that while South African consumers' taste is based on expectations set by the dominant film discourse (Hollywood), Nigerian consumers have had comparatively little exposure to Hollywood cinema.

Okome (2007b) refers to Kenneth Nnebue's film *Living in Bondage* (1992) as the first identifiable Nigerian video film. Okome (2007b) highlights the novelty of this film, and its sequel, *Living in Bondage 2* (1993) in combining traditional storytelling with portraying everyday life. The main character embodies the concerns of Nigeria at that time, the contrast between country life and the corrupting influences of the city. Okome (2007b) also refers to another seminal film in the development of the Nigerian video film, *Osuofia in London* (2003) popularised the comedy as a form in its own right. In analysing the popularity of Nigerian video film, Okome (2007b) draws parallel with the Hollywood industry in focusing on 'manufacturing dreams'.

While gaining a cinema release still dominates the minds of most international filmmakers, the industry in Nigeria is focused on video (and latterly VCD) distribution. Films are watched either at home or in the video parlour (Okome, 2007a), a place where communities come together to watch films. The Nigerian industry relies on a sophisticated distribution network which circulates the hundreds of films which are released each week. Similarly to the success of South Korean films in neighbouring markets, Nigerian films have gained popularity in a number of neighbouring markets and in countries such as the UK and USA through distribution to the Diaspora. While the commercial standing of the Nigerian film industry cannot be called into question, latterly, filmmakers and consumers are turning to questions of quality and calling for an increase in the standards of filmmaking. Barnard and Tuomi (2008) highlight the need for standards of filmmaking and variability in terms of genre in moving forward while highlighting fears among filmmakers that greater regulation of the industry may result in increased censorship.

It can be seen from the above that the Danish film industry has benefitted from state support. Danish film has received critical and commercial success since the late 1980s and although critics have linked an increase in state support with a decrease in creative filmmaking (similarly to critics of Korean state subsidy), it seems that the Danish film industry is focused on developing strong domestic films as well as some of international interest.

It is noted that the global trends in the film industry are towards vertical integration and strategic partnerships. This is so, largely because the

American film industry dominates the global market and presents 'an ideal model' for film industries which aspire to similar commercial success outside their home market. However, it is identified that the course of development for the European film industry contravened the American model when it sought a strategy of fragmentation, through a process of liberalisation and deregulation in the 1980s. Twenty years of undergoing fragmentation and subsequent 'make ups' and 'break ups' between its many small sized firms has resulted in a lack of success for the European industry in challenging American global domination. While the South Korean film industry initially mimicked the vertically integrated structure of the Hollywood industry, latterly, industrial involvement in the industry has focused on film production. The Danish film industry has developed policies in line with the needs of their national film industry, which is a small, linguistically isolated industry. What we can conclude from this chapter is that film policy is important in shaping and developing indigenous film industries and those national film industries serve both industrial and cultural needs within societies.

CHAPTER 5

The Film Marketing Mix

This chapter will begin by introducing the idea of the marketing mix as developed in the wider marketing literature. This will set the scene for a discussion of the key elements which must be considered when offering a film to the market. There are many elements which make up a film, but drawing on existing research on film marketing and film studies and empirical research, key elements of the mix are introduced and discussed with regard to marketing considerations. Culliton (1948) is credited with the original concept of the marketing mix when he proposed the formulation of a recipe for marketing activities. Following this, Borden (1964) developed the term 'marketing mix' which has remained a fundamental concept within marketing management since that time. Although there have been many variations, adaptations and critiques of the marketing mix as a strategic tool, the idea of a checklist of elements to be considered is a useful one. While the marketing mix consists of the various elements to be considered in strategic marketing planning, covering product, price, promotion and place as well as the various additional elements which were added following McCarthy's (1960) original 4 Ps list, the film marketing mix proposed harks back to the original conceptualisation of the marketing recipe. While the particular elements of the conventional marketing mix are not necessarily being retained in this chapter, Culliton's notion of the recipe is being retained and following this, the chapter will outline the key elements which must be considered from a marketing perspective when producing a film.

The film marketing mix proposed in this book is conceived as a recipe for filmmakers and marketers to consider when marketing their film and is presented as a cocktail of clues which consumers look to in order to select films within the marketplace. As will be seen in the discussion of marketing materials later in the book, such clues are culturally bounded (linking to

Bourdieu's, 1984, notion of cultural codes). The film marketing mix comprises of the creative team, actors, script/genre, age classification and release strategy. The creative team incorporates the actors and directors as well as producers, cinematographers and other 'creative' personnel involved in the film. In this way, this chapter moves beyond studies of film marketing which have used the 'star' (namely the leading actor) as a measure of success and of studies of stardom which only focus on the acting talent, overlooking other possible stars which may be recognised by the film's audience. While much of the focus on stars is limited to consideration of casting decisions and star value of actors, this book considers the range of possible 'stars' which a film may contain and argues that different types of film, in terms of genre, budget and so on, determine the identification of the 'star'.

While for big budget, mass appeal films, the star may indeed be the actor, for many smaller films the director, or in some cases the producer, cinematographer or other members of the creative team may play a similar role to that attributed to the actors as stars in works such as Dyer's (2007) seminal book.

THE ROLE OF THE STAR – ACTORS

To date there has been a lot of attention paid to the role played by the lead actor (star) cast in films. This literature can be divided into accounts from film studies academics such as Butler (1990), DeCordova (1985), Dyer (2007) and Kindem (1982) who consider the role of the star in the context of film production and in some instances, film consumption (see Cook, 1979/1980). Within the marketing literature, the star (actor) is generally considered as a variable factored into econometric analyses of film performance at the box office. The literature discussed below does not provide a definite answer as to the marketability of films in relation to 'the star', but it is recognised that the star (lead actor) can often be a point of reference for consumers when choosing particular films. In addition to this, many of the other creative roles can prompt a decision to select particular films from the available offerings; this will be discussed later in this chapter. While this book seeks to go beyond conventional conceptual considerations of the star, the majority of empirical research which examines the star in the film industry is limited to the actor and therefore this chapter will begin with an examination of the impact of the actor on box office success.

Jacobs (1968) divided the factors influencing film choice into five loosely defined areas, with the principal stars seen as the most important factor in attracting an audience. Chapter 2 traced the early development of the film industry and referred to Gomery's (1991) depiction of the independent sector's (which later went on to become the majors) use of stars as a key method of product differentiation. As Balio (1976) and Litman (1998) discuss, the introduction of the stars by the independents at this stage in the industry's development heralded in a new era of product differentiation. In addition to increasing the ability to charge higher fees for films containing stars, the rise of the star system has been seen by King (1985: 46) as a way in which actors can create a 'personal monopoly' through cultivating a unique image. Such an image can be linked to aesthetic factors, associations with certain types of roles or as a sort of quality mark for films within an increasingly crowded marketplace.

The importance of a star's earning capacity is recognised by the *Hollywood Reporter* with their "Star Power" service. It has a database of over 500 actors and actresses around the world, with an indication of their box office potential. This service can be accessed by users who take out various types of subscriptions of the *Hollywood Reporter*. On occasion this appeal is overestimated, as some films do not support big names. A good example of where a filmmaker refused to cast big name stars in a film in order to preserve the integrity of the film was in the case of *Waking Ned Divine* (1998). The writer/director, Kirk Jones was seeking production finance and was offered a deal by a US major on condition that he cast well-known US comedy actors, Jack Lemon and Walter Matthau in the lead roles. Jones refused to make this concession as he felt that the audience would not accept such well-known US actors in the role of farmers from a small village in the West of Ireland. When the film was eventually made, Jones cast Irish character actors Ian Bannen and David Kelly and despite the lack of a well-known Hollywood star, this film was both critically acclaimed in the international marketplace as well as doing well at the box office.

While Jones and his producers were successful in retaining their rights over casting decisions, this can be problematic for filmmakers when trying to secure production finance from the majors who may exert pressure to cast well-known stars in the lead roles in order to increase the attractiveness of the film at the box office. Issues of power and reputation linked to trust can also be seen as playing an important role in determining casting decisions. Kerrigan (2005) showed how in the case of Working Title's film, *Elizabeth* (1998), the marketing team believed that the quality of the script and production values were good enough to support a largely unknown cast and director. In saying this, it must be noted that although the actors cast in this film were, at that time, not recognisable stars, the producers did cast some experienced British actors and a well-known footballer in this film. In using the then Manchester United footballer Eric Cantona in the role of Monsieur de Foix, the producers were accused of stunt casting. However, they were determined to differentiate this film from other British 'frock flicks', the derogatory term used to describe period dramas. This strategy seemed to work and both Geoffrey Rush and Cate Blanchett who starred in *Elizabeth* (1998) went on to become stars after this film was produced. The producers concentrated on casting solid, mainly character actors and some relatively unknown actors in order to give centre stage to the script and cinematography and in this case they were successful.

Their casting strategy for *Elizabeth* was very different to that employed by the producers of another successful British costume drama, *Gosford Park* (2001). In *Gosford Park*, the unique selling proposition was its cast – the producers opting for what is known as an ensemble cast, comprised of some of the most well-known actors in Britain, particularly those associated closely with roles in other costume dramas. This is the more conventional approach to casting for costume dramas and works when there is a strong fit between the brand associations of the actors and the genre of the film. As *Elizabeth* (1998) was not seen as a traditional costume drama, casting actors whose personal brands were heavily associated with this genre would have sent out the wrong message to cinemagoers.

Kerrigan (2005) did highlight the belief of the marketing team and producers of *Elizabeth* (1998) that their track record (having produced some of the most successful independent British films to date) allowed them the freedom to cast as they wished. In contrast to the case of films where recognisable stars may harm the perception and ultimate performance of a film, there are certain types of films which demand the casting of well-known stars. For an example of such a film we can again turn to Working Title, and consider another of their productions, *Notting Hill* (1999). The writer of the film, Richard Curtis, always wanted to make a film about bringing the most famous woman in the world to a friend's house for dinner. In his mind he thought of the actress Julia Roberts or the singer Madonna. When he wrote the screenplay, his first choice to star in the role was Julia Roberts. Julia Roberts has a strong brand as a film star and is associated with lead roles in romantic comedies; in fact, she recently played a character pretending to be Julia Roberts in the film *Oceans 12* (2004). Julia Roberts brand has been established by her playing a number of such roles throughout her career, the most famous of which was the role of a prostitute in the film *Pretty Woman* (1990). In her role in *Notting Hill* (1999), where she played one of the most famous and beautiful actresses in Hollywood, Julia Roberts was both strengthening her brand as a film star and providing a precise fit with the aspirations of the film. The marketing team at Working Title acknowledged that it was a star (actor) driven film and that Julia Roberts was the focus of the film's marketing campaign.

While literature which focuses on the historical development of the film industry highlights the central role played by the studios in establishing early film stars' credentials, Kerrigan (2005) discusses the role of the actor's agent in the power system within today's film industry. Kerrigan's interviewees stressed the control which these agents have over their clients and their instrumentalism in developing their clients' careers. The role played by agents in the US was spoken about during a London Film Festival 2004 panel discussion where producers and directors recounted stories of their first interactions with Hollywood agents. The power of these agents was also discussed in Phillips (1991). Existing film marketing literature which focuses upon predicting earnings in relation to the cast, among other variables, neglects the examination of the relationships which control access to these stars. Therefore, both in terms of casting and in managing actors once they have committed to a film, the importance of maintaining a good relationship with agents cannot be overestimated. If all stars in a particular film are represented by one agent, the act of balancing the demands of one particular star becomes easier than negotiating with a number of different agents all of whom are focused on defending the career and representation of their client. In contrast to the highly contractual nature of relationships between film-makers and actors in the Hollywood system, Lorenzen and Täube (2008) found that stars in Bollywood prefer to work on the basis of trust which sits alongside formal contracts.

The established star (actor) system of the Hollywood studios is seen as one of the key elements of the competitive advantage which the Hollywood majors have over other film industries. Outside of Hollywood, few industries are seen as having such a significant number of film stars. Vincendeau's (2005) account of French film stars highlights the importance of star actors within the economy of the French film industry, while at the same time acknowledging the lack of such a formalised system of managing these stars as is in existence in the Hollywood industry. The importance of the French film stars could be linked to wider discussion of the role of film in French culture and therefore, such well-regarded actors as assured a respected position within French cultural life. As is the case for most non-US actors, only a small number of domestic stars become recognisable in an international context. Examples of those who have gained recognition as stars outside of their domestic marketplace include Juliette Binoche (one of the actors considered by Vincendeau in her book), Penelope Cruz, Javier Bardem, Colin Farrell, Tony Leung and Aishwarya Rai. However, many of these actors from outside the US appear in Hollywood films in order to secure such international recognition.

The appearance of Aishwarya Rai, one of the most well-known Bollywood stars in international films is interesting to consider. Outside the Hollywood system, the Bollywood star system is the only real equivalent in terms of the impact of stars on the industry and Lorenzen and Täube (2008) stress that the star plays a far greater role in the success of mainstream films in Bollywood than in Hollywood while at the same time acknowledging that inclusion of a star does not guarantee box office success. Bollywood stars enjoy lavish lifestyles and widespread acclaim in the same manner as the stars of Hollywood and can be seen as a way into the valuable Indian film audiences. Gurinder Chadha's *Bride and Prejudice* (2004) can be seen as an attempt to bridge British and Indian filmmaking traditions by adapting an quintessentially British story, that of Jane Austin's *Pride and Prejudice* to an Indian context and casting Rai in a film which was essentially made to appeal to Western audiences, the casting can be viewed as an essential marketing element for the film. Rai could attract Indian audiences due to her celebrity and could lend an air of authenticity to the film. Since 2004 Aishwarya Rai has appeared in a number of other Western films, the latest of which being *Pink Panther Two* (2009). Rai is establishing herself as a marketable asset for Western films in the highly competitive Indian market. In contrast to the casting of Rai in *Bride and Prejudice* (2004), in *Slumdog Millionaire* (2008), there was an original aim to cast a well-known Bollywood actor in the lead role, but Loveleen Tandon (casting director/co-director) and Danny Boyle felt that these stars were too good looking and muscular to carry off an authentic depiction of this character and therefore cast a UK actor, Dev Patel, in his first film role. Again, this was an example of casting decisions which took into account the ability of the audience to buy into the characterisation within the film. This need for authenticity in casting decisions was found by Jones and DeFillipi (1993) when looking at the nature of collaboration within the film industry. They cite a casting director who talked about understanding the director's vision in order to create a legitimate look for the film.

Other well-known Bollywood stars include Amitabh Bachchan, who has appeared in over one hundred and fifty films since the 1960s, his son Abhishek Bachchan (who is married to Aishwarya Rai), Shahrukh Khan and Aamir Khan. The second largest film industry in India is known as Tollywood due to the language spoken in the filmmaking region of Andhra Pradesh, Telugu. Tollywood also has a star system, the biggest stars being Chiranjeevi and Rajnikant. Due to their popularity, film stars are often used in political campaigns in India (http://www.deccanchronicle.com/hyderabad/wanted:-actors-election-campaign-780 and http://in.rediff.com/movies/2004/mar/12stars.htm). Also it is common to find film actors change their career to politics later in their careers. Due to their popularity as film actor, the probability of winning election is higher than an intellectual. Therefore, it is also not uncommon to see the film stars of Indian cinema (alongside cricketers) used in the promotion of big brands. Nayar (2009) discusses Indian film stars (and cricketers) in terms of their star power in his analysis of celebrity culture.

The Nigerian film industry, Nollywood, also has an established star system. In contrast to most European film industries, Nollywood is run on very commercial terms. Power is held by the marketers and distributors who finance the films. Here, in addition to actors, the producer is a well-known figure. Genevieve Nnaji has established herself as one of the most popular stars in Nollywood and her film star credentials have seen her crossing over into the music industry as well as endorsing large consumer brands and launching her own fashion label. Kate Henshaw Nuttall who won the best actress award in the African Academy Movie Awards in 2008 and is very popular among audiences for Nigerian films acknowledge her star potential from a commercial perspective on her website where she talks about expanding the Kate Henshaw Nuttall brand with the help of her husband who has a drinks and fragrance distribution company. This open acknowledgement of the brand power of the film star is an indication of the commercial focus to be found within the Nigerian film industry which differentiates it from European film industries. Similarly, Jim Iyke, who has starred in over 100 films, describes himself as an actor, model, businessman and filmmaker on his website. Ramsey Nouah, a former hip hop star is now associated 'lover boy' roles in romantic films. Comedian Nkem Owoh is another popular male lead and has starred in *Osuofia in London* (2003) and *Osuofia in London 2* (2004) and alongside Nouah, Kyke and Desmond Elliot he is acknowledged as a star in the Nollywood industry.

Joke Silva is another well-known actress in Nigeria and has starred in films such as *The Secret Laughter of Women (1999)* a UK/Canadian co-production. In an industry often depicted as suffering from poor-quality acting, film stars such as Silva and her male counterparts Richard Mofe Damijo and Norbert Young are admired for their longevity and acting ability. Within the very crowded Nollywood market, such stars are a key marketing element in differentiating one film from another.

Hong Kong cinema similarly has a number of well-known stars, some domestically and some, such as Tony Leung, Maggie Cheung, Ziyi Zhang and Li Gong who all star in Wan Kar Wai's *2046* (2004). The star power of these actors in their domestic market can be seen by examining the film poster for this film which features a montage of their faces. This contrasts to the posters in other markets where their names are used rather than their faces. This shows the cultural context within which a star is recognised as a star.

Latterly, research has shown conflicting results regarding the role of the star (actor) in the ultimate success of individual films. Wallace et al. (1993)

ascribe positive and negative values to stars in terms of their impact on box office revenue. De Silva (1998), Neelamegham and Chintagunta (1999), Sawhney and Eliashberg (1996) and Sochay (1994) found that star involvement in a film had a positive result on box office performance. Austin (1989), Litman and Ahn (1998) and Ravid (1999) concluded that the inclusion of a well-known star in the cast of a film played no significant role in increasing earnings. Litman and Kohl (1989) identified that the star had a small role in increasing revenue but was not the most significant factor. De Vany and Walls (1999) found that those films which featured a star were more likely to have a longer run on more screens than those without. However, as they point out, this may be linked to the fact that such films are likely to have a greater overall budget than films without stars, which may account for this box office longevity. Evaluating the impact of stars on the box office performance of films is problematic as it is often dependent on the star in question, the image that this star has, and how the intended audience for the film receives them.

THE STAR – THE NON-ACTOR STAR

The star (actor) is not always the main attraction in a film. For many cinemagoers, the director or cinematographer of the film may be a major draw. For example, the films of Quentin Tarantino have a certain style and following. This is true for many directors, Pedro Almodovar, Stephen Spielberg, Gus Van Sant, Lars Von Triers, Paulo Pasolini and so on. In each case, the attachment of such a director indicates a certain style, genre or quality which appeals to the intended audience. Nowell-Smith (1981) refers to this ability of particular directors to establish a particular style of film, as seeing the author's style as inscribing itself in the "text" of the film resulting in the provision of a coherent enabling device which allows the audience to recognise the film as "authored discourse". As film consumption is conceptualised as a service or experience (see Holbrook and Hirschman, 1982), this brings with it, the risk of disappointment. In conventional (and legal) forms of film consumption, there is no option to try before you buy and no money back guarantee. Film consumers must interpret the cultural codes which are communicated through the marketing process in order to make a choice. In addition to a style of film, directors can also imply a 'grade' of film in terms of quality. Lorenzen and Täube (2008) recognise the director star within the Bollywood film industry. They link the rise of the director as star to the gradual shift among consumer preferences for more complex films where writing and directing are important.

A problem can arise when established directorial style is deviated from, as the previous audience can be alienated without the new audience fully accepting the work of such a director. In Europe, unlike in America, writers and directors largely control the direction of the film. Based on his early experience in the film industry, Andrew Macdonald, producer of cult hits *Trainspotting* (1996) and *Shallow Grave* (1994) and a number of other collaborations with director Danny Boyle stated that;

> They (writers/directors) don't make films for anyone other than themselves. They believe that it's important for them to say their thing and then they give it to the producer and the producer is told to raise the money (MacDonald, quoted in Goodridge, 1995).

Expectations set by previous directorial style or association with a particular genre remain with consumers, much in the way that certain actors are associated with certain genres or styles of film. Deviating from a long established style can be dangerous for a filmmaker, similarly to the danger of typecasting which faces the successful actor. Woody Allen, having moved outside his established setting of Manhattan, has received much criticism for his recent films. Allen fans have turned away from his films and his oeuvre can be divided into Manhattan films and post Manhattan films. Similarly, Oscar winning British director Danny Boyle faced a problem in his early filmmaking career when he switched genres following the success of *Shallow Grave* (1994) and *Trainspotting* (1996). These cult successes had earned Boyle and screenwriter John Hodge a following who responded to the dark, edgy film style. Following on from the success of these films, in particular *Trainspotting*, the creative team wanted to try something different and took on a romantic comedy, *A Life Less Ordinary* (1997). This film will be discussed later in terms of the marketing campaign, but in the context of the director as star, it is significant in illustrating the expectations established within the audience regarding directorial style. *A Life Less Ordinary* was not well received as the central fan base for the 'makers of *Shallow Grave* (1994) and *Trainspotting* (1996)' was alienated by the mainstream nature of this film, having expected a style of filmmaking more in line with the previous films. In an interview at Queen Mary, University of London in 2007, Boyle talked about his determination to make different types of films all the time and his desire as a filmmaker to be challenged and to learn. Although this desire to change style was a risky one in the early stages of his career, what has remained constant has been his commitment to making the best possible film within the genre and style that he takes on. Therefore, while Tarrantino fans can retain a certain level of confidence regarding the style of film which they will get from him, Boyle's followers cannot anticipate the directorial style, but rather the grade of film in terms of artistic integrity. Since *A Life Less Ordinary* (1997), Boyle has made a series of films across a range of genres and contexts and with varying degrees of commercial and artistic success. The culmination of his career came in 2009 with *Slumdog Millionaire* (2008) achieving both commercial and critical success across a number of key film markets. An explanation of the directorial style of Boyle may be seen in Stanley Kubrick's statement (cited in Kagan, 2000: 1) that a film is "the result of the way your mind works, imposed on the semi controllable factors that exist at the time you start...".

Although many film cultures are indeed culturally specific, with a particular filmic tradition and style, in the search for new stories, new perspectives and perhaps critically, new audiences, there have been significant movements of directors outside their domestic marketplaces which indicates the global nature of the film industry. Significantly, many non-US directors work within the US. Directors such as Hong Kong's Wan Kar Wai; Mexican director Alfonso Cuarón; Taiwanese Ang Lee, Irish director Neil Jordan and Indian director, Shekhar Kapur have all directed successful films outside their home markets. In the case of Kapur, his first directorial project outside India was *Elizabeth* (1998). Having a non-British director in charge of a very British subject was part of the deliberate decision by the producers to bring a fresh approach to telling the story of a British monarch.

While the actor star may be an obvious signal or cultural cue for many mass film audiences, more sophisticated audiences may respond to the director as cue. This is particularly the case for more artistic films, for films without recognisable actor stars or for films differentiating themselves from the norm within a particular genre. In the foreword for his book on Stanley Kubrick, Kagan (2000) refers to cine-sophisticated reviewers and viewers who find pleasure in examining and tracing the development of directorial style in the films of particular directors. In highlighting the director's credentials, film marketers can signal that this film will appeal to such cine-sophisticated audiences. Dwelling on the risk element in selecting a film due to its experiential nature, film consumers will look for a cue to minimise uncertainty in film selection. Examples of instances where the director signalled product differentiation can be seen in the case of Paul Greengrass in directing *The Bourne Supremacy* (2004) and *The Bourne Ultimatum* (2007). Greengrass was known primarily as a documentary filmmaker, although he had worked on a series of fiction and non-fiction projects prior to this film. The attachment of Greengrass to this film and to the forthcoming Jason Bourne film created much debate and helped to cement the credentials of the Bourne films as serious spy films, rather than fun of the mill action films.

While the director may be the first port of call in terms of classification, decision making and selection of film for the group of film consumers labelled by Kagan (2000) as cine-sophisticates, other members of the creative team may also act as 'stars' in this context. Depending on the type of film, and the cultural capital possessed by the individual creative team members, they can also adopt this role. Cinephiles or cine sophisticated audiences may find cultural cues in the name of a cinematographer, composer, screenwriter or producer depending on their knowledge and the type of film in question. In turn, these creative team members (including creative producers) may be viewed as the star in some films. In this discussion of non-actor stars, the star could also be seen as the unique selling proposition of the film.

Directors of photography are particularly significant for films which break conventional norms of filmmaking. For example, Hungarian born cinematographer Laszlo Kovacs worked on a number of films before establishing his name through his work on *Easy Rider* (1969) which required him to work with limited technical equipment during the 12-week road trip during which this film was made. Italian cinematographer Vittorio Storaro, collaborated with Bertolucci throughout his career starting with Storaro's work on *La Strategia del Ragno* (1970) (*The Spider Stratagem*). Storaro and Bertolucci worked together on *The Conformist* (1970), which is a seminal film in terms of its style of cinematography. Similarly, screenwriters such as Suso Cecchi d'Amico who has worked with great directors such as Antonioni, Fellini and Scorcese since beginning her career in the 1940s can also act as cultural cues, depicting a certain quality of script and sometimes a certain genre. For example, Richard Curtis, writer for *Four Weddings and a Funeral* (1994), *Notting Hill* (1999) and a number of other British films is well-known for writing comedies for film and television. Film music can also act as a cultural cue. The soundtrack for the film *About a Boy* (2002) consisted largely of original songs from Badly Drawn Boy's Damon Gough. In using Gough's music, the producers could signal that this film should appeal to (male) fans of Badly Drawn Boy's music, and in doing so, distinguish the film from previous Working Title Romantic comedies from the same team which were seen as appealing more to female than male audiences. Famously, Miles Davis provided the soundtrack for Louis Malle's *Lift to the Scaffold*, establishing this film as an iconic cultural artefact for fans of Davis Music. The relationship between film and music is well-established, both creatively and in industrial terms, with many record labels having common ownership with film distributors. The role of film producers is often not fully understood by film consumers, but as many actors and directors take on producing roles (sometimes in the form of an executive producing credit), the producer in such cases can sometimes act as a cultural cue in transferring cultural capital gained through previous roles as director or actor.

SCRIPT/GENRE

While creative personnel such as cast and crew discussed above can be seen as tangible, fixed elements of the film marketing mix, this is much less the case in terms of the script and genre of the film. While a certain amount of interpretation may take place in translating cultural cues relating to such personal into expectations of a particular film, this effect is magnified in the case of the script/genre. This is discussed by Stringer (2005) who stresses that genre classification is not a finite result of rational analysis, with a correct identification being arrived at following film consumption. Rather, Stringer (drawing on Jancovich, 2001), proposes that genre classification itself is a process which can be observed and that such observation reveals much about the audience for film and the social and cultural context within which the film is positioned. While it can be agreed that genre identification is not a fixed entity but more of an emergent, collective concept, such identification in the mind of the filmmaker/marketer is essential in correctly positioning the film and targeting the appropriate audience. As the tastes of cinema audiences move with fashion, and one hit in a particular genre can inspire a revival, as was the case with Les Craven's *Scream* films, which heralded a revival of the teenage horror film. In this book, genre is considered alongside the script, as the script can be seen as central to genre identification. As is the case throughout this book, script and genre will be considered from a marketing context. There are extensive studies on scriptwriting and genre from within the film studies field which have informed much of the thinking in this chapter, but in examining the concepts from a marketing perspective, as part of the film marketing mix, this book moves beyond these discussions.

In Litman's (1983) discussion of the film marketing tools, he stressed the importance of the story. The story is told through a script and the scarcity of good scriptwriters in Europe is constantly cited as a reason why European films do not travel as well as those from Hollywood. This is not a recent complaint in the British film industry; in the post-war years Mullally (1946: 18) observed that "there is a dearth of writers capable of conceiving, and constructing, a good strong story for cinematic treatment". The Rank Organisation, in recognition of the difficulty in finding and developing good screenwriters, developed the Scenario Institute in London (MacNab, 1993: 84–85). As a result, Rank was heavily criticised for trying to control access to high-quality screenplays and in doing so, contributing to the anti-competitive environment which existed in the UK film industry at that time.

Such poverty of screenwriting has also been identified as problematic within the Nigerian film industry and in both cases, an explanation of why this is the case may be clarified by revising the structural problems experienced by European and Nigerian filmmakers. In both cases, little development funding is available. In Nollywood, films are made in very short periods of time and therefore little time is devoted to the script development process. Similarly, lack of development funding in most European industries, has resulted in some films going into production before they are ready. As the development process is often undertaken without funding, screenwriting for film is financially unrewarding. Even in the US, where development funding is more forthcoming through the studios, the role of the writer is often seen as undervalued in comparison to that of the director. This was characterised by screenwriter Charlie Kaufman in his film *Adaptation* (2002), where he played himself as a screenwriter.

It is encouraging that European public policy is starting to recognise the role of the screenwriter and the need to support the development process financially, and perhaps this will result in an improvement of the quality of screenwriters working in Europe. European level writers' programmes, such as Arista and Moondance, fulfil the dual role of providing tutoring for aspiring screenwriters as well as providing networking opportunities for European filmmakers.

As will be examined in more detail later in this book, film consumers look for cultural cues in order to establish what they may gain from watching a particular film. There is an element of chance involved in identifying what will attract audiences when the film is completed. Bowser (1990) and Ellis (1995: 102) examined the trademark genres which existed in American film in the 1920s and remain today. The 'western' typified America and the American film of the time. The 'comedy' became very popular in the 1920s when the first comedy features were made. This was the era of Charlie Chaplin, Harold Lloyd, Harry Langdon, Buster Keaton and Laurel and Hardy. Ellis (1995: 104–105) highlights the history of 'genre films' in the following way:

> *Though the introduction of sound required extreme modifications of style and introduced a new group of comics, the comedy, along with the western, the gangster film, and the musical, remains among the most distinctive, indigenous, and important American contributions to film forms.*

Another popular genre of the time was the 'love story'. These were originally referred to as 'women's pictures'. Although the love story had been around since the beginning of the film industry, it reached its popular plinth in the 1920s as, by this time, women constituted the largest cinema going social group. This is in contrast with the situation today where the main target audience for films are young males who are now the most frequent cinemagoers. Such types of light entertainment appealed to the populace as it enabled them to escape from the humdrum of everyday life. This has remained part of the quintessential appeal of the Hollywood blockbuster to date.

Genre continues to be a key determinant for financial success (Litman, 1983; Litman and Kohl, 1989; De Silva, 1998). However, it can be difficult to predict the genres which will appeal at the time of a film's release – as the lead-time between development and theatrical release can be two years or more, the result can be producing in a genre that has run its course or suffered from overkill (Litman 1983: 160). Speed to market is seen as one of the key advantages in the Nollywood film industry where films are produced and released into distribution in a matter of months and therefore can in theory keep pace with contemporary life. However, in saying this, franchise films are very common in Nollywood cinema with the popularity of one film leading to one or more sequels. Ellis (1995) highlights the popularity of adaptations of successful novels and plays during the 1920s and 1930s. This enthusiasm for adaptations has not faded, the recent success of films such as the *Harry Potter* (2001) films, *High Fidelity* (2000) and 2009 Academy Award nominees *The Reader* (2008), *The Curious Case of Benjamin Button* (2008), *Revolutionary* Road (2008), *Slumdog Millionaire* (2008) and *The Dutchess* (2008), are testament that the trend towards popular adaptations has not ceased. However, the success of the original novel alone does not ensure success as was seen by the relative commercial failure of *Bonfire of the Vanities* (1990) or *Captain Corelli's Mandolin* (2001). Alongside adaptations of novels or non-fiction literature, the recent phenomenon of successful films adapted from graphic novels such as *Hellboy* (2004), *V for Vendetta* (2005) and *Watchmen* (2009) can be seen as extensions of the trend for adaptations. The benefit of such adaptations are that they cater to an existing, clearly defined audience who do not need to look further than the title or indication that it is an adaptation in order to develop another key film marketing aim 'want to see'. However, as will be discussed later in the book in considerations of word of mouth, adaptations can also be controversial if they do not keep true to the original source material.

Bhaumik (2004) traces the evolution of the Bollywood film industry in terms of genre. Bhaumik notes that the Adventure romance was the most popular genre during the silent period, giving way to romantic melodrama and social realism with a strong emphasis on music once they moved to talkies. The 1970s saw the establishment of what has come to be known as the *masala* film which incorporates elements of the romance, drama and comedy and contains song and dance sequences, fight scenes and spectacle (Bhaumik, 2004; Lorenzen and Täube, 2008; Srinivas, 2002). Despite the vast diversity of films produced both within the Hindi speaking industry of Mumbai and across the other major filmmaking regions such as Kerala, Karnataka, Tamil Nadu and Bengal, it is the *masala* film which dominates Mumbai film production as well as the minds of non-Indian film consumers. This style of film gained popularity across the Middle East, many African countries and territories where the Indian Diaspora was a sizable presence. This type of film has become a genre of its own and is still popular within India as well as in international markets.

While what does and does not count as a genre is a well-trodden track within the film studies literature, such discussions should not impede film marketers in their attempt to classify films for their audience. Although the term 'genre film' can be used as a term of abuse to indicate a formulaic film, in marketing terms, we can consider genre as an indication of the experience which the film consumer will have upon watching a particular film. In this way, we can treat genre, from a marketing perspective as a fluid concept. Therefore, there is no definitive list of film genres and a number of terms can be used to identify very similar types of film. Table 5.1 indicates a list of conventional genres, but these should not be considered in any way exhaustive as genre from a marketing perspective must be viewed as a flexible entity.

While genre identification is a key element in preparing the marketing strategy and one of the main components of the film marketing mix proposed in this book, genre identification is not a simple process. This returns us to discussions of marketability versus playability. A highly marketable film is one where there is an identifiable genre which is attractive to a core group of

Table 5.1 List of Possible Genre Classifications		
(Romantic/Black)	Comedy	Thriller
Slapstick	Futuristic	Erotic mystery
Period drama	Children's	Western
Love story	Drama	Biopick
Documentary	Psychological	Road movie
Science fiction	Adventure	Fantasy
Musical	Horror	Animated

film consumers and can be easily communicated to them. On the other hand, many highly playable films are difficult to define in terms of genre. IMDB.com, one of the main sites of information for film fans and professionals alike identifies the film's genre, and usually a film will have more than one descriptor. British film, *Plunkett and MacLeane* (1999), proved problematic in terms of having an identifiable genre which could be seen in examining the marketing materials for this film. There was no clear message regarding genre, but instead an attempt was made to highlight the cast and the upbeat tempo of the film. In the case of another Working Title film, *Elizabeth* (1998) as mentioned above, the producers did not want this film to be depicted as a conventional costume drama, but identified the genre as thriller. This influenced the design of the marketing materials which moved away from the soft focus normally associated with costume dramas in favour of a campaign inspired by *The Godfather* (1972).

AGE CLASSIFICATION

Another important, and much overlooked element of the film marketing mix, is age classification or rating. This rating both restricts access to films as well as acting as a signal to film consumers with regard to the type of film on offer. National or state bodies are responsible for assessing the appropriate classification for an individual film. In the UK the British Board of Film Classification was established in 1912 and the classifications it uses can be seen in Table 5.2.

These ratings varying from the US ratings which are governed by the Motion Picture Association of America which has four categories, G which is

Table 5.2 Film Classifications, BBFC (Adapted from http://www.bbfc.co.uk/policy/policy-thecategories.php)

U – Universal, suitable for all

PG – Parental Guidance, some scenes may be unsuitable for some children

12 – No-one younger than 12 may rent or buy a '12' rated film

12A (cinemas only) – No-one younger than 12 may see a '12A' film in a cinema unless with an adult

15 – No-one younger than 15 may see a '15' film in a cinema. No-one younger than 15 may rent or buy a '15' rated video

18 – No-one younger than 18 may see an '18' film in a cinema. No-one younger than 18 may rent or buy an '18' rated video

unrestricted; PG which is similar to the same rating in the UK; PG-13 where parents are cautioned that the film goes beyond the PG rating but is not in the next category, R which requires those under 17 to be accompanied by a parent or guardian and finally, the highest rating, NC-17 where those under 17 are not admitted (http://www.mpaa.org/FlmRat_Ratings.asp). While these ratings are intended as a guideline for parents in assessing the suitability of a film for their children, Litman (1983) emphasised the impact that a film's rating can have upon the success of a film in market terms. Austin (1980), in agreement with Litman, draws upon Brehm's concept of psychological reactance "which focuses on the specific motivational and behavioural response of individuals for whom a given freedom has been threatened or eliminated" (Austin, 1980: 384). When a film is rated R or X in the US (18 or X in Europe) the film has the aura of something forbidden. The publicity gained by such films as *The Last Temptation of Christ* (1988), David Cronenberg's *Crash* (1996) and *Natural Born Killers* (1994) when the censors wanted to outlaw them, was invaluable. This controversy created 'must see', the feeling that one is missing out on an important cultural reference by not seeing a particular film-which is something that every film marketer strives for.

Brehm's (1966: 9) theory predicts that the individual "will be motivated to attempt to regain the lost or threatened freedoms by whatever methods are available and appropriate" – the more a freedom is threatened, the more it is sought. Therefore, when applied to the rating systems of films, the more forbidden it is to see a film, the greater 'want to see' (the industry term for very strong word of mouth, which creates great anticipation for a particular film) is created. To support this belief empirically, Austin draws upon Herman and Leyens (1977) work (Austin, 1981a). In a study of films transmitted by Belgian based French language TV station, RTB, they concluded that "qualifications make the movies more desirable for the television viewers...movies with advisories are watched more than the movies without them" (quoted in Austin, 1981a: 390).

In some cases, age classifications are controllable. For example, in the case of *Notting Hill* (1999), it was possible to re-dub selected parts of the film in order to edit out words which were considered obscene in the US but were seen as adding to the humour of the film for European audiences. Film producers and distributors must understand the cultural differences and sensitivities at play when submitting films for classification as being given the wrong classification can have serious negative consequences for a film's market performance. Such classifications can act as a clear cultural cue for film consumers in selecting a film at the cinema or for home viewing.

RELEASE STRATEGY

In most film markets, films are released through what is known as the windows system. In this system, films are first given a theatrical release (at cinemas) and after a contractually agreed period, they are made available on DVD/Blu-Ray. Following another contractually agreed period, they are available to the pay per view television channels, then free to view. Each window is protected from possible cannibalisation by alternative release formats. The windows system is contentious and there have been a number of attempts to circumvent this by simultaneously releasing a film across all windows, a practice known as 'day and date'. However, so far, this model of distribution has not been disrupted. Needless to say, this section is considering conventional approaches to releasing films as films which are released in non-conventional ways such as internet only distribution will be considered later in this book.

Within the film marketing literature, a number of studies have evaluated the impact of the release strategy on box office success. In a study by Elberse (1999) it was shown that scheduling and release patterns do have a direct impact on the box office performance of a film. Although limited in scope, this study does show that these are important issues to be considered. De Vany and Walls (1996, 1997, 1999), Jedidi et al. (1998), Jones and Ritz (1991), Litman and Ahn (1998), Neelamegham and Chintagunta (1999) and Zufryden (1996) all look at the impact that the number of screens on which a film opens, runs and closes on has upon success. In general, the greater the number of screens a film is released on, the more likely the film is to achieve financial success. But, this explanation is overly simplistic. The number of screens that a film opens on as well as the length of the run that a film achieves is dependent on the budget which the distributors have for prints and advertising (P&A). The cost of each print is in excess of £1000 and one print is needed for each screen showing the film. In this way smaller films with lower P&A budgets will be restricted in terms of the number of screens the film can be shown on at any one time. In addition, according to Kerrigan and Culkin (1999), the major film studios, due to the integrated supply chain at their disposal, can negotiate longer guaranteed runs in cinemas than independent distributors. Just as considerations such as stars, genre and track record of the filmmakers impact on consumer choice (as discussed in the following chapter); these play a role in determining the negotiations for film release. Durie et al. (2000) discuss the types of negotiations which occur between film distributors and exhibitors (cinema owners) in placing a film in the cinema.

Big budget, anticipated films with recognisable film stars/directors attached can book a release date well in advance of smaller films. Such schedules are also subject to change as cinema owners will keep a film which plays well in the opening week or two weeks if there is still public demand for it and this will disrupt the plans for the release of the following film.

Durie et al. (2000) also notes the differences between distributor owned and independent cinemas. In the US, following the Paramount Decrees, there was a separation in ownership between film distributors and exhibitors, but in many territories, this separation does not exist. As Durie notes, this can result in preferential treatment for films which were financed by the cinema's parent company. Since the rise of the multiplex, there has been a clear separation between the 'art house' cinema and the more mainstream multiplex. But as cinema tastes have changed, the distinction is becoming slightly blurred, with some seemingly artistic films being shown by multiplex cinemas, either in recognition of the consumer demand for such films, or as a result of public policy aimed at increasing the diversity of film consumption, such as the UK Film Council's Digital Screen Network. However, in negotiating with cinemas/cinema chains, it is important to match the film's target audience with the demographic profile of the cinema's catchment audience.

A wealth of debate surrounds the issue of whether the major distributors or the independents can secure the most successful distribution deal. While it cannot be denied that the majors are ideally suited to distributing big budget, high profile films, independents and specialist distributors are often more suited to the distribution of smaller films. As they invariably have lower P&A (Print and Advertising) budgets, they are required to execute a more exact and focused distribution campaign than the majors and this is often more successful for these films. Goldberg (1991) summed up this question as whether to aim with a rifle or a shotgun. PACT (1994: 55) found that, in relation to UK productions, films which were independently distributed, recouped a significantly higher proportion of their budgets than those distributed by the majors. The average proportion of budgets recouped, from all media, by independent distributors in the UK and US was 17.75% and 35%, respectively. In contrast, the figures for studio-distributed British films in the UK and US were 6.75% and 20.6%, respectively. The power of the majors to secure preferred play dates, length of run and maximum levels of prints emerged in the PACT submission to the Mergers and Monopolies Commission in 1994. This was especially true for films that were distributed by the majors in the US; a phenomenon that can easily be explained. The majors control the distribution of the overwhelming majority of films in the international market and for this reason it is imperative that the exhibition sector co-operates with them in order to secure a constant flow of product.

While the majors control the main routes to market within the global industry, film tastes change over time and film consumers eventually tire of formulaic films. Blair and Kerrigan (2002) traced this in line with the industrial development of the film industry and indicated the need for the majors to enter into commercial relationships in order to tackle this issue. In fact August 1989 heralded a new era in film marketing in the US when Miramax released *Sex, Lies and Videotape* (1989). According to Perren (2001: 30), "*sex, lies and videotape* helped to set the standard for low-budget, niche-based distribution in the 90s and to lay the groundwork for a bifurcation within the entertainment industry". This led to each of the major Hollywood studios purchasing a specialist distribution company to handle quirky small films. Following this, the studios have bought and sold such specialist distribution companies in what has been a turbulent market.

Traditionally, there were specific times of the year during which particular types of films were released. Art house films were released in spring, blockbusters in summertime. Now, with an increase in the numbers of films on release, the film release calendar has become crowded, making it more difficult for distributors to secure their ideal release dates. With so many blockbusters being released, they are coming out all year round. Christmas has become a popular time to release major films which has caused difficulties for films which rely on a Christmas release due to the seasonal nature of the film. Zygi Kamassa, from Redbus Distributors (sold to Lionsgate in 2005), bemoaned the lack of available screens in the run up to Christmas in 2003 and 2004 for a film which his company backed. As this film had a Christmas theme, this would have been the most appropriate time for release, but they could not wait until Christmas 2005, so released the film in Spring 2004. Western film calendars are becoming more like Nollywood, where films are vying with each other in a very crowded market. Each Friday brings more releases either into the cinemas (for fortunate filmmakers in the West) or through the networks of video/VCD distributors throughout Nigeria and neighbouring markets.

Although there has been an expansion in cinema screens since the mid-1980s due to the rise of the multi- and megaplex cinemas, this has not increased the openings for greater numbers of films to be released year round. This is why analysis of box office figures and length of release of films is a limited method of understanding the dynamics of the film industry. Film distributors understand that impact, i.e. opening a film as widely as possible across the maximum number of territories, will result in box office success, but this strategy is only open to a handful of blockbuster films.

An interesting case which illustrates the power of the major distributors is that of British film. Kuhn (2003) outlined the release strategy for

Four Weddings and a Funeral (1994) in the United States. Having under-taken audience research, Polygram (the distribution company) were conservatively optimistic that they would achieve a level of box office success with *Four Weddings and a Funeral* (1994). But, having a limited P&A budget, they decided to release initially in New York and Los Angeles and to spend heavily on localised advertising in those cities. Hoping that the film would be a success, they planned on using the box office revenue from these cities to finance the gradual roll out of the film across the US. Their strategy of what is called a platform release, worked as planned. Kuhn admitted his naivety regarding the power of the major distributors. When he spoke to Linda Ditrinco, who was the New York representative for the distributor, Gramercy, she had to explain why they had only shown it on a small screen in a multiplex cinema, despite it being sold out. Ditrinco explained that the cinemas have agreements regarding the screens where the major's films are shown. In this instance, as the demand for *Four Weddings and a Funeral* (1994) exceeded that for the other films, the cinema programmer swapped screens, but did not inform the majors of what they had done. For one of their subsequent films, *Notting Hill* (1999), levels of interest were so high that other distributors began to avoid its intended release date. This allowed the distributor to choose the ideal date to release on and they decided to release in May, the ideal time for romantic comedies in both the US and the (Kerrigan, 2005). As the RAS for this film had shown that it was going to be a big hit, it was decided to give it a wide release of 450 prints which was the biggest P&A budget that they had in the UK up to that point. Past experience with *Four Weddings and a Funeral* (1994) had increased their confidence in the romantic comedy genre and they gained additional confidence from the level of audience hype that existed for *Notting Hill* (1999) and so decided on this wide release strategy. In contrast to this, for another of their films, *Elizabeth* (1998), it was decided to use a platform release strategy, whereby, the film is opened in a few cinemas initially and then opened more widely over the following weeks. This helps to mini-mise the initial P&A budget until the performance of the film is evaluated, as was the case for *Four Weddings and a Funeral* discussed above.

Platform release is the normal approach for independent films for a number of reasons. Firstly, independents do not generally have the nego-tiating power of the major distributors which is required to secure a wider release. Secondly, as discussed above, the P&A budgets required for a wide release are prohibitive for independent distributors who rely on good word of mouth to gradually build up the audience for a film and as revenue comes in, the distributors can afford to increase the size of the P&A budget. With the move to digital distribution and exhibition, the cost of prints is being drastically reduced, but with an increasingly crowded marketplace, the need for increased expenditure on advertising (in its various forms) has resulted in the P&A budgets remaining relatively high.

This chapter has outlined the key elements of the marketing mix, namely the star (actor and other), script/genre, age classification and release strategy. There are other elements such as the production values which can be considered, but from a purely marketing perspective, these are identified as the most important factors to be considered in positioning a film within the market and in developing an appropriate marketing strategy. A constant theme throughout this book is the power of the major film distributors over the independents and the power which other actors in the film industry have and this is explored in this chapter in relation to the interplay between the various stars, their agents and filmmakers as well as in getting the film to market through the distribution channels. The marketing mix elements discussed here are the key elements which will be highlighted in the film marketing materials as discussed in Chapter 7. The following chapter will examine consumer selection of films and examine the role of the film marketing mix proposed in this chapter in this process of selection.

CHAPTER 6

Consumer Selection of Films

How and why consumers select the films they watch and how this is influenced by when and where they watch the films that they watch is a much researched, yet it is an inconclusive area of film marketing. Having a chapter which examines consumer selection of films is necessary but does not imply that there is a scientifically proven formula for film selection. What this chapter will provide is an overview of existing studies concerned with consumer selection of films so that scholars of film marketing and filmmakers and marketers can gain an insight into this complex and important area. Similarly to other areas of marketing, most published studies on consumer selection are based on US data. This of course is a major limitation for scholars wishing to understand consumer selection outside the US market. As this book posits that film consumption is culturally bounded, it can be proposed that film choice is also culturally bounded. However, we may be able to make some generalisations regarding the function of film consumption across the global marketplace.

Another key limitation lies in the methods which are used in researching film choice and consumption. The vast majority of studies look at box office data, budget, cast, critical reviews and award nominations and successes in assessing consumer choice. What is missing is a concern with choices expressed by consumers and a more holistic evaluation of film consumption outside of the cinema setting. We have seen from other chapters in this book that films are consumed for a number of reasons. Films can be a form of entertainment, a means of escaping from hum drum life to a fantastic world (Holbrook and Hirschman, 1982); films can be educational, teaching us about other cultures, other historical times, environmental or political issues (UK Film Council/Stimulating World Research, 2007); films may be thrilling, causing our hearts to beat faster and exciting us. Films may give us access to

CONTENTS

other languages, other geographical places. They may make us laugh or cry, be uplifting or cathartic. Much existing discourse around film consumption treats consumers of film as one-dimensional. This chapter presumes that consumers of film are motivated by different wants and needs at different times and therefore may not have consistent patterns of film consumption. Drawing mainly on literature which examines the impact of certain elements of the film marketing mix on film success, the role of critic and word of mouth, this chapter seeks to consolidate existing knowledge of film consumption and in doing so, set a research agenda for examining film consumption in the future.

One tortured question that pervades arts marketing in general and has influenced writing about film marketing is the attempt to evaluate 'quality'. Looking to seminal work by Becker (1982), professional critics are seen as central to awarding status to artists while Bourdieu (1984, 2003) recognised the role of institutions and other members of 'the field' in awarding status or symbolic capital to artists. Such a framework can be used in understanding film consumption. In order to understand the role of such critics and institutions on film consumption by individual consumers and groups of consumers, it is first necessary to reflect on the film industry supply chain as introduced in Chapter 1. While substantial numbers of films are produced each year across the world, only a very small percentage of these films succeed in gaining access to a significant audience. Some will secure theatrical distribution, either domestically or in a number of markets, a small number will gain global theatrical distribution, another group will not benefit from the exposure attached to theatrical distribution but will be released for sale 'direct to DVD/VCD/Video/Blu-ray' and others will not receive conventional release. Of course, the latter method of distribution is the dominant method for Nigerian video films where theatrical distribution does not really exist. As a result of increasing internet speed and advances in new technology, there is a final group of films which will receive internet distribution and gain an audience this way, in so doing, circumventing the traditional windows system of distribution. While the latter group does not necessarily conform to the view of the art world which relies on gatekeepers to validate cultural products, filmmakers involved in the institutionalised film industry do.

This chapter will look specifically at the latter group at a later stage, but the majority of the chapter is concerned with what happens within the dominant structures of the global film industry. The first stage which a film must get through in order to be available to consumers is the financing stage. Where the budget is very low and the filmmaker possesses sufficient financial resources to finance production, they may proceed without gaining permission (in the form of finance) from institutional gatekeepers. In the majority of cases, writers and directors will work with a producer in order to secure production finance. Sources of finance will include pre-sales to film distribution companies, public funds (national and supra-national), venture capital funds, tax incentives and gap funding by financial institutions. A final (and new) form of film financing is called crowd sourcing and this is where small amounts of finance is sought from very large numbers of investors. There are very many ways to finance film production and working out such deals is complex and requires high levels of financial competence from producers. Each element of finance provided can be seen as approval from a key institutional gatekeeper. While some of these gatekeepers may be concerned with the artistic or cultural merit of the film (largely national or supra-national film funds), the majority will invest based on the likely return on investment. In this way, many films without significant projected earnings may be screened out at this early stage. Wallace et al. (1993) used the results of their extensive empirical study of star power and commercial performance to conclude that even Hollywood studios may not be as commercially motivated as they are perceived. They argue that if this were the case, based on evidence of earning potential, they would restrict their output to horror, religious, disaster and science-fiction films as they have higher rates of return than the more commonly produced genres such as biography, drama and romance. Production finance is often contingent on the elements of the film marketing mix discussed in Chapter 5. Once a film is completed, it may have to pass through an additional industrial screening process in the form of festivals and markets, which are discussed in Chapter 8. At these festivals and markets, the film may be sold to additional territories and audience momentum for the film may aid in its being selected by international sales agents or distributors. Exhibitors will look to these festivals and markets in order to assess which films they must show each year and therefore, festivals and markets play an important role in identifying which films are made available for consumers.

MOTIVES UNDERLYING FILM CONSUMPTION

Marketing academics have undertaken a number of studies seeking to evaluate the ingredients required for a film to succeed in the marketplace. Such studies are generally based on psychological or economic analysis of film performance. Studies adopting a psychological approach involve collecting data which considers individual consumer behaviour and choice in order to assess their reasons for selection particular films. Examples of such studies are those undertaken by Eliashberg et al. (2000), Eliashberg and Sawhney (1994) and Zufryden (1996). Economically based studies (see Elberse and Eliashberg, 2003; Jeddi et al., 1998; Litman and Ahn, 1998; Ravid, 1999) tended to use aggregate data from industry trade sources in order to assess the influence of various film attributes on financial performance.

Holbrook (1999) found that consumers consume film for a variety of reasons. Of course, this complicates our understanding of motives for film consumption. However, such complication should not impede our study of such motives, but does imply the need to place boundaries around our enquiry in order to produce some meaningful observations. Wohlfeil and Whelan (2006) correctly note that our understanding of motivation for film consumption may lie in the methods which have been used to understand such consumption. They call for a turn towards more interpretive methods in order to understand consumption of film and illustrate the value of subjective personal introspection as an insight into this consumption. While such research cannot be seen as widely generalisable, a collection of such narrative insights can add richness to existing quantitative analysis of box office figures and extrapolated consumer preferences. While box office figures may provide some insight into how consumers respond to a variety of stimuli communicated through paid for communication as well as word of mouth and wider publicity, we also need to understand consumer satisfaction and how consumption of one film or other cultural product leads to other choices. Elliott and Hamilton (1991) posited that consumers make choices regarding consumption of leisure activities based on simple constructs; however, it would seem more accurate to propose that the nature of decision making is dependent on the specific choice being made and the level of engagement which the consumer has with the particular leisure pursuit.

Wohlfeil and Whelan (2008) also distinguish between film consumption as a collective and an individual act. In doing so, they draw on existing research to posit that consumers of mainstream film consume collectively while 'connoisseurs' do not view watching film as a collective social experience. It may be possible that film consumers move between these states and previous research (for example see López-Sintas and García-Álvarez, 2006) has shown that film consumption can be viewed as a continuum. In an extensive study of Spanish consumers during 1998, López-Sintas and García-Álvarez (2006: 404–405) classified audiovisual consumers into five categories: (1) occasional film-goers, (2) light film-goers, (3) film fans, (4) audiovisual fans, and (5) television addicts. They link their categorization of 'film fans' with those labeled by van Ekjck and van Rees (2000) as snobs whereas 'audiovisual fans' are likened to groups previously identified as cultural omnivores (Peterson, 2005 cited in López-Sintas and

García-Álvarez, 2006). Like many other researchers into film and wider audiovisual consumption, this study examined the link with social class and types of audiovisual consumption. Their findings were unsurprising with film and audiovisual fans being found in higher social classes than members of the other categories.

The significant distinction between upscale and downscale audiences lay not in the level of general consumption of audiovisual products but in the variety of consumption with upscale consumers consuming more broadly than downscale audiences. López-Sintas and García-Álvarez (2006) further distinguish between these groups by pointing out a generational divide between audiovisual consumers in that older consumers tended towards narrower forms of consumption (falling into the film fan category more than audiovisual) than younger fans. This categorization may be even more significant now as the last ten years has seen major developments in how consumers engage with film and television. Finally, in terms of gender and location, the two highest classes in terms of involvement, 'film fans' and 'audiovisual fans' were mainly men and came from larger cities. López-Sintas and García-Álvarez (2006) drew on the work of Bourdieu (1989) in concluding that consumption of audiovisual products is determined by a number of structural factors including access to resources. Without the financial means to pay for cinema attendance, film rental or cable television and living in an area which does not provide a wide range of access to diverse audiovisual products are coupled with behavioural characteristics defined by social class. Therefore, film consumption can be seen as informed by the internalized structures which Bourdieu associated with his conceptualization of 'habitus'. The 'field of cultural consumption' within which film consumption takes place can be seen as informed by demographic factors such as age, social class and gender as well as the patterns of consumption which individuals engage in over the course of their relationship with film.

The UK Film Council's (2007) 'Avids' study, found that 'avids' can be seen to be obsessed with film. They are extensive consumers of film and their engagement with film developed over a period of time. The first stage in an avid's development is where they consume film as a form of entertainment. They engage mainly with films which are considered popular or mainstream. Typically, their relationship with film develops during the teenage years where film is used in order to explore issues of identity. During this stage, avids are likely to develop broader taste in film and to begin to consume non-mainstream films in addition to mainstream films. According to this study, avids can be influenced by friends, parents or teachers during this phase in the development of their relationship with film. Film clubs are also seen as influential in shaping their continuing relationship with film. From the teenage stage, film consumers begin to engage with film criticism and elements of film making in adulthood and some continue to make a career in film making, while others remain as consumers of film. The research developed our understanding of the avid by classifying avids into three distinct categories: summits, specialists and scatterguns. *Summits* are seen as the most knowledgeable and usually work in film or related areas of film education or journalism. They usually combine an interest in the aesthetic nature of film and film as a cultural artefact with an interest in the working of the industry. *Specialists* are classified as obsessive fans. They collect films and memorabilia and are disparaging of films which they do not believe are up to their standards in critical terms. Finally, *Scatterguns* are avids who consumer film alongside other cultural products. While they have a very keen interest in film and may be very knowledgeable, they may be equally interested in other forms of art and media.

What all three categories of avid shared was an appreciation of the accessibility, immersive nature and escapism offered by film. Film was seen by avids as a doorway to other cultural forms which promoted wider knowledge. Many avids used film in order to learn about other cultures or other languages and to explore other interests such as music, art and history.

Before looking at influencers on film consumption, it is necessary to explore motives for film consumption. In increasingly crowded leisure markets, with new media such as online gaming, consumption of video clips on sites such as YouTube, old media such as traditional film may be assumed to be a threatened cultural product. In order to understand film consumption, it is necessary to engage with media reception theories. Staiger (2005) provides an excellent overview of media reception studies and locates this work within political science, linguistics, sociology and psychology. In doing so, she illustrates how taste has been formed within this context and how distinctions between high and low forms of culture are established. Such distinctions should be considered in order to understand the underlying influences of film consumption and how film consumption, similarly to other types of consumption, are informed by notions of the self in society. Staiger (2005) compares psychological and sociological approaches to understanding media reception. In doing so, she highlights the difference between the two in terms of the unit of analysis. While psychological theory emphasises the individual experience, sociological theories of consumption consider how individuals function within a group setting. Much of media reception theory is concerned with internalising media consumption and is concerned with interpreting the media 'text'. In looking at film consumption from a marketing perspective, we are more concerned with how individuals and groups select the films that they watch; how they develop their film consumption tastes and what influences selection and satisfaction or dissatisfaction? Staiger's (2005) discussion of media reception studies is extensive and within this comprehensive overview, she turns to social–psychoanalytical theory and cultural studies in order to explore how emotion influences meaning-making in the context of media reception. In selecting films, consumers can be seen to be projecting a desire to experience emotion be it fear, pleasure or desire. Drawing on Nearing (1997), Staiger (2005: 89) states that emotional reaction to cultural products has been linked to 'low culture' or the popular arts. She talks of the bias in rational analysis of media reception against emotion saying that "supposedly emotions seduce spectatorship" and links this to the privileging of cultural production over cultural consumption. While Staiger's call for a balancing of attention between cultural production and cultural consumption is a laudable aim, as can be seen from the section above, and earlier chapters in this book, film consumption is tightly constrained and consumers of film rely on powerful gatekeepers in allowing access to film.

THE IMPACT OF THE FILM MARKETING MIX ON CONSUMPTION CHOICES

Chapter 5 examined elements of what I have called 'the film marketing mix' and their relevance for understanding film marketing and consumption. In reviewing key literature consulted in Chapter 5, we found that existing studies regarding the impact of various elements of the film marketing mix were often contradictory in their findings regarding the impact which particular elements such as star power, genre and release strategy have on a film's success at the box office. This chapter will not go over this ground again, but it is important to recall that filmmakers and marketers are indeed what Culliton (1948) referred to as 'mixers of ingredients'.

Many studies have looked at which elements of the marketing mix are most influential in commercial terms. De Vany and Walls (2004) found that if a star was in a film, it reduced uncertainty among consumers. However, the study by Wallace et al. (1993) found a much more complex relationship between star power and box office performance. In the case of Nigerian cinema, Esan (2008) found that the stars were a significant indicator on film selection. This is because there is a strong link between the star and the type of film to be expected. The commercial benefit of casting a star depends on the star, if they are on the way up, in terms of earning potential or on the way down. This links Albert's (1998) finding that an actor's previous performance, as evaluated by the consumer, influences the box office earnings of their next film. Popularity of genre is another element which has been studied by a number of authors. Litman (1983) and Litman and Kohl (1989) found that drama did most poorly at the box office, while Fischoff (1998) found that drama was the most popular genre as expressed by consumers. Finally, the power of the distributor is relevant in terms of their ability to negotiate release terms for their film. Wide release has been seen as the most favorable strategy (Elberse and Eliashberg, 2003). However, such a release strategy implies high budgets for distribution as well as substantial negotiating power on behalf of the distributor. Jones and Ritz (1991) noted the importance of opening on as many screens as possible during the first week of release.

Despite the findings outlined in the previous paragraph, films are seen as complex experience goods comprising of various artistic and commercial ingredients, broad scale generalisable studies may not be the best way to capture the essence of how consumers select films. Indeed, such approaches assume that film consumers are rational beings following strict decision making paths and using sophisticated processes of illumination when selecting films. In fact, looking back at the UK Film Council's (2007) Avids study and the López-Sintas and García-Álvarez (2006) study, we can conclude that we first need to understand where on the spectrum of film consumers individuals are located before making assessments of how film marketing mix elements will impact on their choice. Figure 6.1 lays out a tentative assessment of the film consumer based on the above studies.

Figure 6.1 is drawn from the above-mentioned studies and can help in developing further research agendas regarding film consumption. The many studies which have empirically evaluated the demonstrated commercial impact of the various elements of the film marketing mix on success have been invaluable in developing our overall understanding of how these elements impact on box office earnings. However, film marketing scholars need to engage more with scholars from film studies and media reception studies in order to develop meaningful evaluations of how consumers make

Infrequent attendee	Regular attendee (mainstream tastes)	Regular attendee (broad tastes)	Regular attendee (specialist taste)	Film snobs	Film industry professionals/ associated professionals

FIGURE 6.1 *Continuum of film consumers.*

their selections. The continuum above presumes that each of the six categories will behave in different ways in selecting and consuming film and therefore they may each require different studies in order to understand how they respond to the marketing mix. It would be assumed from existing research (discussed above and in Chapter 5) that those in category five 'film snobs', which conform to the UK Film Council's category 'specialists' may be more heavily engaged in their film consumption practices than those in category one. However, as 'infrequent attendees' may be cautious in selecting films which they chose to watch, 'film snobs' may also engage in extensive information search, motivated by their generally high level of engagement. The 'film snob' category may also show tendencies towards consuming film individually rather than as part of a wider social activity (Cooper-Martin, 1991). Hennig-Thurau et al. (2006) discuss various influencers on film choice and find that such influences vary in accordance with the stage a film is at in its release life cycle, as films are released sequentially. Consumers consider risk through evaluating the economic outlay required as well as the perceived risks. Hennig-Thurau et al. (2006) draw on information search literature to illustrate that high levels of uncertainty can lead to expanded information search behaviour common in the service sector. This often leads film consumers to assess 'quality' through clues such as the actors, directors, genre or critical reviews. The following section will examine an extensively researched area of the film marketing literature, the impact of critical reviews on consumer selection.

ESTABLISHING TRUST

The long-term success or failure of a film is dependent upon how well this film lives up to the expectations of the audience in terms of providing the ingredients normally associated with this genre. When these expectations are consistently met, this trust is established. Currall and Judge (1995) refer to trust in terms of willingness to depend on others in given situations, whereas Mayer et al. (1995) speak about trust in terms of belief in the competency or predictability of another in a given situation. McKnight et al. (1998) trace this dichotomy of willingness and belief back to the work of Fishbein and Ajzen (1975). Such definitional differences are important – is trust contingent upon predictability or goodwill? The concept of trust that seems particularly useful in relation to film marketing is that of Lewis and Weigert (1985) as they incorporate confidence into the trust relationship. In an embodiment of both concepts, willingness and confidence, Moorman et al. (1993: 82) defined trust as "...a willingness to rely on an exchange partner in whom one has confidence". They went on to qualify that this trust is a result of a combination of expertise, reliability and intentionality. Grönroos (1997) developed this view of trust as a simplified relationship between a Trustor and Trustee and suggested a scenario where individual actors adopt both roles. This is in line with Sniezek and Van Swol (2001) who expand this concept to incorporate the role of consultation between the 'judge' (who retains ultimate responsibility for decisions) and 'advisor' (a non-responsible person who offers advice) when making decisions.

According to Grönroos' (1997) definition of relationship marketing, marketing is a process including several parties or actors, the objectives of whom have to be met. A mutual exchange and fulfilment of promises is necessary in order to meet these objectives, a fact that makes trust an important aspect of marketing. Trust as a concept has emerged in many areas of the marketing literature from branding (Ambler, 1997; Lau and Lee, 2000), to relationship marketing (Cowles, 1997; Garbarino and Johnson, 1999; Grönroos, 1995, 1997). Kerrigan (2005) found that where high levels of trust existed between filmmakers and film marketers, this resulted in a clearer transfer of creative vision. This trust relationship also applies to that between the film marketer and the consumer and similarly to internal trust, such external trust can also be based on experience. McKnight et al.'s (1998) theory of knowledge-based trust explored how trust is developed through an interaction history. Trust is an important element of many of the relationships which film consumers have. Consumers can develop trust in an actor, director, distributor or cinema, or in the recommendations of particular friends or film critics.

Durie et al. (2000) stressed the need to differentiate between 'want to see' and audience enjoyment. Film marketers can create 'want to see' through the marketing campaign. However, the ultimate aim is to achieve audience enjoyment and therefore 'good word of mouth' in order to sustain the film in the market. Accurate targeting of the film can assist in positive word of mouth. This is where extensive audience research prior to release is valuable. NRG (National Research Group) conducts the vast majority of RAS in the film industry but has been criticised for adopting a formulaic approach to audience research. The results of the recruited audience screening are fed into the development of the marketing materials as discussed later in this book. The remainder of this chapter will consider the establishment of external trust between the filmmakers and marketers and the consumer. Firstly, paid for advertising will be assessed in terms of its effectiveness, then the impact of critical reviews and word of mouth will be evaluated.

THE ROLE OF THE CRITICS

Cinemagoers are influenced by critics and by avids. Much research has been carried out regarding the role of critics in predicting box office success (Austin, 1983, 1989; Cameron, 1995; Eliashberg and Shugan, 1997; D'Astous and Touil, 1999; Holbrook, 1999; D'Astous and Colbert, 2002). Findings here are inconclusive but there would seem to be an overall acknowledgement that good critical reviews can help a film to achieve box office success. In addition, Eliashberg and Shugan (1997) found that the impact of critical reviews could be seen after the first four weeks of a film's release. As an underperforming film will be removed from cinema screens after two weekends, we can propose that the paid for marketing campaign impacts on a film's initial performance at the box office. We could conclude from this that early adopters of film may be less influenced by critical reviews than those more cautious or infrequent film consumers. There has been evidence from Austin (1981) to show how the influence of critics and reviewers only impacted on the more 'esoteric films' and therefore did not heavily impact on box office receipts in the main. Hsu (2006) links discussions of critical reviews with notions of legitimacy. In doing so, she draws on Zuckerman (1999) in highlighting the significance of critics as gatekeepers who screen products offered to audiences and in this way shape consumers consumption habits.

Hsu (2006: 468) is particularly concerned with how critics established belief systems influence which 'market categories' gain recognition within this process. Drawing on Becker's (1984) seminal work, Hsu (2006) examines the struggle which ensues in establishing legitimacy of critical reviews. In convincing the readers (and other cultural commentators) of the validity of one's schema of evaluation, critics increase their own legitimacy and as a by-product of this process, they influence wider notions of legitimacy of genres or classes of film based on the dominant discourse which they have established. Travis (1990) studies the routinization of the practice of film criticism and argues that professional critics are needed in order to read film as a visual artefact. Travis (1990: 53) continues to point out that such application of professional criticism to films results in the establishment of critics as "protectors of 'good taste'" and as tour guides (p. 57). In establishing his argument that the practice of film criticism is routinized, Travis establishes that film critics establish ideal conceptual types of film and use this in evaluating each film. This links to Bauman's (2001) discussion of the formation of aesthetic standards which could be applied to the evaluation of film which formed an essential element of film's transformation into an accepted art form rather than a form of mass entertainment. Travis view may not be seen as closely aligned with that of Eliashberg and Shugan (1997) who posited that film reviewers anticipated the tastes and preferences of their readers, therefore reflecting them based on their findings that critical reviews were in line with future box office earnings. In contrast to Eliashberg and Shugan's (1997) findings, d'Astous and Touil's (1999) findings are in line with Travis. In applying attribution theory to an experimental design, d'Astous and Touil (1999) found that consumers engaged in a 'causal analysis' of the reasons influencing critics' evaluations of films. Their study showed that consumers counterbalanced possible reviewer bias by being more inclined to be influenced by a positive review of a particular film if the reviewer had a predisposition to dislike films by this reviewer.

Holbrook and Addis (2008) revisited the art versus commerce debate in relation to the impact of critical reviews on box office success. By separating out measures of critical acclaim such as awards and critical praise from commercial indications of popularity such as box office earnings, Holbrook and Addis (2008: 89) posit that the critical and the commercial are separate, independent dimensions; industry recognition and market performance. They found that buzz created for a film can be based either on the artistic merit of the film or as a result of what they refer to as 'marketing clout' which the film gains due to its production budget, number of screens it is released on and opening weekend revenue . That which is based on artistic merit may result in increased critical acclaim for a film as indicated by the numbers of positive award nominations and awards and commercial buzz results in increased revenue from consumers seeing the film at the cinema or renting it. This finding links to d'Astous's (1999) evaluation that film consumers consult critical reviews in cases where there is a lot of discussion of a film, in order to understand why. Hennig-Thurau et al. (2001) make the link between positive reviews and consumer expectations. Referring to an earlier study, they claim that such expectations are in turn linked to satisfaction. Although the evidence is a little uncertain regarding the influence of critical reviews on box office success, we can tentatively conclude that consumers may consult reviews in selecting a film in order to minimise risk or to understand high levels of word of mouth surrounding a film. In consulting reviews, consumers may evaluate the review in relation to expectations they have of the reviewers taste and opinion and use this information to make up their mind as to whether to see a particular film or not. The impact of critical reviews seems less for films where they have substantial marketing clout in the form of a large production budget, a wide release strategy and high levels of advertising and publicity. Linked to evaluations of the impact of critical reviews is the notion of word of mouth. The following section will examine the concept of word of mouth in film marketing and draw on existing studies in order to understand the interplay between word of mouth and consumer selection of films.

WORD OF MOUTH

It is difficult to separate the role of the critics from word or mouth as Mahajan et al. (2000) found that they were closely linked. Anderson (1998: 6) defines word of mouth as "informal communications between private parties concerning evaluations of goods and services". Word of mouth has long been a concern for marketers (Czepiel, 1974; Buttle, 1998). Much of the research (Mahajan et al., 2000) on word of mouth derived from studies examining the diffusion of innovation following Rogers (1962). Holmes and Let (1977) showed that product involvement resulted in word of mouth activity by consumers. Studies have shown a link between customer satisfaction and positive word of mouth (Bolton and Drew, 1992; Schlesinger and Heskett, 1991) as well as dissatisfaction and negative word of mouth (Westbrook, 1987). What can be concluded by examining these studies is that word of mouth can be motivated both by satisfaction and dissatisfaction with a product or service.

Film marketing professionals such as Durie et al. (2000) believe that word of mouth is central to the market success or failure of a film. Word of mouth indicates the presence of influencers on choice and in film these influencers are identified as critics and 'avids' (Litman, 1983), the term applied to film fans who influence the decisions of their peer groups. Many commentators believe that it is impossible to control word of mouth. However, identifying the most likely audience for a film and focusing on bringing it to their attention can go some way to ensuring that word of mouth is positive. Durie (2000) also looks at the impact of word of mouth and reviews on a film's success or failure. He differentiates between 'want to see' and audience enjoyment. Film marketers can create 'want to see' through the marketing campaign, this is also known as 'marketability'. However, the ultimate aim is to achieve audience enjoyment and therefore good word of mouth in order to sustain the film in the market. Film marketers can create 'want to see' through the marketing campaign. However, the ultimate aim is to achieve audience enjoyment and therefore 'good word of mouth' in order to sustain a film in the market. Accurate targeting of a film can assist in positive word of mouth.

The experience of Neil Jordan in relation to his film *In the Company of Wolves*, provides an example of where the positioning of a film resulted in its failure at the box office (Jordan, 1997). This adult allegorical fairy tale was distributed in the US by Miramax, who marketed the film as a horror movie and targeted this audience. Audience expectations of a horror movie were unfulfilled resulting in the film being slated by audiences, which ultimately created negative word of mouth and commercial failure; the film was failed by its marketing campaign. Negative word of mouth can undermine the most sophisticated marketing campaign (Katz and Lazarsfeld, 1955).

One of the main problems which has arisen when studying the impact of word of mouth on consumer purchase decisions is how to measure word of mouth. The majority of studies follow Bass (1969) where it is assumed that sales data can indicate the impact of word of mouth. One of the most commonly cited studies on the impact of word of mouth is the study undertaken by Elberse and Eliashberg (2003) which also assumes a causal relationship between word of mouth and box office performance. Such assumptions can be problematic as there are a number of factors which may be seen as contributing to sales which cannot be unpicked using existing research methods. Social network theory has also been used in measuring word of mouth (Bansal and Voyer, 2000). Smaller scale surveys have also been used in order to assess the impact of the group on decision purchases. An example of such a study is that undertaken by Reingen et al. (1984) which examined purchases among members of a US college sorority and found differences in congruency of choice between those that lived together and those that lived separately from fellow sorority members.

De Vany and Walls' (1996) paper found that word of mouth had a significant impact on film performance at the box office. More recently, Moul (2007) concluded that consumer expectations are influenced by word of mouth, although it should be noted that Moul assumed that word of mouth would increase in line with the length of time that a film was on theatrical release, rather than actually measuring word of mouth. Moul and Shugan (2005) proposed that studios engaged in wide release strategies in the current market in order to minimise negative word of mouth. However, this can only be seen as one of the motivating factors behind the wide release.

ELECTRONIC WORD OF MOUTH

The phenomenon of online consumer reviewing has been the focus of a number of recent studies. Chen and Xie (2008: 478) note the difference between "third-party product reviews" and consumer reviews in that the former focus on the technical performance of products while the latter focus on the relevance for customer situational usage. In transposing this to the realm of the film world, online consumer reviews can be seen as less about analyzing the film as a text, with reviews focusing on the fitness of a film for purpose. Is a comedy funny, a thriller thrilling and so on?

While studies of the influence of word of mouth have been hampered by methodological issues regarding the ability of researchers to accurately measure the impact of offline word of mouth, the advent of online reviewing has facilitated new methods of assessing the impact of what is now being termed 'electronic word of mouth' (Hennig-Thurau et al., 2004) or 'online word of mouth' (Brown et al., 2007). Brown et al. (2007) draw on social psychology in order to develop a theoretical framework appropriate for assessing the impact of online word of mouth. In doing so, they cite Rheingold (1993) who stated that online communities resulted from sustained computer mediated public discussions between members of the community. Such interactions also illustrated discernable levels of human feeling and therefore can be considered social relationships. Dellarocas (2003) have indicated the power of online communities to influence a broad range of management activities such as brand development. This echoes the work of Kozinets (1999) in his studies of virtual communities. We can conclude that online, virtual communities should be considered by marketing managers when developing their overall marketing strategy.

Dellarocas et al. (2007) highlight the problems which have existed in measuring word of mouth in the offline context and the possibility of measurement in the online context. In a study which looks specifically at the impact of online reviews on performance of films at the box office, Dellarocas et al. propose a number of diffusion models which can be used in forecasting film performance by factoring in online product reviews which increases the accuracy of the model. This builds on a number of studies based on diffusion models which have focused on forecasting box office performance of films (Jedidi et al., 1998; Sawhney and Eliashberg, 1996; Swami et al., 1999).

Biyalogorsky et al. (2001) found that consumer's word of mouth was restricted to bounded social networks. Such network boundaries may be seen as limiting the impact of word of mouth in the offline context as impact of word of mouth can be seen as linked to the density of the social network within which opinions were transmitted. However, the online environment allows for such social networks to be more fluid and membership is less tied to offline social interaction. Brown et al. (2007) also highlight the need to examine online word of mouth through studying the impact of social structures on the network formation and the impact of this on the transmission of information. It is not enough to examine information transfer in itself, but it is necessary to assess the impact of strength of ties on influencing behaviour.

Holbrook and Addis (2008) and Kerrigan and Yalkin (2009) have both looked to online consumer generated reviews in order to understand the impact which virtual word of mouth may have on film success. These studies are looking at slightly different things as Holbrook and Addis (2008), as mentioned above in this chapter sought to explore the art/commerce divide and therefore were interested in whether share of online word of mouth on IMDB (Internet Movie Database), Rotten Tomatoes and Yahoo Movies translated into either increased returns at the box office, and/or significant critical acclaim in the form of award nominations and wins. They did find a divergence with increased online buzz resulting in increased box office revenue for films with significant marketing support while more artistic films benefitted from nominations rather than necessarily increased commercial revenue. Kerrigan and Yalkin (2009) used a two-stage method of analysis (content analysis of reviews on IMDB and Rotten Tomatoes, and qualitative data on film selection) to explore the impact of user generated reviews on consumer choice. In this small scale study, Kerrigan and Yalkin (2009) found that consumers did not consult user generated reviews in order to make film selections when going to the cinema, but were more likely to consult such reviews as part of their wider film consumption experience. They also found that in the group of consumers studied, offline word of mouth was considered more influential on film selection than online word of mouth. Looking at Voss and Zomeridijk's (2007) conceptualisation of the service experience as a journey, we could propose that film consumption is a cumulative experience, with cultural capital earned throughout a film consumer's life. This cultural capital informs future film viewing choices and word of mouth, in an online or offline capacity which contributes to the amassing of cultural capital.

Taking the concept of the service experience as a journey, we can explore the phenomenon of consumer's repeat viewing of a film. Wolfeil and Whelan (2008) point out that one of the identifiers of a committed film fan is their tendency to build up a film collection. Many such fans return time after time to consume films which they have already watched on a number of occasions. Some films obtain cult status and repeat viewing can be linked to a particular time of year, Christmas for *Its a Wonderful Life*; Halloween the *Halloween* film and other horror films. A less common occurrence appears to be repeat viewing of films at the cinema. Collins et al. (2008) examine instances where film consumers choose to consume the same film a number of times at the cinema. They found that children's films were most likely to be viewed more than once at the cinema, while repeat viewing for films aimed at older audiences were less likely. The most likely to repeat view were 10–14-year olds. They found that likelihood to view a film more than once at the cinema was not significantly influenced by gender, but that the relationship between repeat viewing and gender was linked to the type of film viewed. Collins et al. (2008) examined 2002 CAVIAR data from the United Kingdom and found that repeat viewers of *Harry Potter and the Philosopher's Stone* were balanced between male and female viewers, repeat viewers of *Star Wars Episode 2: Attack of the Clones* were 90% male. From the top ten films which Collins et al. (2008) studied, the eight gaining the most repeat viewings were among the top ten best performing films of 2002. What is interesting from this study is that repeat viewing may not be constrained by income as they found that the only socio-economic group which was statistically significant was C1. Perhaps unsurprisingly, frequent film consumers were marginally more likely to repeat view than infrequent consumers and that they are likely to see a film early in its release rather than later. Collins et al. (2008) propose that the likelihood of younger consumers to repeat consumer may be linked to lack of experience.

WHAT PREVENTS FILM CONSUMPTION?

While the above all address various aspects of what influences consumer selection of films, it is also important to gain further insight into who the cinema goer actually is? Wohlfeil and Whelan (2008) point to the reluctance of some avids to watch films at the cinema due to possible disturbance which may occur as a result of the behaviour of other consumers. While in some contexts, like the Prince Charles Cinema in London's *Singalong Sound of Music* event, require the audience to be boisterous while watching a film at the cinema, many art house cinemas do not allow consumption of food during films. Collins and Hand (2005) stress the need to study micro-data in order to understand which factors combined in order to dissuade individuals to frequent a cinema. We know that the numbers of people consuming film at home is rising and the availability of affordable 'home cinema' equipment may be seen as one of the facilitators of this. Film piracy is a much talked about problem facing the film industry as (particularly young) consumers download illegal copies of films from the internet or buy illegally copied DVDs. There is some debate regarding the magnitude of the problem faced by the industry which has echoes of a previous debate concerning the danger to cinema revenue due to the rise of home video. Collins and Hand (2005) are critical of previous studies which failed to understand the complexity which surrounds the choice of going to see a film at the cinema. Collins and Hand (2005) were able to access CAVIAR data which is data collected on behalf of the Cinema Advertising Association. This data is necessary so that advertisers taking out cinema advertising for their products or services will be able to assess the potential reach in terms of who they will be able to communicate with by taking out cinema advertising. Collins and Hand (2005) took watching videos and watching television as substitutes for watching film. They also assumed that price of cinema ticket does not in itself impact on the choice of going to the cinema or not, but does influence which cinema and time of day/week is chosen. Alongside household income and gender, respondents to the survey were also asked to classify their neighbourhood. They concluded (based only on UK data) that film audiences are indeed younger audiences. In addition, probability of attending the cinema increases in line with income which Collins and Hand (2005: 327) say refutes the claim that film is 'entertainment for the masses'.

What is evident from this chapter is that significant research has been undertaken into consumer selection of films. Despite this, there is little consensus regarding why consumers select films and the information that they use in order to inform this process. However, I will attempt to draw together the different strands of knowledge that we do have about how consumers select the films that they watch. Firstly, we need to repeat the limitations of the studies above. Firstly, as the majority of studies are based on US box office data, their generalisability across other marketplaces can be judged to be limited. Secondly, attempts at producing universal theories of what works and does not work at the box office is problematic for a number of reasons; consumer tastes change over time, film consumption can be seen to be culturally and generationally specific and film consumers may look for different benefits from film depending on their expressed need at a given time. One may conclude, based on the contradictory evidence presented above, that film consumption may sometimes be informed by simplistic forms of decision making as Elliott and Hamilton (1991) proposed as well as at other times consumption choices may be part of an extensive decision making process.

Many further studies are needed which address the psychological and sociological nature of film choice and consumption. It is important to develop culturally sensitive measures in order to understand differences within and between cultural groups in terms of their film consumption. Further large scale studies which incorporate data on home film consumption as well as box office data are required in order to gain a more holistic understanding of how we are consuming film and whether the nature of this consumption, at home or at the cinema, influences our choice of film. This type of research should be complemented by further interpretive studies of actual consumption behaviour. This would enable us to understand film consumption within the context of wider leisure consumption and how the film consumption journey develops. Does the type of cultural capital amassed during the film consumption journey vary according to the type of film consumer (based on the categories outlined in Fig. 6.1 or other categorizations)? How does this cultural capital influence our future consumption? How do our peer groups influence our consumption choices? How will our use of online (non-professional) review and professional reviews change in the digital economy? These are all valid research questions which future research must examine in order for our understanding of film consumption to progress.

CHAPTER 7

Film Marketing Materials

This chapter discusses the materials used in film marketing from a marketing communications' perspective. The material for this chapter is drawn from various international markets and the chapter adopts a comparative approach. For example, marketing materials will often vary from territory to territory in order to appeal to the audience in each territory. This chapter compares marketing materials from a range of films, drawn from diverse film markets and examines how they have been presented to the consumer in the international context. This chapter must be considered in relation to the rest of the book, specifically the chapter on consumer selection of film as well as the chapter on technology. As I have noted in the latter chapter, in marketing terms, developments in new technology have significantly changed film marketing practices. Having said this, depicting these changes as wholesale movement from 'old marketing' to 'new marketing' may be overstating things. For the moment, many of the conventional film marketing practices still survive and may be supplemented by innovative online campaigns. In the case of some very niche films, online may exist in isolation from any offline campaign, but this is more usual for films intended for distribution online rather than going on theatrical release. This chapter focuses mainly on the traditional marketing materials which accompany a film's movement through the life cycle with a specific emphasis on the film marketing materials aimed at the consumer. While the role of the internet will be touched on in this chapter, the impact of the internet and web 2.0 in particular will be discussed in more detail in Chapter 10.

Conventional film marketing materials include posters, trailers, merchandise, electronic press kits and stills. In addition, it is possible to

CONTENTS

distinguish between materials for the trade and those for the consumer. Most attention has been paid to film marketing materials which focus on the consumer rather than on the industry and this chapter will distinguish between these materials and illustrate their importance in the business to business and the business to consumer elements of film marketing. Of course, there is a link between the early film marketing materials which are produced by film marketing professionals for business to business marketing and those used to market to the consumer, and the following chapter will also consider this. This book tries to reflect the diversity of the global film industry in terms of the difference in approach to and execution of marketing depending on the type of film, whether it is an independent film or a studio film, the target audience, the budget, the domestic market for the film and so on. However, in writing in general terms about film marketing and in this chapter about film marketing materials, the focus will be on films with sufficient budgets and projected earnings to warrant a theatrical release and that have secured conventional distribution.

This chapter begins by considering the range of film marketing materials which must be produced in order to support the marketing campaign, both in terms of business to business marketing as well as the final consumer marketing campaign. After discussing some of the key personnel involved in overseeing or producing these materials, the following section explores the notion of visual representation as applied to film marketing. This leads to the considerations of the images used in film marketing materials and the creation and interpretation of film posters. This is followed by a similar process which looks at the other key element of the film marketing campaign, the trailer. These two types of marketing material are given most attention, as many of the practices involved in creating the additional materials such as print and television advertising are derived from practices used in the creation of posters and trailers combined with conventional marketing communication processes. The following section briefly discusses other forms of offline advertising before moving on to looking at media buying and planning and the chapter closes with the conclusions section.

Film marketing materials, like marketing materials for other types of goods and services are produced in order to satisfy the requirements of various stakeholders. In film marketing, when moving through the supply chain, materials are produced at various stages and their production is overseen by different members of the supply chain. Figure 7.1 illustrates the various stages in the film marketing process where film marketing materials must be developed. The inner circle denotes the materials which must be

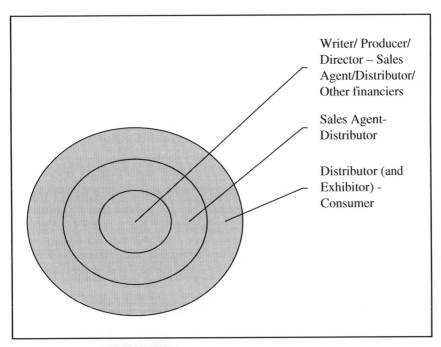

Writer/ Producer/
Director – Sales
Agent/Distributor/
Other financiers

Sales Agent-
Distributor

Distributor (and
Exhibitor) -
Consumer

FIGURE 7.1   *Film marketing materials model.*

presented to a sales agent (or directly to a distributor or other financial backer) in order to enter into an agreement with them. Following on from this, the sales agent (or producer) will provide certain materials to the distributor in order to secure their involvement and then to facilitate with the production of the final film marketing materials which will be used in targeting the end consumer. The activities contained in the central part of the model influence the middle layer which in turn influences the activities in the outer layer.

MARKETING TO A SALES AGENT

As discussed in Chapter 8, securing the services of a film sales agent can result in achieving international sales or not. According to Durie et al. (2000) there are certain rules to be followed when pitching a film to a sales agent. They emphasise the importance of a personal introduction from a respected industry contact when trying to get representation. This contact can either be an agent officially representing the producer or a professional contact who is prepared to vouch for the people involved and believes in the project that they are pitching, but is not involved in the project. The key element of the product at this stage is the script. Firstly, the script can be considered as a film marketing material. While Chapter 5 discussed elements of the script from the perspective of the film marketing mix, this chapter will consider the film script as a marketing material. Chapter 5 emphasised the importance of script quality and the link between the genre and story and the other elements of the film marketing mix. This chapter will depart from these discussions and look at how the script should be presented to possible backers. The script is an essential element of the pitching process and often, the script is the only available film marketing material when looking for production finance.

Alongside the script itself, Durie et al. (2000) recommend that producers provide a short synopsis (1–2 pages) or a treatment of the film, a proposed budget which is as detailed as possible as well as details of any proposed financing or financing that is already in place. A summary of the main characters in the film should also be provided as well as a list of the proposed (or agreed) cast. The above listed materials can help the sales agent to position the film with regard to established genres and target audiences, as discussed in Chapters 5 and 6. Additional materials should be provided in order to reassure the sales agent of the calibre of the creative team behind the film. If casting has been confirmed, a filmography of the principle cast should be provided. Details of the director's track record should also be provided. In preparing the materials to be provided to the sales agent, the focus is on reassuring the agent that their investment, in terms of time and money, will not be in vain. While research discussed throughout this book indicates the importance of the release strategy, the genre, the cast and so forth in estimating a film's performance, Durie et al. (2000) stress that the director is the most important element of the pitching package for an art house film. Therefore, a show reel of the director's previous work may also be provided in order to reassure potential investors. Table 7.1 provides a check list of materials which can be provided to potential investors.

Once finance is in place, marketing activities are focused on getting materials together which can be used by the sales agent and distributors in order to create the final marketing materials to be used in promoting a film to the industry and members of the media during festivals and markets and will also be used during the consumer campaign. This activity runs alongside initial public relations activities as discussed later in this chapter.

Table 7.1	List of Marketing Materials for Potential Financiers
Essential Materials	**Supplementary Materials (if Available)**
Script	
Treatment	
Budget (including proposed finance)	Details of finance in place
Proposed cast (only if it is likely that they would agree)	Cast biographies/filmographies once confirmed/cast photographs
Details of main characters	
Details of significant creative crew (if confirmed)	Crew biographies/filmographies
Director show reel	

THE UNIT PUBLICIST

As film is a visual medium; visual imagery is an essential element of the film marketing materials. In preparing the necessary film marketing materials it is important to attach a unit publicist and a unit photographer to a production in order to produce the most appropriate raw materials which can be used at various times in a film's marketing campaign. Writers on film marketing highlight the need for a unit publicist and photographer to be appointed and the mistake that inexperienced filmmakers can make in trying to cut costs (Marich, 2005; Durie et al., 2000). As discussed earlier in this book, the theatrical marketing campaign is the responsibility, financially and creatively, of the distributor. However, film producers and sales agents must ensure that key materials that will be needed in creating the marketing materials are produced during production and made available to the distributor in order for them to develop the creative marketing campaign to accompany a film's release. This is why it is important for the producer, to be aware of the film's positioning at this stage. The unit publicist is contracted to work on the set of a particular film while a film is in principal photography. At this stage, the unit publicist compiles materials which will be included in the electronic press kit (EPK). Key elements of the EPK are biographies of the actors, director, producer and additional creative talent such as the cinematographer, composer. Marich (2005) notes the importance of conducting recorded interviews with cast and crew at this stage, as to reassemble the cast and crew at a later stage would be very difficult and costly. Video clips may be short scenes from the film as well as scripted interviews with the cast and crew which can be used by art and film review programmes in the run up to a film's general release. In addition to generic interviews to be included in the EPK, the unit publicist can arrange for press junkets to the set in order for cast and crew to be interviewed during production. This may be particularly important if availability of cast members will be uncertain or impossible prior to a film's release.

Along with the biographies (which should appear in full and short forms) and clips mentioned above, the EPK should include a number of other items. Firstly, production notes outlining the key highlights related to the production such as when and where the film was shot and particularly interesting stories which occurred during filming should be included in the EPK. They should be accompanied by a two-page description of the film outlining the plot, indicating the genre and providing a brief overview of the creative talent involved. A full list of cast and crew should be provided, although Marich (2005) notes that this should be marked as preliminary, as this may change prior to a film going on general release. The EPK should also include any write ups that the film has already received in order to highlight the calibre of the film (Marich, 2005). There are many benefits which have accompanied the move to digital EPKs. Firstly, the cost of physically producing EPKs has been reduced as they have moved online. Journalists can now log in and access the EPK material rather than receiving it in a physical pack. This has the added benefit for the journalists of being able to access material in a form which they do not need to convert for broadcast or print publication (Marich, 2005). In addition, it is possible to add materials such as reviews to the EPK at any stage so that as a film moves through pre-release stage to general release and on to release on other platforms, the EPK materials can be supplemented without the cost of producing and distributing physical kits.

THE UNIT PHOTOGRAPHER

Alongside overseeing the publicity strategy for a film, it is important to employ a unit photographer to accompany the unit publicist during principal photography. During filming, the unit photographer should take still photographs of scenes to be used for continuity purposes as well as in preparing marketing materials. On-set photographs as well as photographs of cast and crew between takes and more posed portraits will be used in a number of ways. Firstly, listings of films at festivals and markets will usually be accompanied by a visual image. Finding one image which sums up the central theme of a film is very difficult and having a range of high quality stills to choose from is important. Secondly, editors of newspapers, magazines and websites will want to publish photographs which are of high quality and interesting and therefore in order to maximise a film's exposure it is important to be able to provide these images. Finally, images may be needed for producing film posters and other visual merchandising materials. Durie et al. (2000) note the importance of providing the unit photographer with a clear brief and having a range of colour and black and white stills available. They note the ease of converting colour images into black and white and therefore recommend a split of 60/40 in terms of colour and black and white stills. Schroeder (2002) provides an in-depth and comprehensive account of visual consumption and his book emphasises the importance of the photograph in marketing and consumption, among other spheres. The purpose of film marketing materials such as posters, trailers and advertisements is to position the film in the minds of the target audience, communicate the key benefit which they will receive from consuming the film and differentiate it from competitors. While film is experiential there is a need to be more literal in the advertising of film than for many consumer products. This is inspired by the restricted product life cycle of film. While many consumer goods can benefit from being established in the mind of the consumer as a result of a lengthy marketing communications campaign which allows the consumer time to become familiar with a product and to understand it both in terms of utility and symbolism, this is not possible for a film on theatrical release.

Although throughout this book there is an acknowledgement that things are changing in the realm of film distribution and marketing, the theatrical campaign can be viewed as the debut for a film and in order to sustain itself after the opening weekend, the utility and symbolism of a film must be established and understood by the potential audience over a much shorter timescale than is the case for fast moving consumer goods. While it is important that these materials do not just reflect a film, the marketing materials should be developed in order to present the film in an attractive way so that the target consumer develops 'want to see'. However, due to the power of word of mouth in film marketing, it is important to position the film correctly and to communicate the unique selling proposition so that the consumer expectations are set accordingly. For example, if the marketing communications imply humour, it is important that the film is in fact a comedy.

VISUAL REPRESENTATION

There are a number of considerations when selecting materials to be used in visually representing a film to the consumer. As noted above, although film posters often attain the status of art works, adorning the walls of homes and offices, for the purposes of this book it is important to consider posters as advertising texts. In so doing, we must consider their production and consumption in terms of their ability to communicate the key essence of a film to the target audience. Trailers and television advertising can be seen as extensions of static advertising with the added dimensions of sound and movement alongside the visual dimension. The main marketing materials which are used in this representation are film trailers, advertising (television, print and radio) and posters. Schroder (2002) discusses visual consumption in terms of decoding images. In order to decode these images, Schroder (2002: 37) notes the importance of understanding the 'symbols, conventions, and stereotypes' used in these materials. For this reason, conventional methods of presenting types of film are adhered to so that the consumer is not left in a state of confusion regarding the benefits which may be derived through consuming the film.

One of the accusations levelled at advertising in general is that it is a deceptive medium which aims at convincing unsuspecting consumers to part with their money in exchange for substandard goods or goods that do not meet the expectations of the consumer. Borgerson and Schroeder (2005) provide an extensive discussion of ethics of visual representation in marketing. As film is an experience good, the possibility of deception is even stronger. Webb (2009) discusses the potential for deception which is inherent in the medium of advertising. In her analysis, Webb highlights the difference between deliberate misrepresentation and inarticulateness in communicating the essence of something. As film marketing materials such as posters and trailers may often be prepared before a film is completed, the marketing materials may not be a true depiction of the final film. There is also the possibility of the filmmakers incorrectly anticipating how the film will be received by the target audience. This is why the use of market testing prior to finalising the marketing materials is important. Although scholars of the creative industry such as Hesmondhalgh (2007) are critical of the role of market research in the film industry, such research can prevent the incorrect positioning of a film and aid the consumer in making a more informed decision in terms of whether to consume one film or another. In the experience economy, the film marketing materials can either be the only clue available to the consumer regarding the nature of the product, or they may be one element informing a consumer's consumption choice.

Marich (2005: 14) provides a list of questions to be asked when starting to design the poster image. Firstly, are there well-known stars and will the audience for these actors or director go to see a film on its opening weekend? Being well-known is not enough to convince people to go to see the film. Is the story interesting and original? In terms of the target audience, is it an art house audience where the critics are seen as an important element in decision making or the youth audience which is portrayed as immune to critical reviews? Does the title clearly communicate the essence of a film? For example, *Snakes on a Plane* (2006), and *The Young Victoria* (2009) are pretty self-explanatory titles and therefore the poster, trailer and so on could focus on other elements of the film. If the title is less indicative of the content of the film, such as in the case of *Sideways* (2004), the marketing materials must somehow indicate what the film is about. Is there a central character that the audience will relate to or take an interest in? This can be ascertained through the audience research prior to release and the character or situation can be presented in the marketing materials. Marich (2005: 14) also highlights the need to identify sub-plots which can have appeal for broader audiences. He gives the example of *Rocky* (1976) where the advertising campaign emphasised the romantic story rather than the main focus of the film on boxing. The next question to be asked according to Marich (2005) is whether the film music is memorable and therefore can it be used in the trailers and television advertising? For many films, the music used in the trailer is not from the film as the trailer may be finished before the film soundtrack is finalised or the film music is not seen as effective in communicating the essence of the film in the trailer format. Adorno and Eisler (1994) refer to the notion that music should play a subordinate role in relation to the film itself. Adorno and Eisler question this presumption that film music should be unobtrusive. Rosar (2002) points to the change in film music which happened when popular music began to replace elements of the bespoke compositions and distinguishes between films where the score has been composed specifically for the film in question and those where music is needed in various scenes and individual pieces of pre-existing music are selected. As the major studios are almost all linked to major record labels, the industrial link between film and music is evident. Film can be seen as an ideal vehicle for the promotion of an artist or conversely, a well-known artist being associated with the music for a film can be seen as a marketing hook for the film and can be used in the promotional tools such as the trailer or advertising.

FILM POSTERS

Durie et al. (2000) note the importance of a film poster in positioning a film during a festival. They also refer to the difficulty of securing rights to certain images. The issue of rights clearance and contractual restrictions is an important one when considering film posters. Although the objective of producing a poster is to create 'want to see' in the mind of the consumer through communicating the essence of the film and highlighting the unique selling proposition such as cast, genre or other element, this must be combined with other considerations. Marich (2005) discusses the various contractual considerations which may feed into the creation of film posters. These issues came up during the doctoral research which was the original inspiration for this book (Kerrigan, 2005). It is common for well-known film stars to have contractual clauses regarding the size of their name in relation to the film title, the other actors or director or other key elements. This also relates to the positioning of names on the poster. For example, Marich (2005) notes that the left hand side of the poster is seen as more prestigious than the right side so if names of leading actors are to be placed side by side, in order to achieve an egalitarian presentation of the stars, the name on the right hand side should be elevated above that on the left. When it comes to director's billing, there are similar contractual issues to be considered. According to Marich (2005) in the US, such issues are considered by the relevant guild (actors' guild, directors' guild or other relevant guild). In addition, Kerrigan (2005) found that actors' agents also negotiate with regard to the billing on the poster. For this reason, it can be advantageous for producers to work with actors who share an agent in order to avoid endless negotiations with agents all trying to protect the interests of their clients. In addition to the positioning and size of the actor's name, it is common for talent contracts to contain clauses providing approval over images used in the promotional materials. Again, as an actor's image is central to their career development, this desire for control over its visual presentation is unsurprising. However, this results in a less than ideal situation for the poster designer who must balance the need to communicate the unique selling point to the target market in an appealing way, with the contractual restrictions regarding font, images and positioning.

For this reason, a poster designer must begin by considering the legal requirements and then working around these in order to provide an appropriate visual representation of the film. In the Hollywood system, it is usual for a number of creative agencies to prepare visual images for a film. The studio executives will then consider the visual representation which they believe represents the film most appropriately and this will be used for the theatrical campaign. In addition to using outside agencies, some of the studios also have in-house design. Outside the Hollywood system, independent distributors may have pre-existing relationships with creative agencies that specialise in the creation of film posters. Some may specialise in certain genres while others have competence across genres. A number of industry figures who were interviewed for my doctoral research as well for other projects since then have stressed the importance of thinking about the creation of marketing materials as early as possible. As Durie et al. (2000)

stressed, this is partly due to the problems which may occur in obtaining permission to use logos, images and so on, but also because of satisfying the contractual restrictions and attaining approval from key talent regarding the visual representation in the marketing materials.

Advertising is seen as a key element of segmentation strategy (Schroder, 2002) and this is clearly the case in film marketing. This can include online or offline advertising campaigns but for film marketing there is still a central focus on the film poster. Schroder (2002: 40) makes an important observation that "products complete in the realm of the image". The images presented in the film marketing materials compete with other visual representations and speak to the consumer about what to expect from a film. Schroder urges readers to move away from neural representations of what happens when we consume images and turns to Berger (1998, cited in Schroder, 2002: 47). The four processes which he identifies can help us to situate the design of film marketing materials as well as the process of sensemaking that we engage in when consuming these materials. Firstly, there is the process of resemblance. This is where the images used must resemble the essence of what is being presented. In the case of film marketing, this may be in terms of either 'grade' or quality of film as well as the type of film in terms of genre or style. By highlighting key actors in the communications, this gives the impression of a 'star vehicle', if the director is given prominence then the film may be more stylistically or artistically driven. If a film is linked to an earlier film, book or another known 'property', then this can also be seen as linked to the process of resemblance. The second process is termed 'cause and effect'. This is where a sense of logic underlies the design (and interpretation) process and this can be played out through the narrative structures which can back up claims. For example, in the case of a thriller, the visual communications should depict heightened emotions and tension, in a comedy, humour should be present. Schroder (2002) notes that many visual conventions were established by art history, this can be seen in film marketing as certain colours have been linked to certain types of film as discussed below. Finally, signification is where one act or image indicates another, such as smiling indicating happiness, images of Manhattan indicating a film's location in New York and so on.

MAKING SENSE OF FILM POSTERS

The following sections will explore the visual messages presented in a series of film posters in order to explore the nature of the film poster, design conventions and meaning making among consumers. The poster for Britney

Spears' vehicle *Crossroads* (2002) is a great example to consider when looking at the presentation of a star in a film poster. Firstly, it must be noted that *Crossroads* cannot be viewed as a conventional film. This film could more appropriately be seen as a promotional film for brand Britney as it featured Britney in the lead role as well as featuring her music on the soundtrack. The US theatrical poster (www.impawards.com/2002/crossroads.html) does not appear like a conventional film poster as Britney's name is across the top of the poster and the title appears towards the bottom of the poster. The film could be described as a 'chick flick' or a 'buddy movie' about three friends. This can be understood by looking at the scene depicted on the poster. On first glance this poster shows three girls, arms around each other, looking like they are having a good time. They are casually dressed and are walking across an empty road which appears in the background. On looking at the poster more closely, we can see that the girl in the middle is more prominent, she has blonde hair while her companions have dark hair, and she is wearing a yellow t-shirt which matches the yellow font of the title, while her friends have more subdued clothing. Britney is looking up and her face is clearly discernable while her companion's faces are partially obscured by their hair or sunglasses. So, what we can deduce from this is that the film is a star vehicle for Britney Spears and she is seen as the unique selling proposition. The positioning of this film in the mind of the consumer is consistent with the positioning of Britney at that time, a clean living girl, hanging out with her girlfriends having fun. In order to reinforce the connection between the film and the wider Britney brand, the following text is visible in the lower right hand corner of the poster 'featuring the hit single *I'm Not a Girl, Not Yet a Woman*'. The tagline which appears under the title says 'dreams change. Friends are forever'. Again, this tagline is consistent with the visual imagery used in the poster and the focus on friendship which is central to the film. The same poster was used in most territories for this film as Britney Spears is a well-known brand and therefore the need to tailor the poster to different cultural contexts is less important than it may be for other films. It is interesting to note that the name of the director is not prominent in this film, an indication of the mainstream credentials of the film where the film star and genre are key influencers on film choice rather than the director.

Beside from the contractual issues discussed above, there are some broad rules regarding the creation of film posters. Whether a film is art house or mainstream, it is a dangerous strategy to deviate much from convention in designing a film poster. When promoting a romance, the dominant colours are blue and white. For a perfect example of this type of poster, see the poster of *The Object of My Affection* (1998). This poster presents the conventional romantic drama image (http://media.movieweb.com/teasers/k/g/h/PGduUkfkZg5kgh_d.jpg). This poster has the classic blue and white background with the central characters in an embrace as the prominent image. The lead actress, Jennifer Aniston is wearing a white dress, which at first glance could appear like a wedding dress and Paul Rudd, the male lead is wearing a dark suit. The combination of the pose, the clothes that they are wearing and the way in which Jennifer Aniston is gazing into Paul Rudd's eyes in this poster clearly positions this film as a romance. Although the protagonists are smiling at each other, there is no indication of comedy in the poster which implies that the genre is more straight romance than romantic comedy. Reflecting back on the influence of contractual issues on the poster layout, it is interesting to note that the two lead actors' names are positioned side by side, but Paul Rudd's name is printed in slightly more prominent font. This may be an indication that negotiations were entered into regarding which name took prominence on the poster. Although both names are equally prominent, Jennifer Aniston's face is more visible than Rudd's due to the angle of the image used on the poster. Similarly to *Crossroads* (2002), the unique selling proposition for this film is the genre, signalled by the cast and the design of the poster. Again, the director is not particularly prominent on the poster as the film is a mainstream film targeting the market which looks at stars and genres in choosing a film.

As a film poster should be able to depict the benefit which consumption of the film will have for the consumer, it is important to communicate something about the mood and tempo of the film through the visual imagery used. An example of where this is very well done can be seen in the case of the US theatrical poster for the film *Bride & Prejudice* (2004) (http://www.impawards.com/2004/bride_and_prejudice.html). Again, this poster features the classic colours of blue and yellow. In addition to this background, the title is in gold and the lead actress Aishwarya Rai is dressed in red. The addition of gold and red to the blue and white brings a more passionate and energetic element to the visual portrayal of the film. Again, as is conventional in a romantic film, the lead actor and actress are featured at the centre of the poster, they are equal in terms of size but Aishwarya Rai is more prominent, partly due to the colour of her dress (red as opposed to the cream suit worn by lead actor Martin Henderson) but also as she is looking into the camera lens while Martin Henderson is looking away from it. Although not well-known in the West at the time of making this film, as discussed earlier in this book, Rai is one of the most prominent Bollywood stars and it makes sense that she is more prominent in the poster than Henderson. From the colours and the positioning of the stars, with their backs to each other, it is possible to identify the genre as romantic comedy, but in order to provide further depth to the portrayal of the film, the background of the poster shows a non-descript cityscape with various other minor actors visible. Although the Bollywood identity of the film is not very strongly emphasised in this poster, the formation of the other characters does indicate that this is an uplifting and energetic film as they are depicted as if they are dancing. As the actors are not particularly well-known, and the film was seen as a cross-over film, rather than particularly mainstream, the poster also features an indication of the track record of the director. Gurinder Chadha had a hit in the US with her previous film, *Bend It Like Beckham* (2002) and this was used on the poster for *Bride and Prejudice* (2002). Rather than featuring Chadha's name prominently on the poster the designer put 'from the Director of' so that the link was clear. Chadha's name is on the poster, but is well hidden underneath the title, in very small font, which is hardly prominent. In terms of positioning, both films contained an unconventional love story and reference to multiculturalism so the implication was made that liking one should lead to liking the other. Just in case the imagery and quality mark ('from the Director of') was not clear enough, the poster also contained a reviewer quote saying that the film is "spectacular, romantic, funny and so sexy."

For the Spanish theatrical poster, the central image is present, but this is bordered by a golden arch (http://www.movieposterdb.com/poster/51747a6c) similar to that used in the Italian poster for the film (http://www.movieposterdb.com/poster/e4e82431). In both of these posters the film is depicted more like a clash of cultures film with high-rise modern buildings on one side of the poster, and an Indian temple on the other, in addition, the tagline reinforces the crossing continents concept as it starts with 'From Mumbai to Los Angeles'. The supporting actors are more prominent in the film and a sense of humour is more evident. In both of these posters, the director's name and her last film are given equal prominence under the film title. These posters combine the energy of the film with the an indication of the genre, the director's calibre and the title provides a clue to those in the know, that the film is inspired by the classic British novel, *Jane Austen*.

While *Bride and Prejudice* communicates its cross-over identity by highlighting a number of elements such as the genre, the director and the actors, other films can use nominations of successfully winning awards to indicate their art house or niche sensibility. One example of this is the film *Sideways* (2004). The main marketing hook for this film was the director, Alexander Payne who had a success with his previous films *About Schmidt* (2002) and *Election* (1999). As in the case of *Bride and Prejudice*, the director's name may not be instantly recognisable, but including reference to the previous films on the posters for *Sideways* (2004) signals that this is a non-mainstream film which has a good script and a gentle sense of humour.

The US theatrical poster (http://www.impawards.com/2004/sideways.html) highlights the centrality of the male relationship in this film while also drawing the consumer's attention to the calibre of the director. While Alexander Payne's name is listed at the bottom of the poster as both director and writer, the previous film titles are in prominent font at top of the poster, directly under the title. However, if this was not enough to convince the art house audience, the French theatrical poster also highlights the film's 'quality' through listing the nominations that the film has received. The relatively equal status of the cast and main crew is evident by examining the presentation of their names on the lower part of the film poster, listed in equally prominent font. Durie et al. (2000) indicate that the film poster is the central element of a film marketing campaign in France. The poster for other European markets is similar, featuring the cast having a picnic, raising a glass of wine in a pastoral setting. The use of blue and white as the prominent colours in the poster, when considered alongside the list of US awards and the tagline, 'some go on a journey others take a holiday' gives the impression of something profound happening in this film. What the European poster lacks, apart from the reference to previous films by the director is a clear indication that this is a humorous film.

The above example illustrates the difficulty faced in designing a poster which can communicate the essence of the non-mainstream film without a clearly identifiable genre. Another film which can be seen to have had this problem is the British film *Dirty Pretty Things* (2002). The genre identified on the Internet Movie Database is Crime/Drama/Thriller. The US theatrical poster clearly identifies Audrey Tautou as the unique selling point in the visual communications campaign (http://bp3.blogger.com/_WkKZJVG5wTk/RfJsE4yow_I/AAAAAAAAMd8/N7j-4cfLgH0/s1600-h/dirty_pretty_things.jpg). Tautou was well known following her performance in *Amelie* (2001) which had been a cross-over success. In the US campaign the poster is dominated by a picture of Tautou looking seductively over her shoulder towards the camera. The poster background is black and the font is in coloured lettering across the bottom of the screen. The letters of the title look like they may be cut out of a magazine and therefore resemble a ransom note. These letters are in bright colours and also may be read as slightly comedic in presentation. Above Tautou's head is the tagline 'some things are too dangerous to keep secret'. This returns us to the idea that this is a thriller. However, the overriding image is that of Tautou. The bottom of the poster reads 'The provocative new thriller from the director of "Dangerous Liaisons" and "The Grifters"'. The name of the director, Stephen Frears is not highlighted, but included in the general list of credits at the bottom of the screen, among which 'BBC' and 'Miramax' stand out.

A variation of this poster (but without the brightly coloured font) was used in Spain. The title was written in two-tone font and over the title; in smaller lettering were the names of the three lead actors, Audrey Tautou, Chiwetel Ejiofor and Sergi López. As López is from Barcelona, this may have been used as a marketing hook among local audiences.

In contrast to the black background dominating the US and Spanish posters, the UK poster looks significantly different. The poster is split into two; on the left hand side is a still image of Tautou and Ejiofor looking tense and possibly sad. The right hand side of the poster is on a white background and is dominated by the title in very large black lettering. The words 'magnificent', 'spellbinding' and 'brilliant' are in prominent letters at the top of this section. These remarks are taken from reviews, a key element of positioning an art house film within the realm of the target audience. The actors' and director's names are listed around the title, but are less prominent than the positive review words. This poster may be indicative of the difficulty in visually representing a complex film in an attractive way. While the actors and director may be known, it is important to also give some sense of cause and effect as noted by Schroder (2002).

The above example shows the need to tailor a film to cultural preferences. As signification and convention may differ in different cultural contexts, it is important to situate the visual representation of a film within this context. As the costs of placing media far exceed the cost involved in producing a poster, it is worth considering developing culturally specific marketing communications. Tailoring a film poster to cultural preferences may be important for the film's initial appeal in that market. A good example of this is the Wan Kar Wai film *2046* (2004). By 2004, Wan Kar Wai had built up a reputation as an accomplished film maker. *2046* was a sort of follow up to the earlier *In the Mood For Love* (2000). The US theatrical poster (http://www.joblo.com/newsimages1/2046-poster.jpg) is designed as a montage of scenes which capture the sense of passion and intrigue contained in the film, without clearly identifying this film as a Hong Kong film. The actor's faces are blurred and their facial feature nondescript on the poster. The film's title is at the centre of the poster, surrounded by scenes from the film and under the title; in much smaller font it says 'A Wong Kar Wai Film'. The names of the lead actors are listed along the top of the poster but are not very prominent. The colour scheme is sophisticated, black, red and some blues and greys dominate giving a sense of seriousness to the film.

This poster contrasts with the French theatrical poster (http://www.movieposterdb.com/poster/e6b483d3) which has a more passionate visual image. Tony Leung and Li Gong, the main actors are depicted in a passionate embrace. The colours used in this poster are similar to those used in the US poster, but there is a greater proportion of black, with some red and gold, adding to the feeling of passion instilled by the central image. The title of the film is in prominent font just below the central image and under this again, and in less prominent font is the director's credit 'a film by Wong Kar Wai'. The names of the actors are listed below this again towards the bottom of the poster. In the top left hand corner, in delicate off white font is the ultimate art house mark of quality for a film on release in France, official selection at Cannes film festival. The overall quality of the poster is consistent with the images, rich colours; passionate imagery and the art house credentials indicate that this is a visually rich, artistic film. Most of the European posters for this film contained a similar visual style. In contrast to this is the Hong Kong poster for the film (http://www. moviegoods.com/Assets/product_images/1000/478528.1000.A.jpg).   While red and black are again used as the prominent colours in this poster, with the font in silver, the main difference is that the main actors' faces are shown prominently on the poster. As the main start in the film, Tony Leung's face is slightly more prominent than the others. As these actors are some of the most prominent actors in Hong Kong, their faces are enough of a unique selling proposition for this film. This is a film by Wan Kar Wai and stars the most well-known stars in Hong Kong. The concept being communicated is quite simple.

Keeping things simple should be the main aim in film poster design. If too many concepts are vying for attention in the poster, the consumer will not be able to understand the relevance of the film for them. Of course a clearly identifiable genre or simple concept lends itself well to a simple poster. For example, the film *Snakes on a Plane* (2006) has a straightforward concept. It is a film about snakes on a plane and the chaos that ensues. The poster followed the simplistic concept, the main star Samuel L. Jackson in various action poses with or without a snake. For other reasons, the poster designers for *Kill Bill* (2003) and *Kill Bill, Volume 2* (2004) could afford to keep the posters very simple. By the time of release of these films, the target audience all knew that cult director Quentin Tarantino's next film was called *Kill Bill* and that it came in two parts. All the poster designers needed to do was let people know that the film that they had been waiting for was on release. The poster for *Kill Bill* (http://www.consuminglouisville.com/images/Kill_bill_vol_one_ver.jpg) is very simple; a woman's hand holding a samurai sword down the centre of the poster in front of Japanese script with a tagline 'here comes the bride' across the top and 'the fourth film by Quentin Tarantino' at the bottom of the poster. The woman is clearly wearing a wedding dress and holding a handkerchief with Kill Bill written on it. The poster for *Kill Bill*,

Volume 2 (http://www.filmcatcher.com/uploads/img/product/kill_bill_vol_ two_ver6.jpg) depicts a bride, this time clearly identifiable as Uma Thurman, holding a sword, the tagline 'the bride is back for the final cut' is in the top left of the poster and at the bottom right, in slightly more prominent font is the title, with 'the new film by Quentin Tarantino' in red above it. Again, Japanese writing is evident on the poster, in large but obscured font behind the bride and between the words 'Kill' and 'Bill' in the title. These posters illustrate the poster's role as *one* element of the overall marketing campaign. As the publicity surrounding the release of the *Kill Bill* films was substantial, the poster merely had to remind the core audience that the film was about to be released.

The conventions involved in film poster design also extend to distinguishing a film from what may be expected of it. An example of this is the film *Elizabeth* (1998). As mentioned earlier in this book, the creative team did not want this film being viewed as a conventional 'frock flick'. Rather, they identified the film as a thriller and one of the main methods of communicating this to the public was through the poster campaign. They developed a series of one-sheet posters developing this theme (http://www. imdb.com/title/tt0127536/posters). They feature the key actors individually with the words, 'traitor', 'heretic', 'lover' and 'assassin' along the top. The only other prominent text on the poster was the statement 'a film by Shekar Kapur'. This reinforces two messages, firstly, 'a film by' denotes an artistic film and the director's name was not previously associated with the costume drama genre.

FILM TRAILERS

Traditionally, while the film poster may be displayed in prominent places in order to be seen by the target audience, the film trailer would only be seen by those going to see other films at the cinema, at the discretion of the projectionist. This is in addition to the 'coming soon' features at the start of a video or DVD. With the development of online campaigns, each film will have a dedicated website which will (at the very least) host the film trailer. In addition, film trailers are often available on other peer to peer websites such as YouTube and may be added as links to people's social networking sites such as Facebook or My Space. These developments will be discussed in more detail in Chapter 10 of the book. The following section will look at the processes involved in making film trailers and the link between the trailer and the rest of the film marketing campaign. Trailers are used in order to provide the potential consumer with a taste of the film. The drawback of the poster is that a three-dimensional audiovisual product is presented in a two-dimensional way without the benefit of sound. The trailer can overcome this problem and in so doing give a more developed sense of the film being presented. Short teaser trailers can be shown in the cinema well in advance of the release date and following the technological advances discussed in Chapter 10, these teaser trailers can also be circulated as virals which build word of mouth in advance of a film being released. These teaser trailers can often consist of very general scenes from a film and some character and plot development. However, as teasers are often produced prior to a film being completed, it is unlikely that a clear narrative structure would be presented. The purpose of the teaser is to signal that a film is coming and to begin to transmit a narrative about this film to the target audience. It is more common for teaser trailers to be shown for what Justin Wyatt (1994) refers to as "high concept" films. Teasers can be used effectively alongside initial promotional activities which serve to start speculation about the film and generate word of mouth.

THE PURPOSE OF THE TRAILER

As Kernan (2004) acknowledges in her timely and comprehensive study of film trailers in the US, these trailers must achieve two distinct aims; trailers must at once "withhold the fullness of the cinema event" while achieving a "sense of heightened presence" (p. 24). It is this tension between giving the consumer enough information to persuade them to chose a film, while avoiding the repeated accusation that film trailers give away all the funny bits or give away the story. For this reason, trailer making is a little explored art form. Kernan (2004) engages in a rhetorical analysis which locates the film trailer within the context of film production and consumption in the three historical periods which she studies; the Classical Era (1930s and 1940s), the Transitional Era (the 1950s to early 1970s) and the Contemporary Era (mid-1970s onwards). In setting up her analysis in this way, Kernan positions the trailer as a commercial tool which aims to promote the film to the target audience. Through studying trailers in this way, we can learn about the evolution of film as a dramatic form, the changing cinema audience as well as developments in film marketing techniques. During the classical period, the trailer was a predominant method of promoting film to consumers. During the transitional stage, cinema audiences were moving away in favour of television and the trailers adapted to be more persuasive. Kernan (2004) characterised this phase of trailer making as uncertain and experimental in terms of what the audience wanted, reflecting the studio's confusion at this stage. Finally, the contemporary era sees the trailer lose some of its dominance as film is promoted through such a wide number of methods. However, I would caution that forms of the film trailer are and will gain increasing significance in the digital economy. This leads us to consider the definition of a film trailer provided by Kernan (2004: 1) as "a brief film text that usually displays images from a specific feature film while asserting its excellence... created for the purpose of projecting in theatres to promote a film's theatrical release". In this way while Kernan (2004) acknowledges the ubiquitous nature of the film trailer, she privileges theatrical trailers over those made for other media. Conversely Johnston (2008: 145) promotes a more inclusive notion of the trailer by depicting it as "one of the few visual texts that exist comfortably on multiple screen technologies". In the age of YouTube, where people are developing the practice of consuming short media clips on a range of media devices, the film trailer may be seen as the ideal promotional tool for film. Chapter 10 will discuss this more in terms of how technology is changing film marketing practices so the remainder of this section will examine the film trailer in terms of its form and function.

Put simply, and as a promotional tool, the trailer is there in order to persuade the consumer to watch a particular film in the not too distant future. The trailer is as close to the free sample as we get in film marketing (unless one considers illegal downloads!). In the conventional sense, a trailer is viewed in the cinema. This is the ideal setting, firstly, we are in the mood to watch a film, we have chosen to spend our time in this way and are preparing for the film which we are about to watch. Secondly, apart from when studios add trailers for their forthcoming attractions to the reel of the film about to be shown, trailers are selected by the projectionist. There is usually a connection between the film about to be shown and the type of trailers selected (which sometimes leaves me thinking that I have entered the wrong screen as I try to figure out this link). Another significant advantage of the theatrical trailer is that it allows cinema goers to indicate a desire to see a film while in the company of their likely companions. Although the chapter on consumer selection of film indicates that a number of film consumers go to see films alone, for the majority of consumers, they go with one friend or partner or a small group of friends. When presented with the 'coming attractions' in this environment, it is possible to update the 'must see' list and identify willing companions.

Kernan (2004) identifies the common features which trailers exhibit. She indicates that most trailers have an introduction or conclusion which addresses the audience and provides information about the film. This can be done either through the use of narrative or presented non-verbally in the titles. This is combined with selected scenes from the film which are presented as montages of quick-cut action scenes. These scenes provide a sense of the narrative structure and genre as well as introducing the main characters. While the poster could depict the characters, lack of movement or narrative structure prevents the 'actor' being fully transformed into the character. Marich (2005) states the trend for mimicking trailers for existing films in order to provide a reference point for audiences. Marich also discusses the tension between maintaining the suspense of a film and telling all in the trailer. He notes that 'tell all' trailers seem to score more highly among test audiences. Of course, like all forms of research, these results should not be taken at face value. Who are the test audiences? What sorts of films are being tested? And, most importantly perhaps, how does a 'tell all' trailer impact on audience enjoyment of a film once they chose to watch it? As Kernan (2004) notes, meaning is constantly being renegotiated among audiences and the form of film trailers must evolve in line with this. As (reflecting Schroder's, 2002 analysis of the visual) interpretation is bound up in shared meanings, it is important that the style of the trailer translates into audience comprehension. In reflecting evolving film conventions as well as the conventions of trailers themselves, audience expectations about a film can be established within the 30 or 90 s usually allotted to the trailer.

During the excellent Strategic Film Marketing Workshop (http://www.strategicfilmmarketing.com/home.html) which I attended a number of years ago, we had a session on film trailers. It was very interesting to watch a series of trailers which were identical visually but accompanied by different music and a different voice over style. It is very uncommon to hear a female voice over. For similar reasons cited as to why women are heard less often on the radio, a deep male voice is preferred by film consumers. This may be as a result of deep seated gendered notions of authority, but this would need to be explored more deeply. Explanations aside, the established rule is that the voice over is done by a male, with a deep voice. When this was tested during the trailer session of the workshop, there was consensus among participants that the voice over either convinced us to select this film or that the film was not for us. For English language films, even those not emanating from the US, it is usual to have an American voice over artist, or at least one that sounds American. Again, this may be related to our familiarity with and acceptance of the American voice when consuming film. The most prolific and well-known voice over artist of recent history was Don LaFontaine. LaFontaine did voice over for thousands of trailers as well as other audiovisual products prior to his death in 2008. LaFontaine is associated with the opening line of 'in a world where...' BBC News refers to an interview where LaFontaine explained the need to relocate the trailer audience to the world of the film immediately so that they can immerse themselves in this context (http://news.bbc.co.uk/1/hi/entertainment/7595352.stm accessed 02/05/2009). Although the deep voice and standard lines such as 'he was a man...' are much ridiculed, they persist because they work. Again, referring to Kernan (2004), conventions of film trailers are established in the mind of the film consumer and moving too far from these conventions can involve significant commercial risk.

While the typical trailer for the high concept film will have the deep male voice over and standard phrases, this is not the only style out there. Some trailers include actual dialogue from the film which gives the viewer a sense of the actual film consumption experience. Others only show images and music which evokes the sense of the film. In the case of Wong Kar Wai's film *In the Mood for Love* (2000), the US theatrical trailer (http://news.bbc.co.uk/1/hi/entertainment/7595352.stm) starts with the theme song, Brian Ferry's *In the Mood for Love* playing which over a montage of scenes which give a sense of the plot and the visual nature of the film. The final element of the first part of the trailer is a series of statements and questions which help to contextualise the scenes shown. The combination of the chosen scenes, the text and the music communicate the sense of forbidden passion that underpins the film. Once this scene is set, the trailer changes and follows the more conventional style of voiceover. The voiceover artist (in typically deep tones) highlights the quality element of the film by naming the director. As critical reviews are seen as a key element of the marketing campaign for art house films, a number of reviews in high profile US publications are also cited in cementing the art house credentials of the film. Although there are two distinct parts to this trailer, the message is consistent and the viewer knows what to expect. Although the film's art house credentials are established and the characters are clearly from outside the US, there is no dialogue in the trailer. The voiceover is in English and in an American accent which may act as reassurance to any uncertain potential consumers.

A similar technique is evident in the international trailer for French film *Ne Le Dis a Personne/Tell No One* (2006) (http://www.youtube.com/watch?v=tf1_n-D8Idg&NR=1). This trailer was split into four parts. The opening scenes depicted carefree scenes of a couple in the countryside while Otis Reading's *Precious Love* played in the background. This may give the impression that the film is set in the US as the music has strong cultural associations. The film's calibre is transmitted by the words 'Winner of 4 César Awards' in the opening seconds of the trailer. The trailer then moves to a more tense section where we understand that a crime has been committed and the previously carefree male character is being pursued. A montage of scenes help to reveal the narrative structure of the film and are aided with short phrases (in English) appearing on screen to help to contextualise the scenes shown. The next phase is more uplifting and the viewer is given the sense that things have taken a positive turn for the protagonist, again there is no dialogue, but music is used to note this turn of events. Finally, we return to Otis Reading and the trailer ends. Apart from the reference to the Césars, there is no hint in the film that this is not in English. Even the email that the protagonist receives appears on the computer screen in English. This trailer contrasts with the French trailer (http://www.youtube.com/watch?v=F7zypg6UJ1g&NR=1) which features dialogue to accompany the scenes featured. Although the Otis Reading song is played across the opening sequences of the film, the music throughout the rest of the trailer is much more contemporary and French music is also featured. In this way, each trailer appeals to the target audience for the film. While the international trailer may be seen as deceiving the audience, film consumers would look to other clues in order to understand this film such as the cinemas it played in and the additional marketing communication materials. The trailer may cause 'want to see' but it is unlikely that consumers would end up choosing this film expecting it to be in English.

In contrast to the above example, the US trailer created by Strand Releasing for Fatih Akin's *Gegen Die Wand* (2004) (http://www.imdb.com/video/screenplay/vi2175533337/) clearly shows that this is a subtitled film. The trailer does not have a voice over but like the French trailer for *Tell No One* (2006), it relies on actual dialogue from the film to give a sense of the narrative of the film. In other parts, montages of scenes are shown and music rather than dialogue provides the dramatic movement. Songs from *Jesus and Mary Chain* and *Depeche Mode* are used in the trailer and in the film and they help to set the mood of the film. The opening stage of the trailer is dominated by indications of quality, as the numerous awards received by the film are listed. This establishes the film as a quality independent prior to revealing something about the nature of the film. Despite the clear identification of the film as not from the US, the trailer closes to the sounds of a typically American song which may have the purpose of reassuring the audience and leaving them with a familiar feeling.

TELEVISION AND PRINT ADVERTISING

The main focus of this chapter has been on film posters and trailers. This is because the other film marketing materials such as print and television advertising follow similar patterns to those seen in conventional marketing practice. For this reason the focus was on the visual elements that are specific to film marketing. In addition, considerations that go into planning and executing the posters and trailers are similar to those informing decisions regarding the scenes and images to be used for print and television advertising. In terms of creating these more standard forms of advertising for film, the key element is the segmentation of the market which is possible through these media. As physical newspapers and magazines become increasingly more segmented in terms of target audience and appeal, consumers and subsequently advertisers move online to further segmented spaces and cable, satellite and online television develop more niche audiences, it is possible for film marketers to communicate with more narrow target segments in ways designed to appeal to them. Fill (2009: 485) indicates that the key functions of advertising are to build awareness, induce engagement and to position a brand. Fill also stresses the role of advertising in building and maintaining brands. Kerrigan and O'Reilly (2008) unpick the notion of branding as applied to the film industry and establish that it can be difficult to identify what the core brand is within a film as there are a number of competing brands which coexist within the film and are reflected within the marketing communications campaign for the film.

MEDIA BUYING

Marich (2005) provides a comprehensive overview of the media buying process, drawing his examples from the US market. He notes that media buying used to be 'a robotic exercise' prior to the growth of the internet and subsequent media fragmentation. He now characterises media buying as a creative process and certainly this involves a clear strategy. When it comes to media planning and buying, everything begins with the target audience. While the process of placing media may not be so straightforward now, the possibility of effectively targeting the right audience and evaluating the impact of your communications with them has increased in line with this fragmentation. This has been particularly beneficial for small filmmakers who know that their target audience is a specialised group and do not want to spend enormous amounts on mainstream communication activities. They will develop a much more targeted campaign and access their core audience through very specialised media outlets. As Chapter 10 will cover these issues in more detail it is not necessary to expand on this further in this section.

In saying this, the cost of a theatrical release campaign is still growing. For mainstream film, the main expenditure is television advertising. Although the television and newspaper industries are struggling from downturns in expenditure on advertising, these are still the most popular sites within which to advertise a film. Friedman (2006) outlines the strategy employed by major studios in developing their television campaign. In order to maximise impact, the studios balance 'reach' and 'frequency'. More popular viewing times and advertising opportunities around popular shows may have greater 'reach' in terms of numbers of viewers, but these are the mostly costly slots. Rather than focus just on these slots and in order to engage with the consumer more often, these slots are combined with cheaper advertising times later in the evening or on alternative channels. In this way, it is expected that the target audience will see the advertisement a number of times and therefore be more likely to remember it. Friedman (2006) estimates expenditure on a low end media campaign to be between $8 million and $12 million and for a bigger film costs may be around $25 million. Despite the fact that they studied only films which were released on at least 650 screens, Elberse and Anand (2007) found huge variance in television advertising spend between the lowest figure of just below $250,000 spent on *The Good Girl* (2002) and over $24 million spent advertising *Tears of the Sun* (2002). Elberse and Anand (2007) found that television advertising accounted for 56% of overall advertising spend during the period studied (1 March 2001 to 31 May 31 2003). Friedman (2006) offers good insight into the planning schedule necessary prior to a film's release. Research by Toby Robertson (2003) for the UK Film Council found that increasing investment in television advertising did not seem to result in a significant increase in box office. Robertson found that increasing newspaper advertising did seem to have a slightly positive effect for both mainstream and art house films. However, Robertson (2003) did caution that television advertising may lead to greater recognition later in a film's life cycle and therefore contribute to an overall increase in earnings. The difficulty in attributing cause and effect in terms of evaluating the different elements of the film marketing mix and promotional strategy is a problem for film marketers in planning their campaigns.

In terms of timing, traditionally advertising campaigns would begin around four weeks prior to the release date with an extra push during the week before opening and Elberse and Anand (2007) have studied the effect of pre-release advertising on a film's performance by examining US data and using the Hollywood Stock Exchange in order to inform their analysis. In this study, they found that approximately 90% of advertising spend took place prior to the release date. As the traditional product life cycle of film is very short and dependent on a good opening weekend for large releases such as those studied by Elberse and Anand (2007), this is unsurprising. For smaller films which rely on a gradual release, it would be expected that this expenditure would be more spread over the pre-release and release period. However, with the advent of the internet, online campaigns are beginning much earlier and have moved away from the traditional information exchange model to more engaging processes. What is interesting in looking at Elberse and Anand's (2007) data is that although they found the impact of pre-release television advertising to be minimal, across the high concept films which they included in their sample, only 25% of expenditure was committed to trailer production, online advertising and other types of non-conventional forms of advertising. It would be assumed that for smaller films, this proportion of the budget would be larger as in order to compete in the crowded mainstream film marketing arena, it is necessary to shout the loudest.

This chapter has outlined the main film marketing materials such as the materials involved in preparing for a film festival, the electronic press kit, posters, trailers and advertising. As well as analysing the production and interpretation of these materials, I have introduced the reader to some basic concepts regarding the positioning and planning of media buying. This process is discussed in more detail in Marich (2005) and this would be an excellent source for those wishing to explore this more. As media buying varies from country to country there is a need to understand patterns of media consumption in each market. Consulting with experienced creative and media planning agencies in these countries will allow the film marketer insight into the most appropriate campaign for the film. The underlying conclusion in this chapter relates to the need to understand how film is represented, communicated and understood through the combination of audio and visual imagery produced as part of the marketing communications campaign. This chapter is firmly routed in the traditional approach to film marketing which still dominates for those wishing for a theatrical release. However, throughout the chapter (and the book in general) I have alluded to changes that have already taken place in terms of access to consumers, self-distribution and niche promotion of films enabled by technological developments. This will be explored in more detail in Chapter 10 which will also explore the role of publicity in the online and offline environment in the digital age. This chapter has opened up a marketing trajectory which moves from considerations of marketing and visual consumption, positioning films within the market through to the reworking of the marketing mix.

CHAPTER 8

The Film Marketing Calendar

This chapter examines the key features of the film marketing calendar. This includes key festivals and markets and award ceremonies as well as examining the interplay between release strategy and film marketing and looking at the key industry figures who guide a film through the film marketing calendar. The chapter begins by introducing the key figures in the film industry and examining their role in terms of film marketing. The chapter then moves on to examine different types of release strategy for films before a number of key film festivals and markets are introduced and the relevance of these festivals and markets is discussed. Finally, the relevance of various award ceremonies is discussed. The chapter will provide a key resource for understanding how film marketers should engage with these key events and to develop strategies which will benefit the performance of their film in the market.

KEY FIGURES IN THE FILM INDUSTRY

In terms of gaining access to the market, the key figures for film producers to engage with are sales agents, film distributors and festival organisers. These are the gatekeepers who will guide the film through the choppy waters of the film market or will prevent the film from having life beyond production.

Sales agents

Sales agents take on films and sell them on to international distributors and other relevant clients serving the DVD/Blu-ray and television markets. In addition, sales agents negotiate sales contracts with hotels and airlines for the rights to show their films. While there are sales agents in all of the key film markets, Los Angeles, Toronto and London have been identified as key locations where crucial mass of sales agents can be found. A report by Olsberg SPI and TBR Economics (2006) found that there were 35 sales companies in the UK in 2005. They consisted of three types of companies: companies with a turnover of under £1 million, which the report identified as struggling in the competitive marketplace; a second, slightly smaller group of companies which were performing more competitively and a final small group of seven companies which comprised of foreign representative offices of larger international sales companies.

Sales agents interviewed by Kerrigan (2005) noted the importance for a sales agent to become involved early in a project. For relatively inexperienced producers, using an established sales agent allows them access to distributors using the reputation and previous relationship which the sales agent has with the distributors. The earlier a deal is agreed with a distributor, the less financial risk is involved for the production company, so it is beneficial for producers to attach a sales agent to a project at the earliest possible stage. Many inexperienced producers fail to secure the services of a sales agent which it makes it very difficult for their films to succeed in the marketplace. The Olsberg SPI/TBR Economics (2006) report noted the importance of small UK sales agencies in finding distribution for specialised films. Sales agents build up extensive networks of contacts in the international marketplace and use these networks to negotiate production funding for films through the advance sale of rights in addition to securing rights to distribution (and therefore access to exhibition) once a film is completed. Kerrigan (2005) found that sales agents rely heavily on their established relationships in order to sell films to their clients. While an unknown film producer may have some difficulty in securing meetings with distribution companies and negotiating international deals, sales agents can access their developed networks and therefore have a much higher chance of succeeding in gaining a distribution deal.

The reliance on established professional networks emphasises the need for close long-term inter-firm relationships and inter-firm cooperation. These are the two resultant components of supply chain management according to Min (2000: 93). As the film industry is characterised as high risk (Biskind, 1998; Eberts and Illott, 1990; Finney, 1998; Evans, 2003, Phillips, 1991), such close inter-firm relationships and inter-firm cooperation can provide a level of reduced risk. Sheth and Parvatiyar (1995) illustrated how perceived risk is linked to uncertainty. Such uncertainty of outcome is inherent in the film industry and therefore it is natural to seek assurance through established relationships. Such inter-firm relationships are the norm in the European film industry and the nature of the relationships which have formed out of this fragmented structure are documented by Eberts and Illott (1990), Finney (1998) and Kuhn (2003). In these accounts, much emphasis is placed on risk and the need for close relationships to form, where creative and financial risks could be taken due to the high levels of trust in existence in the inter-firm or inter-personal relationships. This emphasis on reputation fits with Garver and Min (2000) in their assertion that the contemporary salesperson is viewed as a relationship manager. Garbarino and Johnson (1999) have studied this type of trust and see it as customer confidence in the quality and reliability of the services offered. Gwinner et al. (1998) believe that the psychological benefit of confidence and trust is more important than special treatment or social benefits in consumer relationships with service firms.

Sales agents may take a film at any stage. While sales agents may take a film in the early stages of development and help to put the financing deal together, they may wish to wait until the film has gone into production or come on board once the film is completed in order to find international markets for the film. The stage at which the sales agent becomes involved with the film can be dependent on a number of factors, including existing relationships between the agent and the producer, the quality of the film script, the quality and reputation of the writer/director or cast of the film and the genre of the film. UK training organisation Skillset[1] points out that sales agents are unlikely to take on a film from an unknown director prior to its completion. Sales agents are not paid by a producer to secure distribution deals for a film, instead they take a percentage of any deal which they secure. This ensures that sales agents take on films which they are confident that they can secure distribution deals for. Alberstat (2004) pointed out that banks will often require film producers to have an agreement with a sales agent before granting completion finance. In addition to negotiating deals with the distributor, the sales agent is responsible for coordinating marketing materials with the network of distributors that they secure deals with and for overseeing the marketing campaigns that each distributor develops for the film in their territory. They must also, through engaging a collections agency, ensure that all receipts due to the film maker are returned by the relevant distributor. Each distribution agreement is individually negotiated, although there are some governing principles regarding how these deals are structured. In order to secure a distribution agreement, distributors need to agree a fee and also commit to spending a certain amount on print and advertising expenses. Print and advertising expenses will indicate the size of release that a distributor plans and therefore is an indication of the level of confidence

---

[1] See http://www.skillset.org/film/jobs/distribution/article_4156_1.asp (accessed 18/04/09).

that a distributor has in a film. Alberstat's (2004) book provides an excellent overview of film production, distribution and exhibition deals providing in-depth case studies and invaluable financial details.

The sales agent will oversee an agreed schedule of deliverables which must be provided to the distributor. This will include the film master in specified format in addition to the marketing materials developed during the production and post production process (trailers, key artwork, photographs of cast, crew and particular scenes in various formats, behind-the-scenes featurette, articles which can be provided to press, technical production fact sheets, the final script and any other materials agreed during the negotiation of the distribution deal). The Olsberg SPI/TBR Economics report (2006) noted that the national support mechanisms for film producers in France include support for marketing materials, promotion at festivals and travel for directors and actors to support promotion of the film. This report also evaluated support for sales agents in a number of countries other than the UK and came up with the following evaluation. France was seen as providing most valuable support for the sales sector.

Charlie Bloye, Chief Executive of the UK's film sales agent membership body, Filmexport warned that licensing films according to territory is not a simple process (personal communication, 30th June 2008). Negotiating digital rights has become a very complicated area for sales agents. Firstly, there are some problems around identifying what digital rights are being licensed. Secondly, as the internet is a global resource, it is very difficult to place geographical boundaries around territories. The usual process of licensing that a sales agent engages in is where a film is licensed to a partic-ular distributor for all rights in that territory. Usually, distributors will wish to take rights for theatrical distribution, terrestrial and satellite television and digital rights. If internet rights are not included in a deal, then according to Bloye, the distributor will want to ensure that these rights are not offered to a competitor. As the distributor invests in producing the marketing materials for a film, it is fair that they are allowed to exploit the film across a range of platforms. It is usual for sales agents to collaborate with distributors in developing the marketing strategy for their films and they can be involved in negotiations between distributors from different territories in order to share marketing materials.

Film markets are key events for sales agents as it is here that meetings take place with international distributors, films which do not secure distri-bution deals prior to completion are screened and bidding wars may take place. For films in the early stages of development, where the creative team attached to the film is seen as strong, the sales agent sends the script to the main distributors with whom they have a relationship four to five weeks prior to the market so that once they meet at the market, negotiations can begin (Kerrigan, 2005). Sales agents hope that their films will prove attractive to a number of distributors in key territories and therefore result in a bidding war at the film market. During the Sundance Film Festival 2009, Variety reported on a bidding war for UK film *An Education*.[2] Fox Searchlight lost out to Sony Classics for the North and Latin American rights which they secured for a fee of $3 million.

As can be seem from the sections above, film sales agent must possess a wide range of skills, and this is emphasised by Skillset who notes that sales agents not only need to know what is currently selling but also predict what will be popular in the future.

Distributors

As can be seen from the previous section, sales agents have well developed relationships with film distributors. Once a distributor has licensed the film from the international sales agent (or direct from the producer), the distributor has the rights to promote and release a film in a particular country or region, known as a territory. A territory may be a country, or (more commonly) a group of countries. According to the UK Film Council,[3] there are over 90 territories in the global marketplace. Although distributors may chose to license a film just for theatrical release, according to Charlie Bloye (personal communication, 30th June 2008) distributors generally want to gain rights to distribute across a range of exhibition windows such as theatrical, DVD/Blu-ray, pay TV, terrestrial TV, and through the internet.

When discussing film distributors, it is important to distinguish between the majors and the independents. Chapter 2 traced the evolution of the US film industry and discussed the formation of the companies which are now known as the US majors. These companies have vertically integrated supply chains and therefore can provide worldwide distribution for films which they produce. The majors have distribution presence in most major film markets and also own a number of cinema chains in international markets (with the exception of the US, following the Paramount Decrees). In this way, the majors can ensure priority for films which they produce in terms of release strategy and marketing budgets. Major studios will also take on a number of independent films each year which they will distribute through their usual

[2] http://www.variety.com/index.asp?layout=festivals&jump=story&id=2470 &articleid=VR1117998976&cs=1 (accessed 19/04/2009).

[3] http://www.screenonline.org.uk/film/distribution/distribution2.html (accessed 18/04/2009).

channels. As discussed earlier in this book, this vertically integrated system has resulted in these US major studios gaining control over the majority of international markets for films. One of the key benefits which the vertically integrated major studios have over independent filmmakers and distributors is the ability to begin thinking about marketing issues at a very early stage. According to Kerrigan (2005) and Fellman (2006), within the vertically integrated system, the marketing and distribution personnel are involved in the greenlighting process for a film and once a film is greenlit, marketing and distribution will work together on planning the optimal marketing and release strategy for a film. They have access to a wealth of box office information for similar films which can be used in planning the campaign. They can also use their market knowledge of different territories in order to develop appropriate strategies. Marketing materials will be produced, taking advantage of economies of scale.

Independent film distributors usually operate within one territory only and secure the rights to exploit films within these specified territories. As discussed in Chapter 4, the size of the majors means that they can negotiate preferential deals with exhibitors leaving little space for independent distributors in this marketplace. Blair and Kerrigan (2002) traced the development of the market for independent films within the US and according to Berney (2006) this market has continued to flourish.

The final type of film distributor which is evident in the marketplace is the studio-independent (Berney, 2006; Blair and Kerrigan, 2002). These are distribution companies such as Sony Pictures Classic, Fox Searchlight, Miramax and Warner Independent which are owned by major studios but finance, acquire and release films with an independent sensibility which would previously have been released by truly independent distributors. Berney (2006) notes that this provides an additional problem for the true independent distributors as even the relatively small exhibition space open to independent or art house films once the blockbusters have secured their preferred release is dominated by major owned 'indie' distribution arms. However, Berney (2006) also notes that the audience for independent films is increasing and he credits the development of the DVD market for film in growing this market. He also predicts that the development of internet-facilitated distribution will add to this broadening out of film tastes. As consumers are exposed to different types of film, their ability to engage with different types of film develops. This logic underpins many public policy initiatives aimed at increasing access to non-mainstream film such as the policies discussed in Chapter 9.

Charlie Bloye (personal communication, 30th June 2008) noted the problems faced when selling a film to a number of territories sharing a common language. This situation has been complicated with the rise of multi-territory satellite companies such as MNET which started in South Africa as a satellite service. MNET originally broadcasted programmes in English only, throughout the continent of Africa, but have since developed provision in Portuguese for Mozambique and they are adding French to provide for the French ex colonies. This linguistic expansion results in a related geographical expansion as this can spread access to North Africa (due to French provision) which then sees the development of Arabic subtitles to meet the needs of this market which in turn opens up the Middle East market. Charlie Bloye talked about these developments in terms of the need to juggle these overlaps to see if there is a need to provide a discount or to license some rights non-exclusively in order to account for the spread of provision of the satellite service.

According to Fellman (2006) distributors can enter into two different types of agreements with exhibitors regarding share of profit. The first is the firm term agreement where a film is licensed to an exhibitor for a fixed release term and profit share is agreed between the exhibitor and the distributor. It is usual to include a 'holdover' clause in any agreement which stipulates that a film must be held over for an additional week if it achieves a specified box office return during its initial run (De Vany and Walls, 1996). The terms of this sort of agreement cannot be renegotiated once they have been agreed irrespective of the performance of the film once it is released. The alternative is when an initial agreement is formulated and once the original agreed run is completed, further terms can be agreed for an extended run. These terms are influenced by the performance of the film during the initial release period. Under both of these types of agreement, before profits are distributed, the cinema is entitled to deduct a sum of money which covers its overheads. This sum is called the house allowance (Fellman, 2006) or house nut (Vogel, 2001). Vogel notes that exhibitors may agree different house nut figures with different distributors and that this is based on the nature of the relationship that they have. Such differences also reflect the power structures of the film industry as exhibitors must ensure that they develop preferential relationships with distributors with control over upcoming blockbusters and can afford to offer less favourable terms to independent distributors. Research by Blumenthal (1988) and Kenney and Klein (1983) has analysed the process undertaken by exhibitors when they are bidding for films from distributors.

As discussed earlier in this book and confirmed by research by Nikolychuk et al. (2009), film producers have an historical suspicion of distributors. This relates to how profits are shared out between the different members of the film industry supply chain. Revenue is earned from exhibition activities and individual deals are negotiated between the distributor and

Table 8.1	Practices Used to Defraud Producers (Adapted from Vogel (2006: 114–145))
Inflating advertising costs	The exhibitor and distributor may provide false receipts indicating that money was spent on taking out advertising, nationally or locally to promote the film.
Bicycling	Using a single print authorized to be shown in a particular screen at a particular time and showing this in an unauthorized screen in order to gain additional undeclared revenue.
	This term also applies to cases where films are moved from an agreed screen to a smaller screen prior to the end of its agreed run as box office performance is not as strong as anticipated. This would occur in order to allow a more popular film to be shown in the larger screen.
Running a film for additional performances	This is where terms have not been agreed to authorize an extended run, but an exhibitor continues to show the film and does not return the funds earned at the box office to the distributor/producer.
Palming tickets	This is where ticket collectors leave a ticket un-torn and return this to the box office where it can be resold without recording the additional revenue earned.
Changing the ticket roll	This is where exhibitors use the first hundred or so tickets from one ticket roll and a second ticket roll is used and the tickets from the second roll are unreported.
Unauthorised reprinting of the negative	This is where exhibitors (or distributors) make additional, unauthorized copies of a film negative and show these in additional screens, the earnings from which go unreported. In the digital age, this practice can be seen as even more problematic as the cost of reproducing a high quality digital print is much lower than reproducing film.
Product splitting	This is where exhibitors in a local area agree to allocate films which are coming up for release among themselves rather than engaging in a bidding war with the distributor. In this way, the exhibitor can negotiate more favourable terms with the distributor than in an open market context.

the various windows of distribution. Vogel (2006) identifies a list of practices which may be undertaken by distributors and/or exhibitors in an attempt to defraud film producers. Table 8.1 lists these practices.

RELEASE STRATEGIES

The above sections have indicated the roles played by sales agents and film distributors (in collaboration with exhibitors). This section will go on to the release strategy in terms of times of year during which certain types of films are likely to perform well at the box office as well examining the types of release strategy available to film producers. Firstly, the windows system will be introduced and this will be followed by a discussion of the release strategy. Chapter 5 discussed elements of the release strategy linked to the film marketing mix and these will be developed in the following section.

The windows system is the term applied to the various stages of release that a film goes through from theatrical release (in cinemas) through home video (DVD/Blu-ray rental), pay-per-view television, subscription pay television and free (network) television. This is the basic windows model but this will vary according to the territory in question and in accordance with broadcasting practice and regulation in each territory. Drawing on the US market, Blume (2006) outlines the various windows and the length of each window for a typical film (see Table 8.2). Added to the basic model are the final two categories which may not exist in other territories. In addition to this model, modes of internet distribution are entering into the film distribution/exhibition process and disturbing the established window's system.

The key logic underlying the maintenance of the window's system is the fear of cannibalisation of one mode of exhibition on earlier windows. Studies by Nelson et al. (2007) and Waterman and Lee (2002) illustrate that it is in the interest of major film distributors to maintain the existing windows system. When the time between releases is reduced, gains can be made by smaller distributors but not by those distributing very big films. Nikolychuk et al. (2009) found that collapsing the current windows system would allow independent distributors to save money on marketing costs. Under the current system, distributors must embark on a marketing campaign for theatrical release, then wait for a period of six months before putting together a further campaign for home video release and so on. Nelson et al.

Table 8.2   The Windows System (Adapted from Blume, 2006: 335)

Medium	Length of Time in this Window	Time Delay after Theatrical Release
Theatrical	6 months	n/a
Home video	10 years	4–6 months
Pay-per-view	2 months	8 months
Pay television	18 months	12 months
Network television	30 months	30 months
Pay television second window	12 months	60 months
Basic cable	60 months	72 months
Syndication	60 months	132 months

(2006: 305) distinguish between the two stages apparent during this first release window, length of time on theatrical release and the 'out-of-market gap'. As most revenue is earned in the later windows (despite possible decreasing percentage of profit payable to the distributor in these later windows), marketing costs must be paid out long before these costs can be covered by revenue. The period referred to by Nelson et al. as the 'out-of-market gap' is the particularly problematic time for the independent distributor. Although there are reports that the time between windows is reducing from the standard 6 months between theatrical and home video release to 4 months and 8 days (The Economist, 2007), the maintenance of the window's system is further testament to the power of the major distributors as various attempts to simultaneously release films through all windows have met with resistance from the major studios. Nelson et al. (2007) report that the National Association of Theatre Owners (NATO), the membership body for exhibitors in the US, published a position paper putting forward a defence of the existing windows system in order to ensure the survival of cinemas.

Nelson et al. (2007) propose two reasons which may explain the shortening of the time between theatrical and home video release. Firstly, the nature of licensing agreements between distributors and exhibitors means that the longer a film remains on theatrical release, the less income is returned to the distributor/producer (proportionately). Secondly, closing the time between theatrical and home video release can be seen to minimise the impact of piracy. As piracy can be seen as partially economically motivated but partially linked to lack of access to films, shortening the period before which consumers can legitimately watch a film at home may contribute to reducing losses through piracy.

As discussed in Chapter 5, many commentators have indicated that the crowded exhibition marketplace has resulted in many of the conventions of release timing being overturned. However, Berra (2008) notes that in the US a strict release pattern can be observed. From January until Easter is a time for the release of what Berra (2008: 26–27) terms the low profile 'popcorn' pictures, films with formulaic structures, identifiable genres and well-known stars. During February, most media attention in the US focuses on what is going on at the *Sundance* festival in Utah. This allows the independent filmmakers who show their films there the opportunity to benefit from this attention while the Studios release their more low profile films. The summer months of June to August are when the really big studio films are released as this is when film-going is highest among the blockbuster audience. Durie et al. (2000) note that in Mediterranean countries, cinema attendance has traditionally decreased after April as the warm weather led to a move to outdoor activities and therefore this has been seen as a risky period for film distributors. However, they note that the increase in numbers of multiplex cinemas with good air-conditioning systems has minimised this risk since the 1980s. The winter sees what Berra (2008: 27) terms 'more serious fare' released by the studios and Durie et al. (2000) indicate that this is the peak film viewing time in Europe. Kerrigan (2005) learned that there are established release rules for film, but, in agreement with Berra (2008) the independents release films all year round as they have less power in negotiating with cinema programmers for ideal release slots. The section below, which looks at the impact of awards on film marketing practices will illustrate the impact which 'awards season' has on release strategy for films.

Fellman (2006) lists the three options available to film distributors when planning a film's release strategy: wide release, limited release and exclusive or platform release. Wide release is where a film is opened simultaneously on as many screens as possible (within a territory, or as is increasingly the case, internationally). According to Fellman (2006), a wide release in the US would see a film opening on between 700 and 3000 screens. When distributors are confident that a film will perform well and they have invested in a costly marketing campaign, they will opt for a wide release. Much research, specifically that undertaken by Elberse and Eliashberg (2003) and Elberse (1999), has indicated that wide release is the most beneficial strategy for distributors as it means that they can take advantage of a publicity blitz. In addition, De Vany and Walls (2007) conclude that major studios also opt for the wide release to minimise losses due to piracy. However, such a wide release is only possible if distributors possess the necessary industrial power to negotiate a wide release in international markets as well as necessary economic resources required to finance the prints and advertising budget required for this type of release.

Limited release is more usual as this sees a film opening on between 50 and 700 screens in the US (Fellman, 2006). This type of release strategy is used when a specific segment of film consumers is targeted and publicity activities are directed at this group. This would see the film opening in major urban centres first before moving out to smaller cities and finally to rural theatres. Final release would be dependent on the success of the film in the initial urban centres with only the most successful films getting a broader release. The advantage of this type of release is that physical prints can be moved after a film has closed in a particular area and that revenue earned can be reinvested in localised publicity campaigns as the film moves around.

The final type of release strategy is the platform or exclusive strategy (Fellman, 2006) and this is usually reserved for art house films and films which rely on strong positive word of mouth from audiences to sustain the film on theatrical release. This type of release would see such films open on a very small number of specialised screens in major urban areas before moving on in a similar way to the limited release strategy. Fellman (2006) illustrates the importance of having a tailored release strategy that suits the film in question. He provides the example of the successful independent film *Best in Show* (2000) which followed the typical platform strategy in New York, Los Angeles and Toronto but also opened on eight screens in the San Francisco area as Warner Brothers, the distributors believed that it may be popular with audiences there. This proved successful and Warner Brothers then used a similar approach to distributing the film in other markets. This film went on to earn over $20 million.

Although theatrical release gains most commentary and the majority of academic research such as that undertaken by Hennig-Thurau et al. (2001) on film performance considers theatrical release alone, the majority of revenue is earned from subsequent windows. De Vany and Walls (1996) have developed a dynamic model which examines the impact of theatrical release on the other windows and shown that strong performance at the box office acts as a signalling process for consumers in selecting the film later in its release. Waterman (1987) estimated net profits of $1 for distributors derived from theatrical release as opposed to video rental returns of $0.35, pay-per-view returns of $0.20 and network television returns of $0.05 in the US market. A further study by Waterman and Lee (2003) found that cumulative profits could be maximised through the maintenance of an extended theatrical window. Waterman and Lee employed a game theory approach and concluded that although initial revenues could be increased by a competitor in the DVD rental marketplace shortening the window between theatrical and DVD release, thereby taking advantage of the element of consumer surprise and the novelty of having access to a film through the rental window earlier than expected. However, they also warned that it was likely that any benefit earned would be temporal, as other competitors would take advantage of any possible benefits by also shortening this time period.

Aside from decisions about when to release a film, what type of release strategy to engage in and negotiations regarding day and date, film distributors are responsible for the film's marketing campaign. Although as mentioned above, the marketing campaign will be discussed with the film sales agent, and some marketing materials provided by the sales agent, film distributors will develop marketing materials for the territories for which the film is licensed to them. While Chapter 7 discusses the film marketing materials in detail, the following section will elaborate on the types of film marketing activities which film distributors must engage in. As this book

| Table 8.3 | Checklist of Film Marketing Activities (Adapted from Blume, 2006) |

Creation of advertising materials (posters, trailers, television, radio, on-line)
Planning publicity activities (interviews with newspapers, magazines, television, radio, on-line)
Planning of advertising and publicity campaign to coincide with release
Organisation of press junket
Booking theatres and agreeing terms
Test screening of film to determine playability and influence marketing materials and positioning
Delivery of prints/digital film to theatres
Ongoing monitoring of film performance on each screen and negotiations regarding extending exhibition time
Extension/reduction of advertising and promotional activities in line with performance of the film
Negotiation and coordination of commercial deals with consumer goods companies to provide cross-promotion for their products and the film

proposes an holistic approach to film marketing, it is argued that all of the activities from idea generation to final consumption of a film by a consumer are classified as marketing activities, within the film industry, certain practices are considered as part of the marketing campaign. Blume (2006) lists a number of activities as part of the theatrical release. Table 8.3 provides a checklist of activities which must be undertaken by the distributor.

FILM FESTIVALS AND MARKETS

Having looked at the conventional distribution mechanisms for film listed above, this section of the chapter will look at the role played by film festivals and markets in the film marketing process. Gore (2004) notes that Venice is the oldest surviving film festival, having been established by Benito Mussolini in the 1930s. Gore points out that Cannes (founded in 1939, but suspended during the war years) and Berlin (founded in 1951) are also still in existence. Indeed, these three festivals are still the most prominent European film festivals according to Verdaasdonk (2005). Durie et al. (2000: 53) describe the major markets and festivals as "crucial dates in the diaries of film sales and marketing executives". They point to the *Cannes* festival and market, *MIFED* (which no longer exists, but used to be held in Milan in October) and the *American Film Market (AFM)* in Los Angeles as the most important markets for filmmakers, adding that Berlin is seen as a key market for art house films. Turan (2002) highlights *Cannes, Sundance* and *ShoWest* as key markets for filmmakers and distinguishes between festivals and markets. Montal (2006) provides definitions of festivals and markets and this is a useful starting point for an exploration of these two types of events. Montal (2006: 316) defines a festival as "an established venue usually organised around screenings and prizes, dedicated to introducing movies of a certain style to a paying audience". It is the presence of the paying audience which is a key differentiator between the festival and the market. Although acknowledging that festival audiences include distribution executives and journalists as well as a paying audience of consumers, Montal (2006: 316) highlights the importance of receiving awards and associated publicity attached to festival entry for a film. On the other hand, film markets are defined as business venues closed to the public which may be associated with a festival or not. Although there is a distinction between events which are purely festivals and those which are primarily markets, these distinctions are blurring. Unwin et al. (2007) found that members of the public attending a particular film festival felt excluded from core activities by the presence of many industry figures who focused on doing deals usually associated with a market rather than a festival.

Gore (2004) notes the change that has taken place in terms of what a film festival used to be and what it has become. He states that the original festivals were venues for appreciation of film and saw art and politics very much intertwined. He contrasts this with the disposition of many contemporary film festivals which have embraced the commercial considerations of the film industry. In fact, film festivals can be seen to have a number of purposes. Firstly, and the main consideration for this chapter is that film festivals can act as catalysts for distributing those cinematic messages to society that it would be unusual to see on general release. As film distribution is generally commercially motivated, film festivals are one outlet for less commercial film. This category can include very specialist film in terms of certain genres, artistic film with limited commercial potential and the category discussed by Nichols (1994), 'new cinemas', films from a particular country or group of filmmakers seen as sharing a common sensibility. Secondly, film festivals can act as alternative forms of distribution for films trying to enter the film market without the benefit of the vertically integrated studio system. In addition to these film-focused purposes, film festivals may also act as tourism mechanisms, developed in order to attract visitors to an area or have social motives, such as festivals concerned with human rights or other social or political issues.

Montal (2006) believes that festivals are a more accessible route to looking for distribution deals as films are submitted through an open call, they have low entry fees and the outcomes of the festival are publicised. In contrast, film markets may be very costly to attend as they require paying for market passes to attend and the cost of such passes can often be very high. In a market situation it may also be difficult to get attention for an individual project among the many projects which will be pitched over the course of the market. Berra (2008) in his book on independent American film observes that aiming for entry into specific film festivals can influence the film production schedule. Berra (2008) also illustrates the huge importance of festivals such as *Sundance* for independent filmmakers in terms of getting exposure for their films. This can mean that production and post-production activities are truncated, not just for budgetary reasons, but in order to be submitted to the relevant festival on time. Missing the most appropriate festival in a given year would be a terrible blow to the independent producer who struggles to find a distribution deal.

The *Sundance* festival is one of the most talked about festivals in the film calendar. The festival grew out of the Sundance Institute, established by Robert Redford in 1981 and based in Utah. As documented in Biskind's (2004) analysis of developments in independent US cinema after the 1970s, the Sundance Institute was established in order to provide support for independent filmmakers struggling to finance and launch their films in the face of the domination of the major studios. Biskind (2004) tells the story of how Steven Soderbergh's *Sex, Lies and Videotape* (1989) transformed the independent film landscape and the place of the *Sundance* festival in 1989. Although Robert Redford apparently did not favour film festivals, he was persuaded to provide a resource for independent filmmakers to engage in the marketing and promotion of their films, once they had been produced with the help of the Sundance Institute. Biskind (2004) notes that by 1989, *Sundance* had become associated with 'worthy' films and that the best film award was usually awarded to the most worthy film based on subject matter rather than on the filmic nature of the film. This had resulted in the festival being seen as a commercial kiss of death for a film as being associated with *Sundance* inevitably meant that a film had little playability. Independent film distribution in the 1980s as described by Biskind (2004) is reminiscent of the industry in the UK at present, few independent distributors committed production finance to films and many of those who did went bankrupt. Instead, completed films were acquired at festivals. Although *Sex, Lies and Videotape* did not win the Grand Jury Prize, it did win the audience award. This highlights one of the important elements of the film festival. When a film screens at a festival, this may well be the first time that anyone from outside of the business side of the film industry gets to see a film. Although many festival audiences are comprised of a high proportion of industry figures, the presence of informed and engaged film consumers is important in identifying films which may not seem like commercial successes on paper, but which the audience responds to. Since the uncertain first decade of the *Sundance* festival, it has now been established as a key festival for independent films, particularly those from the US. A good response from the *Sundance* audience can motivate a distributor to consider licensing a film that they may have previously overlooked. Montal (2006: 319) refers to *Sundance* as "the hottest venue for independent American films".

Slamdance was created by filmmakers to support other filmmakers in 1995 and also takes place in January in Park City, Utah. *Slamdance* is seen as a direct competitor to *Sundance* as it takes place at the same time in the same place. The difference between *Slamdance* and *Sundance* is that the main competition categories are open to first time filmmakers and films with budgets of under $1 million. *Slamdance* has a particular emphasis on short films.

The most well-known film festival/market is the *Cannes Film Festival* which takes place in Cannes in the South of France in May each year. In the same year that *Sex, Lies and Videotape* (1989) won the audience award at *Sundance*, it won the overall festival prize at the Cannes Festival, the Palme d'Or. Although, as stated above, this festival was originally launched in 1939, the festival did not run during World War II and so was officially founded in 1946. Montal (2006) notes that *Cannes* is viewed as the premier film festival internationally. During the festival, competition films are shown at the Palais and screening of films in the market take place at venues around Cannes. There are European and American Pavilions at Cannes and similarly to the American Film Market, many national film agencies have a physical presence at *Cannes*. *Cannes* is seen as a more mainstream festival than *Venice* or *Berlin* and therefore, Montal (2006) points out that it is seen as a major launching ground for international films. Perhaps its location on the French Rivera and the timing of the festival at the start of the summer are responsible for *Cannes* being seen by some as a party more than a festival as many non-film industry people go to Cannes during the festival to star spot. However, *Cannes* has a very active film market and filmmakers fight hard to get attention for their film during the festival.

Berlin International Film Festival or *Berlinale* as it is also known, is held in February each year. 2010 will see the 60th festival. *Berlinale* has a major film and television market, the European Film Market, as well as the festival. The final element of the overall event is the Talent Campus, a series of events which are held over the course of a week which is targeted at young filmmakers and closely connected to the festival. The top prize at *Berlinale* is the Golden Bear which goes to the best film as judged by the festival jury. Films appearing in competition at *Berlinale* also succeed in gaining press attention, especially if they premier at the festival.

The *American Film Market (AFM)* is held in November each year (having moved from its original time slot in February/March). In contrast to the festivals discussed above, *AFM* started life purely as a market rather than a festival. The event is held in Santa Monica, California each year and delegates must register to attend well in advance. This is the key event for US film professionals and in addition attracts very high numbers of international delegates. During this event, attendees hold meetings, screenings and discuss deals during eight days. Similarly to *Berlinale, AFM* has a programme of seminars which take place during the first days of the market. In 2004 the *AFM* entered into a partnership with *AFI Fest*, a film festival which is held at the same time in Los Angeles.

The *Toronto International Film Festival* is held in September every year and this timing means that many film studios look to *Toronto* for initial publicity for films for which they are seeking *Academy Award* nominations (Kay, 2008). The *Toronto International Film Festival* was established in 1976 and has grown into one of the key festivals for the international film industry (Montal, 2006). *Slumdog Millionaire* (2008) secured its first award of many at *Toronto* in 2008. Montal (2006) points out that what makes *Toronto* unique is how easily accessible the festival is to the general public and the presence of a strong local audience alongside a strong international film market.

The largest film festival dedicated purely to documentary film is the *International Documentary Film Festival Amsterdam (IDFA)* which takes place in Amsterdam each November. This festival was established in 1988. Similarly to other festivals, a series of talks and master classes take place alongside the festival screenings in order to foster the art of documentary making to which this festival is dedicated.

Established in 1969, the *Festival Panafrican du Cinéma et de la Télévision de Ouagadougou (FESPACO)* is the key festival for African cinema and is held in Burkina Faso on a biannual basis. This festival provides a showcase for African filmmakers to show their work. Although this is a Pan-African festival, the focus of this festival on francophone film industries both linguistically and in terms of artistic sensibility has meant that popular West African cinema such as Nigerian and Ghanian video films have not fitted with the overall festival agenda. Olorunyomi (1995) reports the discontent of Anglophone African filmmakers regarding their perception that *FESPACO* is biased towards Francophone films. In addition to the perceived linguistic bias of *FESPACO*, Ukadike (2002) in his collection of interviews with filmmakers from across the continent of Africa, uncovers the perception that French support for filmmaking in former French Colonies has influenced a particular (non-African) style of filmmaking. Since its inception in 1969, *FESPACO* had developed into a full-fledged festival with film awards in a number of categories and now has a film market which runs alongside the main festival.

Pusan International Film Festival was established in South Korea in 1996. Kim (1998) links the birth of a number of specialist film festivals in South Korea in the 1990s with the centrality of film consumption to the youth culture in South Korea. Kim (1998) points to the ambition of *Pusan* to identify itself as a focal point of Asian cinema, competing with the Hong Kong and Tokyo festivals. *Pusan* was first developed as a regional initiative and supported to the city of Pusan government but from 1998 it has been supported by central government (Shin, 2005). Through increased government support and popularity among neighbouring film industries, *Pusan* has succeeded in establishing itself as both a showcase for domestic film and a key centre for wider Asian cinema. Shin (2005) notes that *Pusan* has been central to promoting South Korean films to other festivals as festival programmers are exposed to South Korean films (contemporary and through retrospectives) at the festival and go on to programme these in festivals such as *Berlin*.

There is no clear or commonly accepted definition of what constitutes a film festival. The defining characteristic is that it has to offer something that does not exist for the rest of year and be more than just a screening of a particular film. Over the past decade, the number of film festivals has expanded rapidly. The initial limited number of professional events with a specific function of introducing films and new talents to the commercial distribution sector has developed into what can be seen as an alternative distribution circuit. As Kim (1998) and Nichol (1994) found that through the selections and programming that they engage in, the way they present films and the narratives that they create around films, film festival organisers create very specific persona for the festival. From a business perspective, Montal (2006) and Gore (2004) urge filmmakers to do extensive research before choosing where to submit their film. Once the festival has been chosen, filmmakers and the professionals working with them must plan their festival strategy carefully. Strategic planning will include identifying which distributors will be in attendance at the market and drawing up a short list of the most desirable according to their fit with the film in question. It is preferable to make contact with potential distributors prior to the start of the market in order to provide information about the film and to set up a screening and a meeting at the festival or market.

Film festivals serve the collective purposes of promoting niche films to both the industry and the audience. They can offer an alternative method of distribution outside of the structural constraints of the international film industry, as dominated by the Hollywood majors. Through exhibiting films at film festivals, filmmakers can reach their audience independently of major distribution companies, for festivals which are also film markets, filmmakers can secure distribution rights on the basis of a positive audience reception for their film as was the case for Irish film *Once* (2006) and *Slumdog Millionaire* (2008). Film festivals can increase the number of visitors coming to an area at a particular time and finally, film festivals can focus on particular genres which are underrepresented in the mainstream channels of distribution or showcase national cinemas. In achieving the above aims, there are various marketing functions which are performed. In a purely commercial context, the films themselves are showcased, positioned in line with the overarching festival identity and presented to the audience in an attempt to 'market' the film. Alternatively, the films exhibited in the festival can themselves act as social marketing tools in marketing a social issue, promoting alternative viewpoints about such issues, or in marketing a culture, subculture or region through its film. Finally, the film festival itself can be seen as part of the overall marketing strategy of a place, in positioning the film festival as a tourist attraction or a celebration of local identity.

Awards ceremonies

The final elements of the film marketing calendar which must be considered are awards ceremonies not linked to festivals. Linking back to earlier discussions in this chapter concerned with the role of critics, being nominated for or winning a major award is presumed to have a positive impact on the success of a film in the marketplace, however, the little empirical research which considers this does not show strong support for this assumption. According to Durie et al. (2000), award nominations and successes can play a key role in the marketing campaign of a film, particularly in the case of art house films. They stress the increased media interest that an award nomination (and particularly a success) can bring. In Chapter 7, the use of awards in marketing materials is discussed. Apart from key festival awards such as the Palme d'Or from *Cannes* there are a host of other awards given by film industry bodies, national entities or media organisations. Certain awards can result in a film being classified as an independent film, while others may indicate a level of popular appeal. Simonton (2004) studied films receiving awards or award nominations[4] in order to assess the link between cinematic

[4] Data was analysed from the Academy of Motion Picture Arts and Sciences, Hollywood Foreign Press Association, British Academy of Film and Television Arts, New York Film Critics Circle, National Board of Review, National Society of Film Critics and Los Angeles Film Critics Association between 1975 and 2002.

creativity and achievement. Cinematic creativity was measured in terms of awards bestowed by industry guilds and later film ratings. Although assumptions that industry guild awards and film ratings are somehow detached from the decision makers involved in these award ceremonies may be problematic, the strongest indication found in this study showed that Oscar awards most strongly correlated with other indicators of creativity. In an earlier paper, Simonton (2002) found that film direction and the quality of the screenplay, as measured in terms of Oscar nominations for these categories as opposed to others, impacted most significantly on a film's success. Esparza and Rossman (2006) draw on the institutional theory of DiMaggio and Powell (1983) in stating that awards can help to define what is valued within that field and in so doing, influence future activities.

The most well-known and well publicised award ceremony is the annual *Academy Awards (Oscars)* which are held each year in late February or early March in Los Angeles and presided over by the Academy of Motion Picture Arts and Sciences. Durie et al. (2000) emphasise the benefit of an *Oscar* nomination on its commercial potential. Eligibility for the *Oscars* requires a film to be released in the US between the beginning of September and the end of December of the preceding year and therefore, the *Oscars* may have most impact upon a film's performance in the international rather than the domestic US marketplace, although *Oscar* success can lead to a film being re-released. Academy members vote on nominations for the various awards and Simonton (2004) points out that in the case of most of the awards, the nominations are restricted to those Academy members with most relevant expertise, for example, best director awards are voted on by directors only. Simonton (2004) measured the impact of the nomination as opposed to the actual award, which is voted on by a broader group of industry peers. Simonton (2004) found that the receipt of the *Oscar* was more statistically significant than merely being nominated. While the *Oscar* nomination and ultimate awards are seen as a measure of critical acclaim, which may then be translated into box office success, the nomination and awards ceremony attract a high level of media attention and therefore nominated and winning films can benefit from this publicity. Holden (1993) highlights the political nature of the *Oscar* campaigns and therefore, as Simonton (2004) points out, this sort of activity must also be considered when using such award data to indicate levels of creativity or critical acclaim.

Simonton's (2004) study also found a strong correlation between the award for best director and best film and this is linked to the theory of the auteur in film criticism. As the majority of the films considered for this study were from the US, and a significant number were studio films where filmmaking can be depicted as under the control of the producer or studio executives more than the director, this finding may indicate that despite popular discourse, the director still has a significant impact on the performance of a film. Leenders et al. (2004) studied the impact of award ceremonies based on the composition of their jury and found that the *Oscars* and *Golden Globes* were most influential on films which they classified as 'difficult to evaluate'. This difficulty to evaluate was linked to the absence of identifiable stars in the film. Esparza and Rossman (2006) studied the conditions under which actors received *Oscar* nominations and found that the overall quality of the creative team had a greater impact than the social ties of the actor. This may explain why it is usual for a small number of films to receive nominations across a number of categories each year. Leenders et al. (2004) had assumed that awards voted on by film consumers (measured by the *People's Choice Awards*) rather than industry insiders or professional critics would have a stronger indication of box office performance, but this was not the case. Winning an *Oscar* was found to have a more significant effect on commercial performance than the other awards studied. However, as Levy (2001) noted in his historical analysis of the *Oscars*, *Academy* voters tend to vote relatively conservatively and favour popular films over more challenging fare.

Dodds and Holbrook (1988) investigated the relevance of Oscar nominations as predictors of box office success and found a correlation. Similarly, when looking specifically at nominations/awards for best actor/actress in a leading role and best picture, Nelson et al. (2001) found that success in these categories resulted in an increase in a film's share of screens, average revenue per screen. They also found supporting evidence that films released in the last quarter of the year benefitted more in terms of subsequent earnings than nominees released earlier in the film calendar. Deuchert et al. (2005) found that significantly increased box office revenue derived from the receipt of an *Oscar* nomination, with little additional benefit coming from a win. However, it must be noted that this research (like most of the research in this area) only considers US data and therefore does not account for possible positive effects which an *Oscar* win may have on international box office where films are released after winning the award.

Leenders et al. (2004) found that the impact of the *Golden Globes* and the *Critics Awards* on box office earnings was less than in the case of peer and audience awards. This seems to confirm the view of Levy (2001) that critics may look more to artistic merit than popular appeal with *Academy* members in general voting more conservatively than professional critics. The *Golden Globes* are voted on by members of the *Hollywood Foreign Press Association (HFPA)*. *HFPA* was established in 1943 and the first awards were presented in 1944. Following the informal ceremony in 1944, 1945 saw the first formal ceremony which was held in the Beverly Hills Hotel. Unlike the *Oscars*, the *Golden Globes* have (since 1951) had separate categories for best actor and actress awards in drama and musical and comedy, and since 1955 they introduced awards for television as well as film. The *Golden Globe* nominations and awards ceremony take place at least one month prior to the *Oscars* and therefore are seen as providing some indications regarding possible *Oscar* nominations and successes. However, analysis undertaken by Brevet in 2005 and again in 2007 found that *Golden Globe* winners were unlikely to go on to claim the *Academy Award* apart from in a small number of categories. Table 8.4 contains the award winners for the categories within which Brevet found most likelihood of the same nominee winner in both award ceremonies. Looking back over the last 25 years, there is closer correlation between the winners of 'best film' (72%) and 'best actress in a leading role' (72%).[5] The award for 'best director' coincides 68% of the time while that of 'best leading actor' went to the same nominee 60% of the time. The lowest correlations were in the categories of 'best supporting actor' (56%) and 'best supporting actress' (48%).

There are a number of other significant film awards which go largely unexamined in the marketing literature. In addition to the *Golden Globe*, film critics' associations such as the *Los Angeles Film Critics Association*, *New York Film Critics Circle* and *the National Society of Film Critics* also give out awards on an annual basis. The *Independent Spirit Awards* honour film made outside of the Hollywood Studio system. The various guilds also give annual awards such as the *Director's Guild of America's* annual feature film directing award, the *Producers Guild of America's Golden Laurel Awards* and the *Screen Actors Guild (SAG) Awards*. Little attention is given to awards ceremonies outside of the US such as the *European Film Academy's* annual awards ceremony which has been running since 1988 and was known as the *Felix* until 1996 after the former statuette. The British Academy of Film and Television Awards (*BAFTAs*) garnered little attention until the ceremony moved from well after the *Oscar* ceremony to between the *Oscar* nominations and the awards ceremony. This move has resulted in the *BAFTAs* now being seen as influencing the voting behaviour of Academy members.

This chapter has outlined some of the key events within the film marketing calendar. In this way, it is possible to understand the logic behind release strategy as well as the impact of such a strategy on a film's ultimate

---

[5] This differentiates between cases where the same actress received both awards, but for different roles. In 2009, Kate Winslet won the best actress award in both cases, but for roles in different films and therefore they were treated as different in the analysis.

Table 8.4	Comparison of Academy Award and *Golden Globe* Winners 2007–2009 (source: IMDB, *The Telegraph* and *The Times*)		
	2007	**2008**	**2009**
Best picture (Oscar/Golden Globe)	*The Departed/Babel*	*No Country for Old Men/ Atonement*	*Slumdog Millionaire/ Slumdog Millionaire*
Best director (Oscar/ Golden Globe)	Martin Scorsese (*The Departed*)/Martin Scorsese (*The Departed*)	Joel and Ethan Coen (*No Country for Old Men*)/ Julian Schnabel (*The Diving Bell and the Butterfly*)	Danny Boyle (*Slumdog Millionaire*)/Danny Boyle (*Slumdog Millionaire*)
Best actor in a leading role (Oscar/Golden Globe)	Forest Whitaker (*The Last King of Scotland*)/Forest Whitaker (*The Last King of Scotland*)	Daniel Day Lewis (*There Will be Blood*)/Daniel Day Lewis (*There Will be Blood*)	Sean Penn (*Milk*)/Mickey Rourke (*The Wrestler*)
Best actress in a leading role (Oscar/Golden Globe)	Helen Mirren (*The Queen*)/ Helen Mirren (*The Queen*)	Marion Cotillard, (*La Vie en Rose*)/Julie Christie (*Away from Her*)	Kate Winslet (*The Reader*)/ Kate Winslet (*Revolutionary Road*)
Best supporting actress (Oscar/Golden Globe)	Jennifer Hudson (*Dream Girls*)/Jennifer Hudson (*Dream Girls*)/	Tilda Swinton (*Michael Clayton*)/Cate Blanchet (*I'm Not There*)	Penelope Cruz (*Vicky, Christina, Barcelona*)/Kate Winslet (*The Reader*)
Best supporting actor (Oscar/Golden Globe)	Alan Arkin, (*Little Miss Sunshine*)/Eddie Murphy (*Dream Girls*)	Javier Bardem (*No Country for Old Men*)/ Javier Bardem (*No Country for Old Men*)	Heath Ledger (*The Dark Knight*)/Heath Ledger (*The Dark Knight*)

box office performance. In addition, the chapter considered a number of key film festivals and markets where the business of film takes place. What can be observed in this analysis is that although there were initially a small number of designated film markets where the main buying and selling of film rights took place, the number of festivals developing markets alongside the festival itself, or festivals growing out of markets (as in the case of the American Film Market) is increasing. This increase is indicative of the importance of film festivals as alternative methods of distribution for independently produced film. As the means of film production are becoming increasingly accessible to wider numbers of aspiring filmmakers, we can predict that such informal routes to market will grow. The following chapter will explore some of the issues raised by these new technological developments and illustrate the ways in which these are changing existing film marketing and consumption practices.

CHAPTER 9

Social and Societal Marketing and Film

This chapter will examine the wider impact of film on society and in doing so will look at film in terms of a marketing tool itself – the marketing of cultures, stories, social and political messages. When discussing film marketing and writing about film marketing (and wider arts marketing), the issue of public support for film often arises. Why do we need to support (often uncompetitive) national film industries? Why should we care about issues of representation on the screen? This chapter will engage with these questions and in doing so will illustrate the importance of film as a cultural artefact, a venue for exploring issues of identity and belonging. This chapter will begin by looking at the issue of audience development and participation in film.

In recent years, consumer marketing has taken a more ethical turn. Increasing consumer concerns with the environment and fair trade and consumer resistance to globalisation signal a wider debate in the marketing literature around ethical consumption, the impact of globalisation on consumer choice and related issues. While societal marketing was once an add on following the production, product, sales and marketing concepts much loved by principles of marketing text books, social issues in marketing are now gaining increased attention. However, in this rush to bring the social into marketing analysis and discourse, some confusion over terminology is evident. With this in mind, it is important to begin this chapter by defining the concepts of social, socially responsible and societal marketing and illustrating the relevance of these concepts to discussions of film marketing. This chapter then proceeds to present a framework within which motivations of filmmakers and marketers can be discussed.

While societal marketing is established within the marketing literature as concerned with the ethical or societal implications of commercial activity, social marketing theory refers to the application of marketing techniques in

CONTENTS

communicating social issues, in such areas where the social element of the marketing function is explicit and where marketing techniques can be used in order to affect social or behavioural change (Bryant, 2000). In addition to this, some research (Özbilgin and Kerrigan, 2002) has also focused upon the ability of marketers to have a secondary social impact. Shaping social issues and impacts may not be the explicit intention of the marketer but merely a by-product. Debates regarding motivation of filmmakers are generally located in the art versus commerce as discussed earlier in this book. However, this chapter introduces the important and often overlooked area of the social role and impact of film. Schaefer and Kerrigan (2008) have discussed how the film industry has begun to examine societal issues such as environmental impact of film, however, the film industry is far behind many other industries in terms of their focus on the environment and related issues (see the criticisms levelled at the makers of *The Beach* (2000) due to their alleged destruction of the natural environment when filming). However, film does have a role to play in social marketing. Social arts marketing can be defined as the use of the arts in advancing social causes and influencing social change. Documentary filmmakers have long been engaged in just these activities and film marketers have entered this realm through their efforts to increase the audience for such films as well as for feature films which highlight social issues in an attempt to influence social change.

SOCIAL AND POLITICAL IMPACT OF ART (FILM)

The wider social and political impact of the arts is much debated and film is no exception to this. The clichés of 'art for arts sake' and 'art for social good' have attracted many proponents and detractors (Navaie, 2004; Fillis, 2006). As Radbourne (2002: 50–51) acknowledges, Keynes expounded the view that the Arts Council in Britain was necessary in order to 'create an environment to breed a spirit, to cultivate an opinion, to offer a stimulus to such purpose that the artist and the public can each sustain and live on the other'. Creative and commercial interests should not be perceived as mutually exclusive particularly in the context of the film industry.

Sir John Drummond (2000) once attributed a notional responsibility to arts professionals in shaping and expanding the tastes and consumption choices of the audience. Therefore, this chapter proposes the need for film marketers to assume an educative agenda, which informs consumer choice, as well as to fulfil their traditional concept of meeting current and expressed demand. Currently it is difficult to separate the political, cultural and commercial elements of filmmaking. Bourdieu (2003) did not initially consider film as an art form, and latterly in his work he conceded that certain, more artistic films were in fact art. The approach to film taken in this book considers film as more than just an industry and this chapter examines the social and political impact of film on society. In doing so, there is a dual focus on marketing evident, firstly, film can be used as a social marketing tool, inspiring attitude or behaviour change, and at the least, increased awareness. Secondly, if film has wider social and political impact, then issues of social inclusion, representation on screen and access to a diverse range of films must be viewed through a marketing lens.

Film plays a significant social role that embraces political, artistic and commercial spheres. The earliest forms of film were purely commercially motivated as film was seen as mass entertainment of the lowbrow variety (Kerrigan and Culkin, 1999). As filmmaking grew more sophisticated, the social and political roles became evident and films were used in order to instil political ideologies or to express artistic vision. An example of such films is *Battleship Potemkin* (1925), which was used to propagate the communist ideology. This chapter seeks to explore the continuum of motivation, which exists in the marketing of films by examining the varying motivations which filmmakers and film marketers have in offering their films to the market and in doing so, presents a typology of film marketing motivation which is developed from Kerrigan and Özbilgin (2002).

FILM AS EDUCATOR (THE SOCIAL MARKETING FUNCTION)

As discussed in Chapter 6, film was used as an educative medium in the United States from its inception. Film was seen as an essential tool in teaching early Americans what it meant to be American and how they could achieve the status of 'good Americans' (Kerrigan and Culkin, 1999). Today, feature films are primarily viewed as forms of mass entertainment and the social element is often overlooked. For example, the film *Forrest Gump* (1994) was critically acclaimed and commercially successful but underlying the entertainment element was a clear socio-political message which re-inforced the concept of the American dream where success is possible for anyone who works hard enough. Similarly Madichie and Ibeh (2006) found that members of the Nigerian Diaspora look to Nollywood films in order to instil a sense of Nigerian culture while living and raising children abroad. In this sense, the role of film as an educator is recognised.

Kula (2004) noted the formal endorsement of the significance of film by 1980 when UNESCO adopted the *Recommendation for the Safeguarding and Preservation of Moving Images*. Kula (2004: 1) highlights the first premise of this recommendation that *all* moving images are "an expression of the cultural identity of peoples ... and form an integral part of a nation's cultural heritage, as well as constituting important and often unique testimonies, of a new dimension, to the history, way of life and culture of people." Therefore, it argues, the "safeguarding [of] *all* moving images of the national production should be regarded as the highest objective." Moreau and Peltier (2004) undertook an extensive analysis of diversity in terms of supply and consumption of film in the US, South Korean, France, the European Union (including French data), Hungary (then not an EU member state) and Mexico and found that demand for film adapts to supply, rather than supply being based on demand. They also conclude that increased vertical integration decreased diversity in both supply and consumption terms and that protective policy relating to film production and promotion could be seem to result in increased diversity of films offered to consumers as well as those actually consumed. However, citing the case of South Korea, there was a note of warning regarding the types of films favoured when quota systems were in place, saying that many of the films produced and consumed during this period were derived from video games or based on Hollywood genres.

Until recently much European film policy focused on enhancing and supporting the artist and political or social elements of film. Latterly there has been recognition of the need to re-orientate public policy related to filmmaking to consider issues of commercial viability in addition to the artistic or social motivations. Hence, filmmaking is becoming more of a balancing act between these traditionally oppositional aspirations.

This is true in the case of European filmmakers who are not affiliated to major US film companies such as Warner Brothers, Disney or Paramount. Such 'independent' filmmakers by necessity must finance their films through a variety of public and commercial funds and therefore are becoming, through requirement, more aware of the need to address both the commercial and the artist and social considerations. While it is clear that independent European filmmakers must address such considerations, Hollywood filmmakers, due to the power which they exert over distribution channels, are often depicted as having a commercial role in filmmaking devoid of the social/political or artist element. This can be disputed as according to Said (1994), writers have an implicit social/political role due to the nature of their work. Art represents and reflects reality and art forms such as literature and filmmaking take place in a socio-political context or environment. In this way, filmmakers either reinforce social norms or challenge them. This idea links to Lazarsfeld and Merton's (1948) seminal work on mass media which concludes that mass media serves to reinforce societal norms and values.

This leads us to consider issues of representation which are bound up with considerations of the political and social impact of film consumption. O'Reilly (2004) has shown how listening to popular music and other forms of cultural consumption play a role in forming or expressing identity, but to date, this has focussed mainly on internal identity. Hargreaves and North (1997) found that one of the social functions of music was the management of self-identity. However, one of the impediments to serious considerations of the wider impact of film on society and on individual identity is the perception of film as purely a form of escapism. This fits with Holbrook and Hirschman's (1982) discussion of arts consumption as escapism.

According to Giddens (1994 in du Gay et al., 2000), life consists of a series of 'passages' and in moving through these various life passages, loss and gain play a substantial role. Giddens argues that modernity has resulted in individuals being faced with a myriad of complex choices, which shape the individual. Lifestyle choices, according to Giddens (1994 in du Gay et al., 2000: 256) "…are decisions not only about how to act but who to be." Choices regarding cultural consumption are pertinent in dictating such aspirant identity and to date research has been concerned mainly with the consumption of consumer goods in forming aspirant identity. However, consumption of artistic products such as film, even in its most popular forms, seems to offer ideal venues for the consideration of identity. Staiger (2005) traces the history of theories of film consumption and in doing so, highlights the shift from considering film consumption from a male perspective (citing Metz, 1975) to Mulvey's (1975) analysis of gendered readings of film in her seminal essay, *Visual Pleasure and Narrative Cinema*. Staiger (2005) draws on film and cultural studies as well as sociology and psychology in discussing (among other issues) the impact of film consumption on identity formation. She provides conflicting viewpoints on the impact of film consumption on such identity formation, concluding that many elements effect identity formation other than the 'reception' of film. Film consumption and its role in identity formation should be viewed within its wider social and cultural context. Webb (2009) discusses the power of film in shaping perceptions of society and groups within society. In identifying film as one of the key 'cultural industries', Webb states that the cultural industries are "very important in the production and institution of ideologies, because it is the signifying, or symbolic, systems that provide us with the means for understanding the world" (117).

Struggle for balance

If we accept the importance of film in terms of shaping social and political representations as well as informing individual identity, there is a need to examine the industrial frameworks which govern the film industry. Film marketers play a role in informing and satisfying customer demands for film consumption by packaging films in a certain way, targeting particular segments and controlling the volume and variety of films that reach an audience. On the one hand the alternative, art house, UK and European films, which are marginal to the mainstream, are often associated with an educational role for film marketers in shaping consumer choice, and on the other hand those mainstream, formulaic genre films from the US, are associated with the role of marketers in foreseeing and satisfying demand for such films. These two marketing approaches have long been considered as irreconcilable poles in the literature and the marketer–consumer interface was assumed to be radically different for these types of film. Tzokas and Saren (1999) argue that value is created through the interaction between customer and marketer, but develop this further by suggesting that particularly in relation to cultural products value is only created if perceived by the customer. Applying this to the suggested continuum, value as perceived by film audiences can range from the enhancement of social awareness to the provision of escapist entertainment.

Mathieu and Standvad (2008) provide a typology of film production regimes based on an institutional and production system analysis. They conclude that the types of films produced are influenced by the production structures in their country of origin. In doing so, they present three ideal types of production system, the 'high concept' Hollywood system, the 'auteur' model and the 'high contextual framework model' which is based on the Danish system. In presenting such a typology, they acknowledge the existence of many varieties of film production system but in drawing on Crofts' (1998) analysis of the intersection between type of economy and type of film industry which exists (industrial, cultural or political) they illustrate the influence which the state has in shaping the film production environment. As discussed in Chapter 4, the film industry and film output are influenced by state intervention (or lack of intervention) and such intervention influences the type of films produced in each system.

MARKETING PRACTICE AND SOCIETY

Marketing practices do not occur in a vacuum free from business politics, ideology and the economy. Dominant business ideologies have shaped marketing practices in the UK. The classical business ideology was influential in the last two decades (Henderson, 2001). This ideology, which refers to a specific point in history, argued for the minimisation of government intervention in the economy and exalted the consumer as the sole arbiter of marketing decisions. The work of authors such as Smith (1776) and Friedman (1962) formed the theoretical basis for this ideology. Capturing the reality of marketing practice, since the Thatcher years of the 1980s, this dominant ideology has informed marketing practice and public policy in the UK.

One of the underpinning assumptions of this pervasive ideology was that the sole role of managers, marketers in this context, was to understand and satisfy demand (Chrissides and Kaler, 1993). This assumption fails to recognise that marketers may play a socially responsible or ethical role in shaping or informing demand (Kerrigan and Özbilgin, 2002). Since the early 1990s, this ideological approach to management has been criticised due to its blinkered focus on customer demand, and narrow definition of utility and profitability (Heeler and Chung, 2000). This approach could be criticised for naively assuming that the customer possesses perfect knowledge in terms of the potential utility of a product. This criticism resonates with Smith and Quelch's (1993) argument that manufacturers of products inherently hold far greater knowledge of the potential utility of their product than their customers. Reverting back to the case of the film industry in the UK, two questions could be posed: Should the marketers note the criticisms levelled at the dominant classical business ideology? And should they assume a role to educate the public in order to inform their choice of film consumption that transgresses their classical role of meeting expressed consumer demand?

When evaluating the historical transformation of the focus of marketing practice, many mainstream marketing texts classify various stages in the evolution of marketing from the early production and product eras, through the sales concept to the marketing concept of the 1960s. Fullerton (1998) disputes this view, asserting that the marketing concept was present alongside the product, production and sales concepts from the outset. He draws attention to conscious demand stimulation and the role, which marketers had in driving change. Thus, it can be argued that contrary to the common wisdom, which is also evident in some marketing texts, demand stimulation or education of the customer has been a recognised practice in the film industry. Therefore, reconciliation of these two supposedly oppositional roles may be easier than it is suggested earlier. However, one note of caution would be that, demand stimulation and educative roles may be assumed by the marketers for different ends, again ranging from pursuit of financial exploits to selfless altruism.

The exchange relationship

The practice of the exchange relationship and its trajectory in the UK may provide an explanation for the varying roles of marketers in meeting or shaping demand. The exchange relationship, referred to by Baker (2000: 1) as the 'true essence of marketing', rests at the core of marketing practice and refers to an on-going mutually beneficial relationship between a marketer and the customer. However, dichotomous models of the exchange relationship between the customer and the marketer exist in the current marketing literature, suggesting either that 'customer is the king' or that the power relationship between the marketer and customer occurs in equilibrium. As the nature of the power relationship between these two parties determines the marketing approach taken by the practitioners, the recognition of the nature of this power relationship is instrumental in understanding what kind of approaches marketers take in terms of consumer demand.

As it is debated that the emphasis on the exchange relationship has been transforming during the last two decades, some authors have been hailing the emergence of a more balanced power relationship between the marketer and the consumer, while some others have been arguing that the extent of this transformation, particularly in the commercial film sector, may be overstated. While these discussions about the direction of progress continues, it is certain that as Jobber (1998) so succinctly expresses it, atomistic and individualistic view of marketing fails to ensure protection of consumer welfare:

> 'A second limitation of the marketing concept concerns its focus on individual market transactions. Since many individuals weigh heavily their personal benefits while discounting the societal impact of their purchases, the adoption of the marketing concept will result in the production of goods and services which do not adequately correspond to societal welfare. Providing customer satisfaction is simply a means to achieve a company's profit objective and does not guarantee protection of the consumer's welfare. This view is supported by Wensley, who regards consumerism as a challenge to the adequacy of the atomistic and individualistic view of market transactions. An alternative view is presented by Bloom and Greyser, who regard consumerism as the ultimate expression of the marketing concept, compelling marketers to consider consumer needs and wants that hitherto may have been overlooked' (Jobber 1998: 11).

The relationship marketing literature (Grönroos, 1997, 1999; Gummesson, 1997) heralds the transformation of the exchange relationship, arguing that the traditional approach, which elevated customer demand, is slowly being replaced by a concern for equilibrium of the power relations between the customer and the company. However, this claim may not be substantiated in the film industry, because the industry appears to focus upon maximising the 'push' factors, being more concerned with providing a constant stream of films, rather than paying attention to consumer tastes and demand. Therefore, the practice of film marketing diverges from the marketing theory that underpins practice in other industries. The gap between the film industry and other industries is worrying as satisfaction of expressed customer demand is a well-recognised determinant of sustainable business success.

Sustainability

The paradigm shift in the exchange relationship, which is evident in other industries, is borne out of a belief that single-minded pursuit of satisfaction of customer demand would not be sustainable in the long term (Grönroos, 1997; Gummesson, 1997). Mainstream literature referred to above has recently started noting that for the sake of long-term sustainability, it is necessary not only to meet the articulated demands of the customer but also to expand their horizons by introducing new products that will challenge and develop their tastes. The reflection of this conception in the film industry results in a widespread assumption that the upshot of providing a continuous stream of films, which simply seek to satisfy the current consumer demand or indoctrinate customer demand through fad and fashion, will be sustainable. One off box office successes in particular genres of film, have frequently led to many, often sub-standard, copycat productions. An example of this can be seen when following the success of Lock, Stock and Two Smoking Barrels (1998), Honest (2000) and Gangster No. 1 (2000) were released. Both of these films underperformed at the box office. These productions have sought to cash in on the popularity of the originals but are often met with viewer apathy. Critics of the Nollywood and Bollywood films have focused on the need for more sophisticated stories in order to satisfy developing consumer tastes. This is a further illustration of the need for filmmakers and marketers to challenge and develop tastes rather than just satisfying expressed tastes of the audience. The experiences of failure in the industry have caused a general feeling of caution and a search for innovative approaches to marketing and a new role for marketers which transcend their traditional approach of pursuit of profits through manipulation of demand towards an approach where they become purveyors of strategic direction and informed customer taste and choice in the British film industry. Since the decline of the British film industry during the late 1980s, the need for sustainability has been high on the agenda for film producers and policy makers in the UK. This chapter engages with these issues through providing a typology of marketer/filmmaker motivations and level of consumer engagement. While social marketing has an important role in educating and informing customers, societal marketing may indeed offer a solution to the formation of a long-term sustainable film industry, due to its dual focus on social issues and entertainment in pursuit of commercial gain.

Fact and fiction – Blurring the boundaries

Currently, there is a blurring of the traditional separation between fictional films which are viewed merely as entertainment and documentary films which had an educative purpose. A series of fictional films such as *Michael Clayton* (2007) and *Blood Diamond* (2006) have raised serious social issues within a conventional fictional format. Both films had recognisable stars attached to the films and were marketed and distributed in conventional manners. At the same time, traditional issue based documentary films such as *Black Gold* (2006) and *An Inconvenient Truth* (2006) have been marketed more like conventional art house or mainstream fictional films and enjoyed cinema releases.

These developments illustrate the value of film (from documentary to fictional film) as a tool of social marketing. In addition, discussions regarding how societies, individuals and issues are portrayed in film illustration the potential for filmmakers and marketers to engage in societal marketing. Recently, critics of the film *Slumdog Millionaire* (2008) referred to it as 'poverty porn', the same filmmakers in the past have been criticised for 'glorifying drug taking' in their film *Trainspotting* (1996). These claims may be refuted, but the societal impact of bringing such issues into the public consciousness may be valuable. *Persepolis* (2007), a French/US co-production which looked at the Revolution in Iran from the perspective of the main protagonist as she grew up in Iran and France, provided a human insight into a subject which is normally considered from a political perspective. Similarly, Lebanese production *Caramel* (2007) provided an alternative view of Lebanese society than that portrayed by news stories focusing on political tensions in the region and Brazilian *Linha de Passe* (2008) sought to address the portrayal of life in Brazil's favella as drugs and crime fuelled. Discussions over the authentic nature of such portrayals aside, such films have a clear societal role in educating and informing us about other social, cultural and political contexts. This links to some of the issues raised in relation to film and other forms of media by Webb (2009).

Kula, in his discussion of the (long term) cultural role of audiovisual products, paid special attention to films which were intentionally in opposition to existing political systems such as Michael Moore's *Fahrenheit 9/11* (2004) and *Bowling for Columbine* (2002). These films were seen by audiences both inside the US, the political system which was being criticised in these films and in other territories. He also looked at the importance of films in debating interpretations of political events, drawing on two oppositional views of the Israeli military campaign in Jenin in 2002. Muhammad Bakri's film *Jenin, Jenin: A One-Sided Movie* (2002) depicted a massacre where 500 Palestinians were killed and the town destroyed while an alternative view was proposed in Martin Himel's *Jenin: Massacring the Truth* (2004), which draws on a United Nations investigation that refuted the idea that a massacre had taken place.

In an earlier paper by Kerrigan and Özbilgin (2002), a bi-polar continuum ranging from free exploitation of consumer demand to indoctrination in terms of desirable consumption patterns was defined. Elements of this are discussed in the chapter looking at consumer selection of films. This continuum presents a dubious and even dangerous tightrope for practitioners and policy makers. It is dubious and dangerous because it precariously defines the role of the marketing professional in a vacuum, divorcing them from any social or ethical responsibility. In this chapter, this framework has been modified to include a middle ground approach, ranging from social marketing through societal marketing to commercial exploitation. Table 9.1 illustrates this range of motivations which exist in filmmakers and marketers.

Each item on the model signifies a different level of engagement between marketers and customers, ranging from no engagement to high levels of

Table 9.1 Continuum of Roles and Motives of Marketers in Addressing Consumer Demands Modified from Özbilgin and Kerrigan (2002)

Ethical continuum of marketing motives	Marketers' Intentions to Engage the Consumer		
	No engagement	Moderate engagement	High level of engagement
Commercial exploitation of demand	1	4	7
Enlightened self-interest or societal marketing	2	5	8
Altruism or social marketing	3	6	9

List of films examined: 1. *American Pie* (1999), 2. *Erin Brockovich* (2000), 3. *The Idiots* (1998), 4. *Pearl Harbour* (2001), 5. *Mrs Brown* (1997), 6. *Bloody Sunday* (2002), 7. *Captain Corelli's Mandolin* (2001), 8. *Bread and Roses* (2000), 9. *Injustice* (2001).

engagement, and identifies the motivational factor in the exchange relationship, from exploitation to altruism. The first category denotes a market driven approach, which relies on maximisation of profits by meeting the needs of the customer. Therefore, this category suggests that the marketer seeks to predict the audience tastes but does not attempt to challenge or shape them in any way. Examples of films that yield to this kind of marketing practice include teenage orientated 'gross out' films such as *American Pie* (1999). The second category is similar in the sense that the film is marketed as a mainstream film and while the subject matter is of societal interest but there is no call to action associated with the film or implied by the marketing campaign. Consumer welfare issues are incorporated in so far as they contribute to commercial success of the film. Films in this category may include films such as *Erin Brockovich* (2000) which highlighted issues of corporate power and public health in the US and was based on true events. This film did not simply seek financial gain but its subject matter incorporated elements of awareness rising.

The third category is outside the commercial realm film marketing, focusing on public good over box office revenue. By definition, films that are included in this category are generally not well-known due to their lack of commercial focus. An example of such a film is Scandinavian Dogma film, *The Idiots* (1998). A group of Danish film directors who wanted to overturn commercial filmmaking practices united and produced a series of films shot using hand-held digital cameras and low budgets. These films were known as the Dogma films and this style of filmmaking from proved surprisingly popular in the late 1990s. *The Idiots* (1998) was the first and most controversial of these films due to its subject matter – it looked at issues surrounding the portrayal of people with disabilities – and scenes of a gratuitous sexual nature. Despite lack of an apparent public demand for such a film, the filmmakers felt that these issues were pertinent for the social welfare.

The films in the fourth category straddle the continuum in so far as marketers play a role in shaping public tastes while acknowledging commercial considerations. Films, which manipulate historical events and act on public sentiment, fall under this category. One obvious contemporary example is *Pearl Harbour* (2001), which was criticised due to its false historisation of the events leading up to the bombing of Pearl Harbour during World War II and was marketed in a way that tapped into nationalistic sentiments of the public thus moderately shaping customer choice. If social marketing underpinned the motivation of the filmmakers, historical accuracy would have been of paramount importance, practically deeming the film a historical documentary. However, due to the societal marketing focus elements of historical accuracy were traded for the enhancement of entertainment value.

Category five is curious in that as this chapter predicts, the number of films in this category is likely to increase. In this category of films, the filmmakers have moved beyond purely commercial considerations as they wish to engage with a specific political, social or historical issue and in doing so to engage the consumer and shape their perceptions. *Mrs Brown* (1997), which displayed the private face of the publicly austere Queen Victoria, fits into this category.

Bloody Sunday (2002), which dramatises the events of the Bloody Sunday shootings in Northern Ireland, is an example of category six films. While the film was marketed in a way which sought to shape public opinion, film commentators were critical of the fact that public funding was made available to this film from Irish and UK film bodies. Due to its politically loaded nature, such funding was viewed by some as controversial. Films in this category are likely to attract controversy of this kind. Motivation for making and marketing this film did not derive from a commercial ambition, rather the desire to highlight this social issue to the public and in doing so, to engage them and shape understanding of issues in Northern Ireland.

Category seven films are underpinned by commercial motivations and rely on heavy consumer engagement in order to achieve success. This category includes films which are eagerly anticipated as they are adaptations of successful books or sequels. The marketer is marketing the film to an existing target audience and requires their engagement in order to ensure commercial success. *Captain Corelli's Mandolin* (2001) is a good example in this category. The marketing campaign for this film was built upon the extraordinary success of the book of the same name. The film was shot on the Greek Island where the book was set to maximise the link between the book and film. Despite appearances – in terms of the marketing campaign – the film was not true to the story as told in the book and for this reason, many of those who had an emotional engagement through the book were disappointed with the film and word of mouth suffered. This category also includes children's films which seek to maximise pester power by using child focused marketing communication techniques. An obvious example of this is *Pokemon: The First Movie* (1999). The title itself indicates the desire to create a number of sequels in order to benefit from the success of the Pokemon phenomenon. Another example of this can be seen in the *Harry Potter* (2001) films.

High engagement and enlightened self-interest are crucial in category eight. An example of a film, which is positioned in order to shape and inform social likes and wants in addition to engage commercial considerations is

Bread and Roses (2000). This film was concerned with ethnicity and trade unionism in the American context. It achieved public acclaim and its marketing practice involved informative techniques. Ken Loach, the director of *Bread and Roses* (2000) has a definite if limited following in the UK but his concentration on American issues in this film expanded the reach of this film beyond his captured audience. This category assumes an engaged audience who wish to learn more about an issue.

The final category is the most prominent example of social marketing by filmmakers. In this instance, marketers seek to influence the public over irrespective of commercial gain. Film is used as a communicative medium through which public opinion is shaped. The danger for films contained within category nine is that they may transgress from altruism to propaganda. Indeed the judgement of this transgression is hard to make and is often dependent on the subjective evaluation of the individual filmgoer. A recent example of this is *Injustice* (2001), a low budget independent production that sought to highlight the number of people who died under mysterious conditions while in police custody in the UK. The film could not initially be shown in conventional exhibition venues due to an on-going legal battle between the filmmakers and the police authorities. Despite this, many underground showings of the film were reported and word of mouth surrounding both the film itself and the events, which it depicts, can be viewed as evidence of this success. Following this period of guerrilla showings, the film eventually won the right to be shown in cinemas.

SOCIAL AND SOCIETAL MARKETING

The historical divide between fact and fiction is continually blurring and following Baudrillard's (1983) *simulacrum*, in the post-modern age it is increasingly difficult to distinguish reality from fiction. This distinction may be further blurred through the development of genres of the 'mockumentary' which deliberately set out to present fiction as if it were fact. Such developments coupled with decreasing funding for film (and traditional documentary in particular) and the repositioning of some issues based documentary film may usurp the social role of film marketing. An interesting development occurring within the social film marketing arena can be seen by examining Nigerian film *The Gift*. This film was financed by a charity and tackles the issue of mother to child transmission of HIV in order to tackle this issue and raise awareness. What distinguishes *The Gift* from other films which could be classified as engaged with social film marketing is the presentation of these issues within the narrative framework of a conventional Nigerian feature film. Filmmaker Paul Nwulu wanted to avoid the preaching style of conventional public health films, instead wishing to communicate social issues through conventional narrative forms which would be familiar to (and entertaining for) the target audience. What further distinguishes this film from conventional feature films which seek to raise awareness as well as entertain (and therefore qualifies this film as social film marketing) is its lack of a profit motive as it was fully funded through a charitable trust. Where there is a profit motive, albeit linked to a social motivation, such films can be classified as examples of societal film marketing.

Trajectories of business ideologies, exchange relationship and customer tastes in the film industry indicate a growing recognition of the significance of the stakeholder model (Freeman, 1984) in understanding, addressing and shaping customer demand (Whysall, 2000). Historical transformation of these industrial structures bodes well for the recognition of the societal marketing concept in film marketing. The societal marketing framework, as defined by Armstrong and Kotler (2000), suggests an interplay between consumers' wants, human welfare of society and company profit. This concept emphasises the determination of needs wants and interests within target markets and the delivery of superior value to the customers such that both consumer and society benefit. This new 'win-win' approach is a radical departure from the earlier 'win or lose' depiction of an imbalanced exchange relationship between marketers and customers.

However, it is important to add a note of caution here: It would be naïve to assume that without the support of the enabling social, political and economic changes described above, societal marketing will flourish in a competitive industry run with liberal economic drives for profitability and growth. Although, the societal marketing model distinguishes between short-term wants and long-term welfare issues, this model is based on a static understanding of short-term wants. The model can be criticised in that there should be scope for marketers to play a social agent role, which does not simply reinforce the snapshots of short-term wants of consumers reflected in marketing surveys, but also seeks to shape them with a view to inform their opinion, in ways that will enhance their long-term welfare.

Strategies for change

This chapter has explored the impact of the complex interplay of dominant business ideology, exchange relationship and social considerations on marketers' engagement with customer needs and demands in the film market. Proposing a framework that illustrated different levels of customer engagement and types of motives for marketing practice nine categories of film types are identified. This framework underpins an assumption that the roles marketers play vary according to both their motives at the outset and also the degree to which they aim to inform, shape or forecast customer tastes and demands. This formulation challenges the traditional approaches that demarcate and polarise marketers' roles in terms of the exchange relationship, highlighting that a synergistic approach, which combines these two traditional roles, is also possible.

It is important to formulate a strategy for the future direction of the exchange relationship and marketer engagement in shaping customer demands. It is possible to combine both commercial and social aspirations and varying levels of engagement in the exchange relationship. It is also evident that moderate levels of engagement and enlightened self-interest, which amalgamates social welfare and financial gain considerations, i.e. societal marketing, are possible to implement. Considering the macro-social trends, which drive the film industry towards sustainable practices, recognition of social welfare issues and the broadening of access for audiences, it is reasonable to expect that film marketing practices which manage to reconcile these different and often conflicting stakeholder interests will be more sustainable in the long term.

Each of the nine categories in the framework was defined and explored using examples from the UK and world cinema that are consumed by UK audiences. These categories were instrumental in formulating a strategy for the future direction of the exchange relationship and marketer engagement in shaping customer demands. As discussed earlier in this chapter, perceiving varying roles of marketers as irreconcilable is indeed counterproductive. The above framework demonstrates that it is possible to combine both commercial and social aspirations and varying levels of engagement in the exchange relationship. It is also evident from the framework that moderate levels of engagement and enlightened self-interest, which amalgamates social welfare and financial gain considerations, i.e. societal marketing, are possible to implement. Considering the macro-social trends, which drive the film industry towards sustainable practices, recognition of social welfare issues and the broadening of access for audiences, it is reasonable to expect that film marketing practices which manage to reconcile these different and often conflicting stakeholder interests will be more sustainable in the long term. Therefore, it can be reasonably argued this category (five) provides the most feasible route for marketing professionals in terms of balancing necessary commercial considerations with social welfare issues.

It is necessary to combine both approaches to create a synergistic affect which recognises the need to meet existing demand as well as to educate and broaden customer tastes in order to provide individual satisfaction as well as sustainable social welfare. However, in order to understand the nature of this synergistic effect, a broader systematic evaluation of film marketing, which falls under all categories specified in this paper, would be useful. Further study of these espoused categories should be carried out in order to fully appreciate the complete spectrum of interaction in exchange relationships in film consumption. Further exploratory study on the impact of the consumption of a variety of films on consumer demand could be instrumental in understanding what shapes consumer tastes.

While the main focus of this book is on how films are marketed, this chapter highlights the need to look more closely at the impact which the marketing of film to consumers has on society and the individual film consumer. While the societal role of film consumption has been a concern since the early years of the film industry, the blurring of fiction and non-fiction and the use of film (both fiction and non-fiction) in programmes of social marketing are consistent with the post-modern age. Film as a popular art form, with widespread consumption, has the potential for societal good but also the potential for great harm. Harking back to the earlier chapter on policy and film marketing, this chapter further strengthens the case for public support for the film industry and film marketing practices, while at the same time, acts as a warning about the power of film in contemporary society.

CHAPTER 10

The Impact of Technology on Film Marketing Practices

The film industry has always been a technologically driven industry. As I explored in the early part of this book and is well established (see Balio, 1985; Gomery, 1991; Thompson and Bordwell, 2003), early developments in the film industry were all motivated by access to technology. This chapter will not go over this well trodden ground but will attempt to examine more recent technological developments which have a direct impact on film marketing practices. The key issues to be considered when looking at such technological developments are on the supply side as well as the demand side. Firstly, the opening up of access to filmmaking as a result of ever higher quality film-making and editing equipment has empowered those outside the closely guarded inner circle of the film industry to produce relatively low cost films. Secondly, increased access directly to consumers has been facilitated by the growth of the internet. This has taken place within the context of ever increasing levels of convergence between media organisations. On the demand side, we can see changes in consumer behaviour on a number of levels. Firstly, technological developments have significantly changed the nature of advertising, moving from a passive form where advertising messages were designed by companies and broadcast/projected to consumers towards interactive forms where consumers are actively engaged in promoting products and services, whether consciously or unconsciously. Secondly, and profoundly, the lines between the producer and consumer are becoming blurred. In some cases it may be possible to identify the producer and the consumer; a film is shown at the cinema, the filmmakers are the producers, the viewers are the consumers. However, there are a number of collaborations which will be referred to later in this chapter which make these distinctions difficult; if a consumer directly finances a film, are they a producer or a consumer or a prosumer? If they provide content which is

CONTENTS

then used in a film or their image is used, the same question applies. Finally, if they participate in research which informs the state of the final film, how does this question apply? Finally, new technologies have made the process of duplicating and distributing film faster, easier and most importantly, cheaper than ever before and therefore film piracy is seen as a troubling issue facing the film industry. This chapter will examine these issues and draw on a series of specific film cases in illustrating how these technological changes are impacting on film marketing practices within the context of the wider film, media and entertainment industries.

CONVERGENCE IN THE CREATIVE INDUSTRIES

Henry Jenkins' (2006) book *Convergence Culture* provides excellent insight into what is happening in the media industries and in this analysis, Jenkins posits that the media industry goes through paradigm shifts all the time. In saying this, Jenkins (2006) points to the rhetoric of the digital revolution where commentators pronounced the death of old media in favour of new media during the dotcom bubble, but following this, these predictions were retracted. Jenkins (2006) highlights an important element of the new phase of media convergence which is occurring now when recalling the events of the New Orleans Media Experience in October 2003 where old and new media people came together but were unsure of how to interact with each other. While previous phases of convergence in the media sector have seen powerful media conglomerates come together to create even larger, vertically and horizontally integrated entities, the current phase is less homogenous in nature. While this sort of activity is evident, looser networks of relationships between old and new media organisations are forming in the struggle to find 'new business models'. Everywhere I go now, I hear people talking about business models, the need for them, changes to them and finding new ones. In a recent presentation at the EPSRC (Engineering and Physical Sciences Research Council) funded IMDE (Innovative Media for the Digital Economy) Springboard Event, Charles Leadbetter characterized his vision of the future of the media industry as a beach with a small number of very large boulders and lots of smaller pebbles. The large boulders represent a small number of very powerful media conglomerates and the pebbles are the very many extremely small media organisations which fill the spaces around them.

While the media sector has always had a significant degree of convergence in terms of the media conglomerates which own film studios, music labels, television stations and so on, the internet age has seen the introduction of a new set of actors in the film sphere. The early movements in this stage of media integration were motivated by the need to access content. The internet could provide infinite spaces for interaction, commercial and social engagement, but the mantra 'content is King' loomed large. The only way to attract people to your website was through the provision of interesting content. The possibility of having internet protocol television relied on accessibility of interesting content. As producers had content and problems in accessing the market and the internet providers now had a means of access to the consumer, it seemed logical to enter into mergers and contractual agreements regarding sharing these resources. The most high profile of these mergers at that time was the Time Warner/AOL merger which was announced in January 2000. Thompson (2003) described the AOL Time Warner merger as 'keiretsu', a Japanese term denoting a confederation of firms from different industries with interlocking ownership and a shared strategic vision. The expansion in mergers and strategic alliances in the media industries that is occurring at this time is reminiscent of the early days in the development of the film industry. In recognition of the concepts expressed by Levitt (1960), present day media companies are recognising and exploiting possible areas of business that can be accessed by entering into strategic relationships. The problems in terms of overvaluation, faced by AOL/Time Warner following their merger have, however, acted as a warning to media companies of the danger of overvaluing the results of such a merger.

The new media landscape

The media landscape as we move towards the end of the first decade of the twenty first century seems to be one where old and new media are co-existing and the spaces between them are becoming less evident. This environment is one in which some large 'old' media organisations such as newspapers (see Graham and Hill, 2009a, 2009b; Graham and Smart, 2009), television and traditional record labels are in financial trouble due to huge overheads, ever declining advertising revenue and piracy. Stuart Till, UK Film Council chairman depicts the future for the film industry through creating an engaging narrative where a character called 'Brit' (representing the British Film Industry) stands are a fork in the road wondering which way to turn (http://www.screendaily.com/news/opinion/film-industry-faces-its-own-epic-adventure/5000875.article). To the left, Till depicts a desolate landscape with abandoned buildings where "the only building that seems inhabited and active has a large black flag with a skull and crossbones fluttering from the roof". The alternative view, to the right, is very different, the landscape is lush, there is a cinema with long queues of people waiting outside and "half a dozen sustainable producers" are close by. Brit feels something holding him back from taking this attractive route and realizes that he is holding a crumpled piece of paper in his hand, it reads: "How do you exploit the opportunities offered by the new digital world and equally ensure the pirates do not destroy your industry?" Till (2009) has posed the most pertinent question facing the film industry. There are many possibilities offered by the digital world to producers, but this digital world also exacerbates the problems of piracy. In a study undertaken by Nikolychuk et al. (2009), the issue of how to compete with free came up repeatedly. When consumers get something for nothing, how can the industry expect them to pay? At the same time, there are examples of successes in terms of new business models which are allowing producers and distributors to engage directly with consumers through the internet or via a content aggregator.

The threat of piracy

The UK's *Digital Britain* report (DCMS/BBER, 2009) outlines the possibilities and the challenges facing the creative industries in the digital age and much discussion followed the report regarding the threat of piracy and possible solutions. Looking towards lessons from the Chinese cultural industries, Montgomery (2009) posits that Chinese cultural producers are finding appropriate revenue streams which are appropriate for the digital age. Montgomery (2009) highlights the fact that concepts of individual intellectual property were in conflict with the collectivist principle which dominated Chinese society since the People's Republic of China (PRC) was founded in 1949. The 1980s signalled the beginning of economic reform in the PRC but this was linked to strict censorship laws which prevented many cultural products such as music and film from being distributed inside the PRC. According to Montgomery (2009), the combination of these factors led to the development of a relatively vibrant and unchallenged music industry. This policy environment is similar to that in which South Korean cultural products such as film, television series and music gained popularity. In her analysis, Montgomery (2009) explores arguments that Intellectual Property protection benefits developed economies with established cultural industries and that government protection of indigenous industries is one route to establishing and growing both cultural production and consumption of domestic cultural products. Looking at this research, it is clear that there is a move in the music industry in the PRC (and elsewhere) towards the live performance and exploiting other revenue from artists and their music rather than the traditional income stream of the recorded music sales. Looking to the music industry, and to territories where there are high degrees of piracy can be instructive for the film industry during this period of soul searching for new business models which will overcome the 'competing with free' problem. One of the problems with discussions around finding new business models relates to the dynamic nature of such models. As industrial structures and consumption practices change, it is important to develop means of responding to these changes which are appropriate.

There seems to be widespread recognition within the film industry that similar problems to those already encountered by the music industry will need to be dealt with in film (Till, 2009). What is not clear is what will replace the current dominant industry structures discussed earlier in this book. Tshang (2007) draws on earlier research to conclude that as industries such as film and video games mature, they enter a process of rationalization which can reduce levels of creativity. The high levels of risk involved in film production and distribution tend to lead to risk adverse behaviour typified by establishing 'safe' genres and formulaic film as is identified by Wyatt (1994). Mezias and Mezias (2000) found that specialist firms which focus on innovative development of film types differentiate themselves from the major studios out of the necessity to develop creative product and inability to compete in the established genres. In light of this, it is interesting to examine the various approaches taken by the mainstream, established media giants and incumbents in negotiating the digital era for film production and consumption.

Legal ways to access film for free

As one of the reasons behind film piracy is lack of access to a wide range of film through the conventional distribution routes. Prior to the development of affordable and workable digital routes to distribution, issues of capacity and storage informed films shown at the cinema or available to rent or buy on video/DVD and now Blu-ray. However, we are now in an on-demand world where consumers want to watch what they want when they want. The best route to this is through the internet and the lack of legal alternatives saw consumers utilize bit torrent technology in order to broaden their tastes. A number of national film support bodies like KOIC in South Korea and the UK Film Council are now involved in developing online film access systems in order to tackle issues of piracy (Noh, 2009; Ward, 2009). What is encouraging is that consumers seem to be taking up the opportunity to pay for this content rather than downloading for free. These services are committed to providing consumers with alternatives regarding how to access this content legally and not have to compromise on quality. This allows consumers to search for the film that they wish to watch and the type of viewing experience they want. However, the digital age means more than just watching film, in an age where user-generated content can be uploaded to hosting sites and viewed by millions of consumers within minutes, the distinctions between producer and consumer, watching and creating are breaking down. More than just wanting access to films from a viewing perspective, filmmakers and fans want deeper levels of involvement with film and similarly to movements in the music world, prosumers are mashing up various elements of culture such as film and music in order to create their own creative products, either in their own right or as an homage to the original source.

THE FUTURE OF DISTRIBUTION – DEALING WITH DECREASING REVENUE AND PIRACY

There seem to be three types of approach to tackling the problem of piracy and linked reduced revenues that may come from film production. This is also linked to the problem of access to distribution. Firstly, for many of the mainstream Hollywood studios, they are signalling improved special effects such as 3D technology as a means of safeguarding the legal consumption of film. Kay (2009) provides an interesting insight into this vision of the future among industry leaders and commentators on the future of the media. Two viewpoints seem to dominate regarding the future of theatrical exhibition. On the one hand, the mainstream cinema experience is seen as moving more towards special effect such as 3D and IMAX as well as enhancements such as vibrating seats and devices offering interactivity to film consumers. This helps in tackling the piracy issue as watching at home, on a computer or other device cannot come close to the cinema experience. On the other end of the spectrum, Kay (2009) found predictions regarding niche theatres which will cater very specifically to certain types of film consumers. Linked to this was the idea of small, select 'viewing clubs'. Such viewing clubs could be akin to large book clubs and involve a social element. In terms of the future of art house and non-English language films (in the US marketplace), there was general agreement that they did have a theatrical future, and that this would be linked to strong word of mouth campaigns. This is similar to the current situation within the film industry as discussed earlier in this book, and highlights the importance of word of mouth in the online environment. The benefit of online is that it can easily be monitored and systems which allow film fans to express their interest in seeing a film in a particular cinema's catchment area can build a strong commercial imperative for showing that film. In terms of the nature of the home cinema experience, Kay (2009) found the belief that this experience would also develop in terms of sensory enhancement. The internet was seen as the dominant mode of distributing film to the home and developments such as contact lenses which scan images directly will enhance the experience of home viewing.

The second approach is also routed in more commercial approaches to filmmaking based on risk aversion. Again, looking to the Chinese creative industries, Montgomery and Fitzgerald (2006) illustrate an alternative business model being developed by the Huayi Brothers. This privately owned domestic company developed out of a parent advertising industry. This experience in advertising inspired a move into film and television production which relies heavily on product placement in its funding model. Unlike conventional approaches to product placement in film, where products are placed in films and cross-promotion of the film and product is paid for by the consumer goods company, the Huayi Brothers exchange production finance for a prominent role for the clients' products with the film or television programme. According to Montgomery and Fitzgerald (2006) this has two main benefits, firstly, the client is satisfied whether a film is distributed legally or illegally as they are interested in product exposure and secondly, this finance removes the need to rely solely on exhibition revenue. In addition to sourcing production finance in this way, Montgomery and Fitzgerald (2006) note that Huayi Brothers also pay monitors to oversee ticket purchases at cinemas when their major films are released. As electronic ticketing is not established in all cinemas, it is possible to engage in some of the practices outlined in Chapter 8 which can be used by exhibitors to deprive film producers and distributors of their fair share of box office revenue. While such a funding system has obvious implications for creativity, due to high levels of commercial placements and conservative approaches to innovation in high concept films, there may be little difference between the films produced under either of these business models. The difference is that obtaining increased financial input during the production phase of the film reduces the risk during the exploitation phase.

The third approach is that adopted by filmmakers acting outside the established commercial realm. Access to affordable means of film production and editing capabilities, large numbers of independent filmmakers are ignoring the conventional routes to market and accessing audiences directly through the internet. Gubbins (2008) highlights the fact that 'straight to online' is no longer seen as a statement of failure in the way that 'straight to video' has been. Rather, this can be seen as a solution to the problem of oversupply which has typified the film industry for decades. Large numbers of films are produced each year with very limited numbers achieving theatrical release. The assumption was made that there were no audiences for the other films; however, the reality may be one of two alternatives. Audiences may exist for some of these films, but these audiences are small in number and geographically dispersed. Alternatively, the audiences for the films may be among the group of active film consumers who do not see films on theatrical release. In both of these cases, the logic for 'straight to online' is clear. Unlike films aiming for theatrical release, the straight to online film faces very low barriers to entry. Barriers related to cost are low as are those related to access to the consumer.

New routes to market

There appear to be two groups of filmmakers who are utilizing the internet as an alternative method of distribution. Firstly, those labelled 'net natives' by Gubbins (2008) who have not operated within the conventional structures of the film industry who are finding ways of creating revenue streams through internet distribution or are developing and distributing films this way as calling cards which they can use to develop their reputation within the film industry. In addition, some established filmmakers have turned to online distribution in order to quickly gain exposure for their film. The following section will look at how the studios are embracing social media in enhancing their marketing campaigns.

SOCIAL MEDIA AND FILM MARKETING – WHAT ARE THE MAJORS DOING?

While ten years ago, major studios had websites with information about forthcoming releases and films on general release (Johnston, 2008), things have changed now. Online and viral marketing campaigns are now as important as the conventional practices discussed in Chapter 7. As Johnston (2008) found, film trailers are easily transferred from one technological medium to another allowing consumers to view and share trailers while on the move as well as watching in the cinema. Before the development of social media sites such as Facebook and mySpace, it was difficult for consumers who were not technologically savvy to watch and share trailers and film clips in 'unofficial' spaces. What is happening in relation to film marketing can be referred to as 'intermediality'; where narratives move across various media (Nikunen, 2007). What is specific about these campaigns is the nature of the relationship between the media organisations and the consumer. As Jenkins (2004) noted, the development and success of these campaigns are reliant on consumer innovation as well as compliance with the aims of the media organisation. While media organisations can develop online activities for consumers, they will only succeed if the consumers avail of these facilities and develop their own word of mouth building activates. Dobele et al. (2005) note that viral messages need to be engaging to inspire consumers to pass them on. Nikunen (2007) draws on a range of studies to show the centrality of media to the development of fan culture. Online trailers must be selected by consumers for viewing rather than being shown to passive cinema audiences (Johnston, 2007).

In addition to online activities, studios are developing ways in which to deepen their relationships with consumers through strategies based on simple CRM (Customer Relationship Management) systems. In 2006 social networking site MySpace and Twentieth Century Fox launched their 'Black Curtain Screening Series', http://www.myspace.com/blackcurtain. This allows consumers to sign up for advance screenings of films through their mySpace page. In return, they must add Black Curtain as a friend. They then select films which they would like to preview and if successful, they will receive an email inviting them to the screening. This and other schemes which allow consumers to sign up to receive news of film releases and enter competitions allow the distributor to find out more about their preferences which can be used in targeting them for future campaigns. This use of database marketing by distributors which can help to target their upcoming campaigns can lead to more focused campaigns in the future.

The major studios are developing online games to accompany films. *Resident Evil: Extinction* (2007) had an online game alongside online advertising. This activity was an attempt to get consumers to engage more with the film prior to release in the hope that this would generate want to see. Much talked about *Snakes on a Plane* (2006) incorporated a viral campaign where fans could personalize a telephone message spoken to Samuel L. Jackson which invited them to see the film. In addition to this, blogs and social networking sites were used in order to release and spread rumours about the film in an attempt to build up pre-launch word of mouth for the film. Event films have always been keenly anticipated with fans looking for leaked information and discussing this in various fora. Johnston (2007) indicates the types of online chatter which can accompany the release of these high concept films.

The Cloverfield campaign

One particularly successful and adventurous film marketing campaign that has emerged from a major studio recently is the campaign for *Cloverfield* (2008). This campaign began with a trailer which was shown in cinemas and on selected sites which showed scenes from the film, but without a title or release details. This led to very significant numbers of consumers going online to search for information about the film, which led them to a series of clues. The official website had material gradually added to it which was date stamped, allowing the viewer to figure out the film narrative. Some of the pictures had notes on the back which could be accessed through shaking the computer mouse. The initial film poster still did not have the film title but used the image of the Statue of Liberty looming over New York in order to link to the earlier campaign. This initial campaign appealed to the core audience who were online and liked the intrigue of working things out. The core target audience were the science fiction audience and could be expected to add the trailer to their social networking pages and generate online word of mouth about the campaign. Prior to the film's release, an additional, conventional trailer was released which gave a sense of the narrative of the film (http://www.youtube.com/watch?v=IvNkGm8mxiM). This trailer revealed the name of the film. The official website was released at the same time; this had the basic contents to be expected of a website: trailer, poster art, synopsis, links to Facebook and MySpace pages for the film as well as files which could be embedded into social networking sites of consumers. There was a competition for free tickets to screenings of the film, where the person creating the most attention for the film through their own sites (judged by how many of their contacts adopted the widget for the film which they posted) would win the tickets. This online campaign ran alongside a traditional advertising campaign in the weeks before release. The particularly innovative element of the campaign was a more interactive element in the form of an alternative reality game which saw fans producing their own fake advertising for a fictional product, Slusho and following clues related to the film, some posted on a MySpace blog of the main character. This carefully targeted campaign mixed reality with fiction in a way which appealed to the core audience and resulted in the creation of significant word of mouth.

FINDING ALTERNATIVE ROUTES TO MARKET

Established filmmakers

Gubbins (2008) refers to the release of Wayne Wang's *The Princess of Nebraska* (2007) which, following appearances at a number of film festivals including its debut at Telluride Film Festival had an internet release on the 17th of October 2008 (http://www.imdb.com/title/tt1092411/releaseinfo). Scott (2008) raised the question of the benefit of releasing a film online for free, but reflected that this manner of distribution achieved a significantly greater audience during its 'opening weekend' on YouTube than would be expected for the opening weekend on theatrical release in key art house cinemas. However, *The Princess of Nebraska* (2007) was reportedly made on a very low budget with money saved during the production of *A Thousand Years* (2007) to which *The Princess of Nebraska* (2007) serves as a companion piece (Lim, 2008). *The Princess of Nebraska* (2007) was released in the YouTube Screening Room, a YouTube initiative which was launched in 2008 to showcase high quality short films and also allow some feature length films to debut on the site. An upgraded version of the regular site, the Screening Room is pitched as more like 'event viewing' for film. Drilling down deeper into the motivation of 'giving your film away for free', it is interesting to look at the case of *The Princess of Nebraska* (2007) in light of an interview with director Wayne Wang. Hart (2008) points out the Wang saw the internet release much in the way in which theatrical releases have been viewed, as loss leaders which showcase films for the subsequent windows. Releasing through the YouTube platform did not require significant expenditure on publicity, but in fact generated publicity due to the novelty of the release strategy.

Finding alternative routes to market, the 'Net Natives'

However, at the recent Power to the Pixel conference in London, significant resistance to the entry of YouTube was evident among digital filmmakers. YouTube is perceived as located within the corporate commercial space and as such, may be seen as in opposition to the beliefs of significant numbers of filmmakers who are determined to operate outside that sphere. What is interesting about these filmmakers is that they are commercially savvy. While they do not seem motivated by money, therefore adhering to the dominant discourse of the 'starving artist', these filmmakers recognize the need to access funds in order to develop sustainability and continuous output.

The first of these new breed of film maker/marketer hybrids that I will discuss goes by the name of M dot Strange, writer, director, producer, editor, actor and music supervisor of *We Are the Strange (2007)*. M dot Strange encourages aspiring filmmaker/marketers to build a cult around their film and to become the cult leader (M dot Strange, 2008). M dot Strange used crowd-sourcing (Howe, 2008) a process where the public are recruited in order to provide input and resources to solve a problem or provide content, in order to facilitate the making of and subsequently the marketing of his film. Hunt (2009) posits that the wuffie factor, a product of social capital that harnesses social networks in order to build business in the online environment. Hunt (2009) emphasises that community interaction results in increased levels of social capital. This is precisely the logic which has underpinned M dot Strange in his film making/marketing practice. M dot Strange (2008) highlighted the alienation which film consumers can feel from mainstream film. M dot Strange placed a video advertising for extras on video sharing site YouTube and asked people if they wanted to be an extra in his film. All they were required to do in order to become an extra was to send him an image of themselves which would then be incorporated into the film, a democratic form of casting. M dot Strange (2008) talked about "the importance of being important", and that this was what he was tapping into in his search for extras. He received six to seven hundred photos in the first week of casting which backed up his perception that people want to be involved. M dot Strange (2008) differentiated between old and new media by highlighting the ability of wealthy media conglomerates to spend huge sums on expansive marketing campaigns which can deceive the consumer. Conversely, M dot Strange believes that new media practitioners have a much harder time if trying to lie to consumers.

While established media organisations continue to debate the problem of copyright in the film industry, M dot Strange, among other filmmaker/marketers prefers to encourage other filmmakers to offer outtakes and clips from their film online so that others can create mash ups by using this material. Not purely motivated by artistic altruism, M dot Strange (2008) pointed out that filmmakers could learn a huge amount about their 'fans' through offering them these materials. Through observing the style of film created as well as the music provided on the soundtrack of the films produced, M dot Strange felt he could develop a more successful marketing strategy based on the preferences of his fan base. In addition to the research potential provided here, M dot Strange uses the internet as an advertising and promotional space and he talks about the 'new P & A' for the digital age. This involves exploiting low cost and highly creative opportunities wherever possible. M dot Strange believes in building a WOMA (word of mouth army) committed to promoting the film. He mobilized this army in a number of creative ways. M dot Strange read books on marketing and branding in order to understand something about building this online community and believes in being open about this. For months prior to the film previewing at Sundance, M dot Strange leaked behind the scenes films and short clips on YouTube and build up this core WOMA. As people began to comment on his YouTube clips he could gain an understanding of who his audience was by looking at their account information. This could tell him how old they were, which other types of clips and music they viewed and other psychographic information.

Once the film was accepted for the festival, he posted the trailer on YouTube and when the film was shown at the Sundance Film Festival in 2007, M dot Strange conducted video interviews with audience members leaving the film. Although the reactions of the majority of audiences were negative, the audiences that reacted negatively were relatively mainstream audiences which were not the core audience for this film. By posting these negative responses on YouTube, he once again mobilized his WOMA who increased their efforts to assist the film in connecting with a wider audience. What works in the case of M dot Strange is that he sees himself as part of his online community, not apart from it. His core fan base seem to also be creative animators who use his content in creative ways and respond to what he has done with *We Are the Strange* (2007). Because of this, he communicates with his fans through various web 2.0 platforms and for the follow up film to *We Are the Strange* (2007), he is continuing to use crowd-sourcing to attract cast and crew to the film. His revenue model seems a very fair one. *We Are the Strange* (2007) is available to watch for free on YouTube and a DVD is also available to buy through a number of online retailers. The DVD has a range of special features which is the reason why many fans chose to buy it. There are two specific elements to this business model, firstly, the filmmaker/marketer is seen as and believes himself to be part of the community that he is marketing to. Secondly, consumers are asked if they want to provide payment once they have watched the film, therefore removing the risk involved with film consumption through traditional channels of distribution. In terms of sustainability, it will be interesting to watch how this progresses over time, as according to M dot Strange, his strategy works due to his authenticity as a member of the group rather than a filmmaker admired by the group.

When listening to M dot Strange discuss his position within his WOMA, there are clear links to Muniz and Guinn's (2001) seminal article where they identified three key elements of community. The first of these elements in shared knowing of belonging, secondly, they point out the presence of shared rituals and traditions and finally; a sense of moral responsibility. These elements are clearly present in M dot Strange's WOMA. Analysis of this WOMA necessitates reflecting on the oppositional positioning of brand communities such as that depicted by Schouten and McAlexander (1995) in their study of Harley Davidson fans. This oppositional identity can be seen as sitting alongside a level of commercial awareness that typifies the postmodern consumer. Not quite consumer, not quite producer, definitely not just a customer. The relationships established by M dot Strange are in line with Thompson et al.'s (2006: 50) characterization of branding strategies which "use narratives and tactics that demonstrate an empathetic understanding of customers' inspirations, aspirations, and life circumstances and that generate warm feelings of community among brand users". Not only does M dot Strange allow access to his creative products for free (as well as the opportunity to buy enhanced products), he offers community members practical advice and encouragement regarding the filmmaking practices that he engages in. By operating with a pseudonym, M dot Strange has bought into concept of branding. He has branded himself and is mobilizing this brand by developing relationships with his WOMA (see Fournier, 1998).

This analysis of the relationship between M dot Strange and his WOMA has echoes of the findings of Thompson et al. (2006) in their study of Starbucks where respondents distinguished between Starbucks, depicted as a large soulless corporation, and local coffee houses where the owners were seen as committed to the community, their staff and their customers. Although both have a commercial imperative, deep suspicion for those operating within the corporate system were viewed with suspicion while independents were seen as connecting more with the community. Thompson et al. (2006) are concerned with the concept of the 'Doppelgänger Brand Image' by which they mean the circumstances through which alternative narratives are developed from the core brand narrative which previously existed. If M dot Strange is seen as harnessing his WOMA too cynically or suddenly seems apart from his core fan base, he could find himself facing a similar loss of authenticity.

NEW ECONOMICS IN THE FILM INDUSTRY

While M dot Strange is looking to crowd sourcing to assist in production and promotion of his films, others in the industry are looking at new economic models in order to take advantage of the benefits derived by social media as well as tackling the problems faced by filmmakers in terms of getting their films produced and distributed. Turning to cooperative models or ways in which skills and time can be exchanged between networks of filmmakers, filmmakers such as Arin Crumley are trying to establish organisations or structures to facilitate these types of activities. Crumley has set up TheOrganism.org (www.theorganism.org). TheOrganism aims at formalizing these practices and providing assistance to filmmakers wishing to work in this way. They have provided a number of templates for documents which producers can use in order to set out the terms of collaboration they are entering into. TheOrganism is currently conducting a pilot study to investigate the practicalities of such a system and it will be interesting to look at how this turns out.

While the activities of the filmmakers discussed above are focused on harnessing fan resources as a means of bypassing conventional distribution routes, there are others who are working with the system to change things. An example of this can be found in looking at the work of Lance Weiler and Stefan Avalos who moved into digital filmmaking once they had discovered how to make digital look like film during postproduction. Weiler and Avalos' film *The Last Broadcast* (1999) was made for a very low budget and the majority of time spent on the film was in the post-production stage of the film. Kirsner (2008) recounts the trouble which the filmmakers had in persuading a digital projector manufacturer to sponsor the film's debut theatrical release in a Pennsylvania cinema in March 1998. At the end of the 1990s, as mentioned earlier in this chapter, it was possible to make digital films, but exhibiting them without spending thousands on converting to film was practically impossible. When Weiler and Avalos did manage to secure the use of a digital project for their one week run, they had to operate it themselves as this sort of equipment was not used by cinema projectionists. Weiler and Avalos did not passively wait for someone to make digital distribution possible, knowing that what they needed was technically possible; they proceeded to lobby technology companies in order to support their digital distribution dream. Kirsner (2008) recounts the interactions between filmmakers, technology companies such as Texas Instruments, exhibitors and distributors which took place at the end of the 1990s and illustrates the uncertainty that they faced in moving to digital projection. Snobbery or fear among filmmakers in addition to uncertainty over the most appropriate technology to invest resulted in sluggish move to digital. Kirsner (2008) juxtaposes the success of *The Blair Witch Project* (1999) with Weiler and Avalos' *The Last Broadcast* (1998), illustrating the huge difficulties faced in overturning industry norms.

The final example of filmmakers finding new ways to engage with consumers and to explore new revenue streams comes from the aptly named *Steal this Film* (2006). This is a documentary film which examines issues of copyright from an interesting perspective. Jamie King made this documentary from the perspective of the Swedish organisations which aim to facilitate file sharing among peers such as The Pirate Bay, this film interviews a series of key figures at the cold face of intellectual copyright issues such as those in the major studios, producers of content and consumer. The Pirate Bay is a BitTorrent indexing site which allows consumers to access BitTorrent which allow them to download and share media files. In April 2009 Pirate Bay owners Peter Sunde, Fredrik Neij, Gottfrid Svartholm and Carl Lundström were found guilty of assistance to copyright infringement, sentenced to a year in prison and fined 30 million SEK (approx. 2,385,000 GBP or 2,684,000 euro). The defendants are currently appealing against this verdict (Kiss, 2009). The Pirate Bay website is still running. An interesting comment is made in the film by filmmaker Alex Cox who points to fears that video players which allowed taping of film of television would see the end of the film industry and proved unfounded. Cox highlighted the move in the legal system from considering the consumers to protecting corporate interests. What is evident from this film and other activities going on in the film industry is that efforts to cling to intellectual property rights as they currently exist are futile. As an aside to this discussion, the determination of large film studios to safeguard all their revenue streams and protect their property was evident during the preparation of this book. Attempts were made to include images of film posters to be included in Chapter 7. In order to secure these rights, I would have had to employ a lawyer, pay very substantial sums of money and negotiate separate agreements for separate territories. In some cases, electronic rights could not be granted, and as it is now convention to have books available in printed form and electronically and as such, to distribute worldwide, this was impossible. In one case, all text referring to the film would have to be approved in advance. Such determination to control and exploit all revenue opportunities can be seen as counterproductive.

Steal This Film (2006), in the spirit of the film was distributed through BitTorrent. In 2007, *Steal This Film II* was released and during the Pirate Bay trail in the early part of 2009, a companion film was released. During the *Power to the Pixel* in 2008, King stated that making money was not a motivating force behind the film, exposure was. They asked those who downloaded the film to send $1 to them if they liked the film and said that a significant number of people did send this money. For the second film they asked for donations of $15 and offered mystery gifts in return. King posited that revenue earned in this way was significantly better than through You-Tube (although his films are also available there). King also raised the difficulty of asking people to pay for a film before they see it, saying that this created friction (King, 2008). This leads to a very important conclusion; it could be proposed that films which people like will be successful financially in the future as they will pay after watching. This does not mean that people will no longer go to the cinema to see a much anticipated film, but they may do so either as the film is a sequel or adaptation so that there is some risk minimisation; the director or other creative personnel are trusted to produce a film which reaches the expectations of the consumer and a reordering of the existing windows system. Films may initially be released on the web and only gain a theatrical release (and be released in the subsequent windows) once sufficient positive word of mouth has been earned.

What seems clear from looking at the new breed of filmmaker/marketers is that they want to develop relationships with their audiences, whether this is linked to involving them in the filmmaking process, mobilizing word of mouth to generate publicity for the film or in mobilizing around issues. This, linked with a renewed focus on commercial issues which is not about amassing great fortunes and protecting intellectual property, but about creating sustainable filmmaking, is succeeding due to its authentic nature. At the same time, campaigns for high concept films, funded by major studios are engaging audiences in other ways. Drawing on developments in the user driven environment of social media, studios are developing marketing campaigns in the online environment which harness the interests and behaviours of their target audiences. Young audiences who are the digital natives expect more than 'one to many' communication. Through developing online games and portable applications which consumers can embed into their own web pages, filmmakers are benefitting from the online sphere.

Alongside the harnessing of social media by established media organisations, the digital natives are developing filmmaking/marketing practices which are appropriate for the digital age. Espousing a more democratic notion of filmmaking and consumption, these filmmakers are either forcing change within the existing structures of the film industry or circumventing these structures in order to access the consumer or build up online fan bases. This movement has seen a resurgence of creativity within the marketing function of film alongside the filmmaking activities. These filmmakers do not see 'marketing' as oppositional to the creative practice of filmmaking, but seek to use marking activities in order to offer their films to an audience. These filmmakers have the advantage of authenticity among their fan bases as they are generally part of the fan base that they are marketing too. However, it is not proven that such approaches will be relevant for all types of film. While the genres of science fiction, horror and documentary (which deals with issues) may inspire feelings of community which can be accessed in order to find an audience for films of this sort, this may not be true for other sorts of film. What is clear is that film marketing in the digital age can no longer remain as marketing as numbers, as each film needs to develop their audience in a way which is more appropriate for the target audience and the type of film.

CHAPTER 11

Conclusions

Throughout this book I have used the term 'film consumption' and the notion that films are consumed. I have deliberately used this term rather than the often used term of 'watching a film'. For me, to watch seems like a passive activity, which does not really reflect the nature of our engagement with film. When we consume a film we watch it, listen to it, think about it, decode it and are sometimes changed by it. For this reason, we consume the film, we take it inside ourselves and it has an impact. Consuming film can alter mood, change perception, irritate and annoy us, but we are never exactly the same having consumed a film.

CONTENTS

LIMITATIONS

While this book covers many elements of film marketing, I have to acknowledge that there are a number of omissions from what would have been the ideal book. Firstly, I did not include very specific details regarding marketing, budgeting and campaign planning. This is due partly to the fact that the many 'how to' film marketing books do this better than I could. As many of the authors who have written these books are film marketing practitioners, their expertise in this area would put mine to shame. Secondly, rate cards change, the media landscape changes and there is significant difference across countries in terms of the predominant media. My book would be vastly extended and quickly out of date if I dedicated significant space to these issues. Another shortcoming of the book is its reliance on data from the US and UK. It was my dream to produce a book which had a much more global identity, but I was restricted by the material that I had access to. I have searched hard to find the information that I have included from outside these countries, but there is a general lack of data pertaining to many film markets. This is partly due to the mechanisms of academic journals in the UK and US which privilege data emanating from these or similar, countries. Secondly, in some very interesting film industries such as India and Nigeria, it is very difficult to gain access to reliable and comprehensive industrial data. Thirdly, my personal resources in terms of time, financial means and linguistic ability restricted my ability to collect and analyse primary data in these countries. And finally, although there are increasing numbers of scholars who research the film industry from a marketing perspective, this remains a relatively under-researched area.

Another area which I have not focused on in this book is that of product placement in film. I see this as a separate area from the core concerns of film marketing as presented in this book. Although such placements and linked promotional opportunities can be key elements of film finance, this leans more towards 'film and marketing' than 'film marketing'. There is also the linked area of merchandise which has moved from low-cost items such as t-shirts to other audiovisual products such as video games. My lack of attention to this area may be a weakness, but this signals the distinction between the high concept film where development of ancillary products, high degrees of product placement and tie in promotional deals are both possible and expected, and the lower cost films which are further towards the independent realm. This increasing merger between film and 'the market' may be reflected in the rise of Branded Entertainment (see Lehu, 2007) where film and other audiovisual products can be viewed as promotional tools for mainstream product. As access to film finance becomes increasingly hard and media fragmentation makes it difficult for mid-range mainstream drama to attract funding and audiences, we would expect the focus on branded entertainment to increase. However, for very many independent filmmakers, product placements and other commercial activities remain difficult. All of these omissions will mean that this book is not 'the complete guide to everything you ever considered when you thought about film marketing', however when I lamented the limited nature of my book to a friend, they smiled and said 'you can put that in the next book'. Of course all academic work has limitations and omissions and hopefully these limitations and omissions can provide a programme of work for scholars in film marketing, myself included.

LOGIC OF THE BOOK

Now I have gotten the limitations of the book out of the way, I can reflect on what has been covered within the preceding chapters. In order to understand the logic of the book, it is important that I explain the positioning of the book.

My intention was to produce a book which filled a gap in the marketplace. As noted earlier in this book, there are a number of very insightful and highly practical books on film marketing aimed at practitioners and students. In addition, there are a series of books by academics or journalists which deal either implicitly or explicitly with film marketing issues. However, what is missing is a book about film marketing which locates this discussion within the marketing literature. While there are significant differences between marketing films and marketing fast moving consumer goods, it is still possible to make sense of film marketing and to explore film marketing practice within frameworks developed and tested by marketing academics. In saying this, it has been important to look outside marketing as well in order to find appropriate frameworks within which film marketing practices could be understood. In this aim, I am indebted to the countless film historians, cultural studies scholars, sociologists, psychologists and even the odd enlightened economist as well as the general management scholars and geographers who have posed and answered many of the important questions about the film industry and marketing practice within this industry. Inspired by marketing scholars who look outward in developing insight into the world of marketing and consumption, I have tried to do this in this book. Of course, my use of these literatures may be seen as limited as I have applied the gaze of the marketer to the issues under consideration rather than attempting to be a psychologically grounded cultural sociologist film historian. I have looked around for literatures and frameworks that help me to understand and hopefully explain the various elements of film marketing covered in this book.

Setting the scene

The structure of the book also indicates how I conceive of film marketing. The introduction to the book introduces the reader to some general marketing theories which have influenced how I think about film marketing practice. This whistle stop tour of marketing thinking is not supposed to be exhaustive in any way, but positions the book within the relevant theoretical context in relation to marketing. I start by bringing a number of mainstream approaches to and concerns of marketing together with the literature on supply chain management as this informed my early research on film marketing. After introducing the film industry supply chain, I progressed to a discussion of what constitutes film marketing, bringing in considerations of film consumption. Chapter 2 examines the origins and development of the film industry. My approach to film marketing calls for consideration of the historical context within which studies of film marketing are set. I started by outlining the nature of Hollywood's global domination of the box office before introducing the historical evolution of the film industry. This chapter signals my understanding of film marketing practices as wedded to and grounded in their historical, political and social context. Film marketing does not occur in a vacuum (a favourite saying of mine). In order to understand why film marketing practices have evolved as they have done, why access to the market is strictly controlled, why film consumption choices are limited, why consumer tastes are so aligned and so on, it is necessary to look at the macro-environment. While film studies scholars and geographers have provided much more in-depth analyses of the industrial formation of the industry, my précised account is necessary in order to contextualise the remainder of the book. Having provided this overview I then looked at some of the reasons why this domination still persists.

New product development and research

Chapter 3 sees a move from the general (the evolution of the film industry) to the particular. In this chapter, some key film marketing concepts are introduced and discussed. The first of these are marketability and playability. Here I discuss the difficulties faced by films which may play very well and get good audience response and films which sound appealing. In general, more mainstream and identifiable films in terms of genre and style are more straightforward to market. If the concept is simple, it can be communicated in a simple way to the consumer. However, if the concept is innovative, it can be difficult to get this point across to the consumer. As film is an experiential product, it can only be evaluated once it has been consumed. This leads on to a discussion of the role of market research in the film industry. Again, the starting point for this discussion is an historical account of the development of film marketing practices both in terms of intentional film marketing activities as well as practices derived from the use of film as a form of social research which have now been subsumed into market research practices in the film industry. The next section in this chapter introduces ideas of new product development and applies this to the development process in film, allowing for the classification of types of film in accordance with theories of new product development. Later in the chapter, the types of research undertaken in the film industry are explored with particular focus on the recruited audience screening.

Policy and film marketing

Following this examination of the development and research practices involved in the film industry, Chapter 4 returns us to the macro-level of analysis as the impact of the wider policy environment on the formation of the film industry and subsequently, film marketing practices is examined. The focus of the early part of Chapter 4 is on the US and the role of policy in establishing the US film industry. This is followed by a discussion of the efforts made to support the film industry at the pan-European level. The chapter then looks at specific developments in the UK, South Korea, Denmark and Nigeria in order to illustrate the impact which specific policy environments and industrial and societal context has upon the evolution of the film industry. This evolution also informs the types of film marketing practices which will follow. Each of these specific film industries has evolved in a particular way and this has informed the way in which film is consumed in these countries as well as the types of films chosen by consumers.

The film marketing mix

Chapter 5 follows this by proposing a 'film marketing mix'. The key elements which need to be considered by the film marketer in order to offer a film to the market are considered. I was drawn to the 'mix' notion by the idea of the marketer as a mixer of ingredients. This is precisely the case for the film marketer as each time a new film is produced and intended for the market-place, the marketer must assess the collective of these ingredients in order to identify the unique selling proposition of the film as well as considering the need for consistency between the mix elements. A film is indeed the sum of its parts. A good script poorly acted, an interesting idea badly communicated, inappropriate casting, all of these things can mean that the final film is not playable. The role of the star is considered in this book, but in thinking about 'film star', the notion of the star as other than the actor is explored. Although research in this area is inconclusive, the power of the actor to attract audiences is established. In Chapter 5, the different star systems in Hollywood, Bollywood and Nollywood are considered. Similarities and differences between these systems are examined. Other than the actor stars, certain directors or cinematographers may also indicate a certain sort of identity for a film. It seems that the further we move from the High Concept (Wyatt, 1994) film to the more obscure, the more likely it is that the director is the star rather than the actor.

Once the role of the creative personnel has been discussed, attention turned to the script and the linked element of the genre. While the term 'genre' has sometimes been used to denote a film which lacks imagination and merely mimics other successful films, in marketing terms it is essential to define a film's genre. A selection of possible genres is presented and discussed in the chapter as is the notion of creating a genre if one does not exist. Genre identification or creation deals with the 'what is it?' question.

This question will be asked during pitches for funding, meetings with potential distributors, journalists, agents, actors, director and so on and the answer can influence either a positive or negative outcome. Inability to articulate the essence/purpose of a film may result in a lack of finance to produce the film or the lack of an audience for the film once it is made. While casting, identifying key crew, developing the script and the genre are largely controllable factors, we now move to slightly less controllable elements of the marketing mix. Firstly, the age classification awarded a film can provide key shorthand regarding the target audience for the film, as can the release strategy. However, particularly in a global film industry, ability to control both the classification of the film and the ability to negotiate the desired release strategy for the film may be more difficult.

These essential signalling elements are important in positioning a film for a particular audience. For example, looking at *Persepolis* (2007), this animation film was given a 12A rating in the UK which may indicate that it is a film pitched at children, or at least young teenagers. However, as this film was exhibited in mainly art house cinemas, not known as catering for the young teenager market, the combination of these elements of the film marketing mix could act as a signal to the potential audience. What is important when considering the mix of elements which influence the positioning of the film within the market is that the message is consistent and authentic. Casting a well-known star in a very small film can feel incongruous both in terms of the message being communicated as well as play-ability. The discussion towards the end of the chapter which considers how films are released and where they are shown leads us towards considering the consumer and their response to film marketing. Further research which examines the interplay of these elements of the film marketing mix is needed, specifically in relation to how branding frameworks can be applied to film marketing. Kerrigan and O'Reilly (2008) have begun to conceptualise this but there is a need to empirically assess the interplay between the different elements of the film marketing brand and how the consumer interprets these different brand messages.

Consumer selection of film

This concern with the consumer and how they choose their films is the focus of Chapter 6. This is the most well researched area within film marketing, from a 'marketing' approach. The chapter draws on the numerous studies which have been done, looking at the focus of the research and the methods used. The majority of studies in this area draws on box office data and therefore makes assumptions about why people make the choices that they do. By analysing aggregate data in this way, film consumers are treated as rational beings and little acknowledgement of the context within which films are chosen. Interpretive researchers have looked at the film consumer in a more holistic way and in doing so can shed some more light on the range of influences that come to bear on the selection of film to be consumed. The UK Film Council's Avids study served as an interesting insight into how film consumers develop their consumption over the course of their life. From this study we can start to distinguish between film consumers in terms of their relationship with film and the benefits that they wish to derive from their film consumption. The elements of the film marketing mix act as signals to the consumer when deciding on whether a film is for them or not and this information may be combined with word of mouth, in the online of offline context and critical reviews of films. The chapter ends by looking at impediments to film consumption which is under-researched and yet is an important area to consider.

The film marketing materials

Understanding how people select films leads on to an examination of the key film marketing materials in Chapter 7. This chapter considers the key film marketing materials such as posters and trailers as well as looking at the people involved in overseeing the production of these materials. The chapter examines the types of visual images that need to be produced in order to market the film, both to the industry and to the end consumer. The importance of the Electronic Press Kit is discussed and the key ingredients of the EPK are considered. Following a discussion of how film can be visually represented and communicated to the consumer, various film posters and trailers are analysed in terms of what they are communicating to the consumer and how they are positioning themselves. From this, the clear conventions of film marketing are understood. In order to position a film to the target audience, they must share an understanding of the visual messages which are being communicated. The need to tailor film marketing materials to incorporate cultural preferences and shared cultural meaning is also explored in this chapter. The adaptation versus standardisation debate which is ever present in the international marketing literature is also present in the realm of film marketing.

Further research examining interpretation of film marketing materials would deepen our understanding of how consumers in different cultural context read film marketing materials and give us insight into what consumers are looking for, both from the marketing materials and from the film itself. Looking back to earlier discussion in the book, the analysis of marketing materials in Chapter 7 highlights the difficulty in producing appropriate marketing materials for more complex films. In star driven vehicles, the star is prominent, for more artistic films, the director as artist is promoted through the use of 'a film by'. The film's context and genre should be presented through the poster, but if too many messages are contained in one poster, the consumer may not be able to understand the overriding message. Trailers can provide a more complete sense of the film as they have sound, movement and the opportunity for character or plot development and through the growth of the internet and mobile technology, the opportunity to see film trailers is increasing. It will be interesting to undertake further research on how consumer tastes are developed through greater access to trailers in this way. As consumers become more accustomed to watching short clips on various devices, the nature of the film trailer could change. The chapter ends with a discussion regarding the process of media buying and different forms of advertising that film marketers can consider when planning their campaigns.

The film marketing calendar

Chapter 8 looks at key events in the film marketing calendar. The main focus of this chapter is upon film markets and festival as well as major award ceremonies. The chapter begins by introducing the role of the sales agent in getting films into the international marketplace. The role of distributors is also discussed in this chapter and distinctions are made between the independent and the major distributors. They operate in very different ways in terms of placing film with exhibitors and both types of distributor can be seen to have their own inherent advantages and disadvantages. The majors have power within the industry and therefore can negotiate with exhibitors to secure favourable conditions. On the other hand, independent distributors are accustomed to developing campaigns which are tailor made for the film in question. By necessity, they cannot reply on a painting by numbers approach to the marketing campaign. Relationships between film producers and distributors are often characterised as lacking trust. There is an inherent suspicion of distributors among filmmakers as distributors are seen as dishonest in accounting for profit share. Chapter 8 discusses the nature of such deception (taken from Vogel, 2006). A key element of the film marketing calendar is the release strategy. The difficulties of the windows system for independent filmmakers and distributors is discussed as well as the problems in securing a suitable (if any) release date. While a number of studies have indicated that opening a film on as many screens as possible and across as many platforms as possible is a good way to maximise returns, such analysis ignores a number of key impediments. Firstly, such a global release would require a very significant print and advertising budget. Secondly, this would require extensive coordination between a number of international distributors (unless the film was being released by a major studio in all markets). Thirdly, this strategy assumes that it is possible to secure exhibition slots on such a wide scale. Therefore, film distributors plan release strategies that balance considerations of power, resources and timing.

Timing may also be linked to certain film festivals, markets or award ceremonies. The number of film festivals in existence has been increasing steadily. While some cater to general tastes, many are very specific, focusing on a particular genre or target audience. In Chapter 8, my focus is primarily on prominent festivals which either have associated film markets or are seen as having a significant commercial element. For independent films, these festivals and markets are a crucial route to market and a positive audience reaction to a film in a major festival can result in it securing a distribution deal. While there is increasing interest in film festivals as commercial sites, research in this area is very limited. Winning an award at a major film festival such as Cannes or Sundance can positively impact on the market potential of a film, and generally identifies the film as of artistic or intellectual merit. However, the level of publicity attained for festival awards is limited compared to that associated with the Academy Awards and Chapter 8 discusses these award ceremonies in terms of film marketing concerns. This is an area which has benefitted from a number of published studies. However, the majority of these studies make assumptions about the link between the award and box office revenue which may not necessarily be the case. Further research regarding exhibitors' willingness to programme award winning films, unsolicited media attention and consumer awareness or perceptions should be undertaken in order to understand the relationship between the award ceremonies and consumer choice.

Broadening the scope

Chapter 9 moves on to look at the wider impact of film on society. The ethical turn in both consumer behaviour and marketing research opens the door for considerations of such issues in film marketing. While the majority of this book is concerned with how films are positioned with regard to the industry and consumers, and how consumers select films that they wish to watch, Chapter 9 considers the impact which this consumption may have on individuals and society. The social, political and educative nature of film is explored. Film is a form of representation and the notion of representation in film is explored in Chapter 9. In this exploration of the social and societal impact of film, the blurring of fact and fiction is discussed. The move towards theatrical distribution for non-fiction films and the adoption of non-fictional styles of filmmaking in portraying fictional stories is interesting in exploring the impact of film on society. An example of this may be Micheal Winterbottom's film *In this World* (2002) which is shot in the style of a documentary following two men in their journey from a refugee camp in Peshawar to the UK. The blurring of fact and fiction in this film happens on a number of levels. Firstly, although this was a fictional film, the stories and experiences depicted in the film mirror the actual stories and experiences of many illegal migrants. The style deliberately mimicked documentary and the viewer constantly questions the fact/fiction divide. This fact/fiction blurring is extended when we learn that one of the actors in the film actually made this journey after the film was completed. Telling fictional stories in a factual way can provide different ways through which the film consumer can engage with an issue. It is more established to fictionalise true events, but our suspicion of the fictional elements may distract us from exploring the issues raised in the film. Chapter 9 proposes a continuum of roles and motives which bring ethical issues and commercial aims together. Further research regarding filmmakers' motives and the link to the marketing strategy would deepen our understanding of the social and societal motives of filmmakers and marketers. This also implies a need for more audience research which examines the transformational nature of film. How does film consumption change people's attitudes and beliefs? Are people more receptive to social messages when consuming factual or fictional film? These are important questions, not just from a marketing perspective, but in terms of understanding the wider social impact of film.

New technology and film marketing

Finally, Chapter 10 looks at technological developments and film marketing. While technology has driven innovations in filmmaking and film marketing practices since the origins of the film industry, there have been significant technological changes which have impacting on film marketing over the last decade. Chapter 10 looks at these practices in more detail and considers how these changes affect both filmmakers and consumers. Chapter 10 considers the impact of digital media convergence on the film industry. While the media sector has always had a significant degree of convergence in terms of the media conglomerates which own film studios, music labels, television stations and so on, the internet age has seen the introduction of a new set of actors in the film sphere. The early movements in this stage of media integration were motivated by the need to access content. The internet could provide infinite spaces for interaction, commercial and social engagement, but the mantra 'content is King' loomed large. The only way to attract people to your website was through the provision of interesting content. The possibility of having internet protocol television relied on accessibility of interesting content. As producers had content and problems in accessing the market and the internet providers now had a means of access to the consumer, it seemed logical to enter into mergers and contractual agreements regarding sharing these resources.

Chapter 10 considers the impact of these new technological developments on three fronts. Firstly, as is well-documented, filmmaking is now much more accessible to non-professional filmmakers and to independent filmmakers with limited resources. Increasing access to the supply side does not guarantee an audience for your film. Early discussions of digital filmmaking centred on the problems of getting access to the audience. Most film festivals did not have digital projection facilities ten years ago and neither did cinemas. If a film was shot on digital, it must be converted to film stock before exhibition was possible. Ten years ago, film marketing practice was behind many other industries in terms of their use of the internet as a marketing tool. Film websites were very much like shop windows showing potential consumers some visual and textual information about the film but nothing more. Since then, change has been rapid in these two areas. Filmmakers can now self-distribute through the internet as a result of web 2.0 technology and filmmakers and marketers can use the internet in order to build brand communities, research film marketing materials, conduct audience research and so on. There have been two significant shifts due to these changes. Firstly, the producer consumer divide is now longer, a useful framework in the practice and research of film marketing. As consumers become filmmakers through affordable and easily mastered mobile phone and digital recording technology, the reified position of the producer is being challenged. How do we define filmmakers when anyone can make and distribute 'a film'? This change is having an impact on the conventional structures of the film industry and Chapter 10 explores the tension between the enormous media conglomerates, with their access to finance, research and a distribution network and maverick filmmakers who are now not only making film, but finding new routes to market for these films.

Chapter 10 discusses this in terms of emerging business models. The second shift is regarding how consumers (if we can still use that term) engage with marketing communications. Consumers are increasingly used to passing on viral marketing clips. This can be motivated by a desire to support a particular product (in this case a film) or because the viral content is worth consuming in its own right. The line between the commercial and the social is being eroded through the growth of social media and consumers' adoption of such social media. Official websites must be part of a more comprehensive online marketing campaign. This higher level of consumer engagement has brought with it the risks associated with increased consumer voice. Controlling online activities and opinions is as difficult as controlling these offline, but the reach of online word of mouth may be further. Chapter 10 discusses some of the key change that we have seen over the last decade and highlights a number of successful film marketing campaigns which have embraced the online environment and in so doing, have shaped film marketing practices in the digital age. In addition to this, Chapter 10 considers the role of maverick filmmakers who are harnessing the internet in order to build brand communities, supporters and consumers of their films as well as to foster collaboration. Finally, Chapter 10 questions how these developments, alongside increasing piracy, are impacting on the film industry and film marketing practices before questioning the notion of the 'new film marketing' as sounding the death knell of established marketing practices.

SUMMARY

Overall, this book has aimed at providing an holistic overview of film marketing. This extends to the need to consider the historical industrial context as well as the current policy environment on the film industry, marketing practice and film consumption. This leads to the need to think about film marketing as a process which begins once the idea for a film is being formulated and ends somewhere after a film is consumed. There is a need to consider the filmmaker, the film marketers and the consumer in conceptualising film marketing. In this way, we can see that establishing relationships and shared meaning is central to film marketing practice, yet understanding these relationships can be very complex. Within the film marketing landscape, individual consumers have relationships with actors, directors, film composers, distributors, particular cinemas, websites and other consumers. Filmmakers have relationships with other filmmakers, other industrial figures, audiences, actors and communities. What makes this picture so complex is that these relationships are influenced by a number of factors, other consumers, reviewers, agents, casting directors and so on. A consumer may have a strong bond with a particular actor or director while never having actually met in person or having a sense of them outside their cultural products. Actors, directors, distributors, studios and so on may all be seen as having their own brand identity and negotiating this film brandscape

(Kerrigan and O'Reilly, 2008) may be complex. There is a tension between the mainstream and the innovative, both in terms of types of film being offered to the consumer as well as the ways in which filmmakers are providing their films to the consumer. These changes mean that there is a great deal of uncertainty within the film industry regarding the future of the industry in its present form in addition to the continual uncertainty underpinning film as an experiential product. While the development of user generated content and increase in film piracy may be seen as a threat to the future of the industry, looking to the UK Film Council's Avids study, these developments may result in a greater number of people having the resources to develop a relationship with film than was previously possible. As our tastes are shaped by what we consume, broadening access to a range of film in this way may mean that film consumers become more discerning.

As film marketing practices become more innovative and arguably more creative moving further into the digital age, it will be interesting to see how this changes both perceptions of film marketing as well as the practice of film marketing. Film marketing is the bridge between the creative practice of filmmaking and the act of film consumption. As the barriers between making and consuming are coming down, the nature and ownership of film marketing will also change.

References

Adorno, T., Eisler, H., 1994. Prejudices and bad habits. In: Dickenson, K. (Ed.), Movie Music the Film Reader. Routledge, New York, pp. 25–35. 2002.

Aksoy, A., Robins, K., 1992. Hollywood for the 21st century: global competition for critical mass in image markets. Cambridge Journal of Economics 16, 1–22.

Albert, S., 1998. Movie stars and the distribution of financially successful films in the motion picture industry. Journal of Cultural Economics 22 (4), 249–270.

Alberstat, P., 2004. The Insider's Guide to Film Finance. Focal Press, Oxford.

Alvarez, J.L., Mazza, Carmelo, Pedersen, J.S., Svejenova, S., 2005. Shielding idiosyncrasy from Isomorphic pressures: towards optimal distinctiveness in European filmmaking. Organization 12 (6), 868–888.

AMA, 2004. http://www.marketingpower.com/live/content21257.php accessed 24/04/2009.

AMA, 2007. http://www.marketingpower.com/Community/ARC/Pages/Additional/Definition/default.aspx accessed 24/04/2009.

Ambler, T., 1997. How much of brand equity is explained by trust? Management Decision 35, 283.

Anderson, R., 1985. The motion picture patents company: a reevaluation. In: Balio, T. (Ed.), The American Film Industry, second ed. The University of Wisconsin Press, Wisconsin, pp. 133–152.

Anderson, E.W., 1998. Consumer satisfaction and word of mouth. Journal of Services Research 1 (1), 5–17.

Armstrong, G., Kotler, P., 2000. Principles of Marketing. Prentice Hall, London.

Austin, B., 1980. Rating the movies. Journal of Popular Film and Television 7 (4), 384–399.

Austin, B., 1981b. Film attendance, why college students choose to see their most recent film. Journal of Popular Film and Television 9, 28–49.

Austin, B.A., 1989. Immediate Seating: a Look at Movie Audiences. Wadsworth, Belmont, CA.

Baker, M.J., 2000. Marketing Theory. Thomson Learning, London.

Baines, J., 2004. Talk given to MA film and television producing. University of London, Royal Holloway.

Bakker, Gerben, 2003. The decline and fall of the European film industry: sunk costs, markets size and market structure, 1895–1926. Working Paper. London School of Economics and Political Science, London, UK.

Balio, T. (Ed.), 1976. The American Film Industry. The University of Wisconsin Press, Wisconsin.

Balio, T. (Ed.), 1985. The American Film Industry, second ed. The University of Wisconsin Press, Wisconsin, pp. 133–152.

Bansal, H.S., Voyer, P.A., 2000. Word-of-mouth processes within a services purchase decision context. Journal of Service Research 3 (2), 166–177.

Barnard, H., Tuomi, K., 2008. How demand sophistication (de-)limits economic upgrading: comparing the film Industries of South African and Nigeria (Nollywood) Industry and Innovation 15 (6), 647–668.

Barr, C. (Ed.), 1996. All our Yesterdays: 90 Years of British Cinema, third ed. BFI Publishing, London.

Bass, F.M., 1969. A new-product growth model for consumer durables. Management Science 15, 215–227.

Baudrillard, Jean, 1983. Simulations (Paul Foss, Paul Patton, and Philip Beitchman, Trans. Semiotext[e], New York.

Baumann, S., 2001. Intellectualization and art world development: film in the United States. American Sociological Review 66 (3), 404–426.

Becker, H.S., 1982. Art Worlds. University of California Press, Berkley.

Betts, E., 1973. The Film Business, a History of British Cinema 1896–1972. George Allen and Unwin, London.

Berney, B., 2006. Independent distribution. In: Squire, J.E. (Ed.), The Movie Business Book (International third ed.). McGraw-Hill, Maidenhead, pp. 375–383.

Berra, J., 2008. Declarations of Independence: American Cinema and the Partiality of Independent Production. Intellect, Bristol.

Berry, C., 2003. What's big about the big film? De-westernising the blockbuster in Korea and China. In: Stringer, J. (Ed.), Movie Blockbusters. Routledge, pp. 217–229.

Bhaumik, K., 2004. A brief history of cinema from Bombay to 'Bollywood'. History Compass 2 (1), 1–4.

Biskind, P., 1998. Easy Rider, Raging Bulls: How the Sex-Drugs-and-Rock 'N'Roll Generation Saved Hollywood. Simon and Schuster, New York.

Biskind, P., 2004. Down and Dirty Pictures: Miramax, Sundance, and the rise of Independent Film. Simon and Schuster, New York.

Biyalogorsky, E.E., Gerstner, Libai, B., 2001. Customer referral management: optimal. Reward programs. Marketing Science 20 (1), 82–95.

Blair, H., Rainnie, A., 2000. Flexible films? Media. Culture and Society 22, 187–204.

Blair, H., Kerrigan, F., 2002. A new era or a recurring pattern? An analysis of current trends in European and British film making. In: Advances in Communication and Media Research, Vol. 1. Nova Science Publishers Inc., New York.

Blume, S.E., 2006. The revenue streams: an overview. In: Squire, J.E. (Ed.), The Movie Business Book, (International third ed.). McGraw-Hill, Maidenhead, pp. 332–359.

Blumenthal, M.A., 1988. Auctions with constrained information: blind bidding for motion pictures. Review of Economics and Statistics 70, 191–198.

Bogozzi, R.P., 1975. Marketing as exchange. Journal of Marketing 39, 32–39.

Bolton, R.N., Drew, J.H., 1992. Mitigating the effect of service encounters. Marketing Letters 3 (1), 57–70.

Borden, N.H., 1964. The concept of the marketing mix. Journal of Advertising Research, June, 4, 2–7. Available in Schwartz G. Science in Marketing. John Wiley & Sons, NY 386–397.

Borgerson, J.L., Schroeder, J.E., 2005. Identity in marketing communications: an ethics of visual representation. In: Kimmel, A.J. (Ed.), Marketing Communication: New Approaches, Technologies and Styles. Oxford University Press, Oxford.

Bourdieu, P., 1977. Outline of a Theory of Practice. Cambridge University Press, Cambridge.

Bourdieu, P., 1984. Distinction: a Social Critique of the Judgement of Taste (R. Nice, Trans. Harvard University Press, Cambridge, MA.

Bourdieu, P., 2003. Distinction, a Social Critique of the Judgement of Taste. Routledge, London.

Bowser, E., 1990. History of the American Cinema. Charles Scribner's Sons, New York. vol. 2, 1907–1915.

Brown, S., 2006. The Marketing Code. Marshall Cavendish, Singapore.

Brown, J., Broderick, A.J., Lee, N., 2007. Word of mouth communication within online communities: conceptualizing the online social network. Journal of Interactive Marketing 21 (3), 2–20.

Brehm, J.W., 1966. A Theory of Psychological Reactance. Academic Press, New York.

Brevet, B., 2005. Golden Globes vs. Oscars: how do the winners compare? http://www.ropeofsilicon.com/article/golden_globes_vs_oscar_how_do_the_winners_compare accessed 20/04/2009.

Brevet, B., 2007. Globes vs. Oscars: the 2007 update! http://www.ropeofsilicon.com/article/globes_vs_oscars_the_2007_update, accessed 20/04/2009.

Brownlow, K., 1979. Hollywood: the Pioneers. Collins, London.

Brown, S., Kozinets, R.V., Sherry, J.F., 2003. Teaching old brands new tricks: retro branding and the revival of brand meaning. Journal of Marketing 67, 19–33.

Brown, S., 2006. The Marketing Code. Cyan Communications Limited, London.

Bryant, C.A., 2000. Social marketing: a new approach to improved patient care. Social Marketing 7 (4), 161–167.

Buscombe, E., 1977. The idea of genre in the American Film. In: Grant, B.K. (Ed.), Film Genre: Theory and Practice. The Scarecrow Press, Meuchen, N.J.

Butler, J.G. (Ed.), 1990. Star Texts: Image and Performance in Film and Television. Wayne State University Press, Detroit.

Buttle, F., 1998. Word of mouth: understanding and managing referral marketing. Journal of Strategic Marketing 6, 241–254.

Cameron, S., 1995. On the role of critics in the cultural industry. Journal of Cultural Economics 19 (4), 321–331.

Castells, M., 1996. The Rise of the Network Society, second ed. Blackwell, Oxford and Massachusetts.

Chambers, R., 1947. The need for statistical research. Annals of the American Academy of Political and Social Science 254, 169–172.

Chantan, M., 1994. What was GATT about? Vertigo, Spring.

Chen, Y., Xie, J., 2008. Online consumer review: word-of-mouth as a new element of marketing communication mix. Management Science 54 (3), 477–491.

Chrissides, G.D., Kaler, J.H., 1993. An Introduction to Business Ethics. Thomson Business Press, London.

Christopherson, S., Storper, M., 1986. The city as studio, the world as backlot: the impact of vertical disintegration on location of the motion-picture industry. Environment and Planning D: Society and Space 4, 305–320.

Clark, M.G., 1996. Canadian culture not protected under NAFTA. The CCPA Monitor, September.

Collins, A., Hand, C., 2005. Analysing moviegoing demand: an individual-level cross-sectional approach. Managerial and Decision Economics 26, 319–330.

Collins, A., Hand, C., Linnell, M., 2008. Analyzing repeat consumption of identical cultural goods: some exploratory evidence from moviegoing. Journal of Cultural Economics 32, 187–199.

Cook, P., 1979/1980. Star signs. Screen 20 (3/4), 80–88.

Cooper-Martin, E., 1991. Consumers and movies: some findings on experiential products. Advances in Consumer Research 12, 372–378.

Cowles, D.L., 1997. The role of trust in customer relationships: asking the right questions. Management Decision 35 (4), 273–284.

Crofts, S., 1998. Concepts of national cinema. In: Hill, J., Gibson, P.C. (Eds.), The Oxford Guide to Film Studies. Oxford University Press, Oxford, pp. 385–394.

Culliton, J.W., 1948. The Management of Marketing Costs. Graduate School of Business Administration, Harvard University, Boston, Mass.

Currall, S., Judge, T., 1995. Measuring trust between organizational boundary role persons. Organizational Behavior and Human Decision Processes 64, 151–170.

Czepiel, John A, 1974. Word-of-mouth processes in the diffusion of a major technological innovation. Journal of Marketing Research 11 (2), 172–180.

Dale, M., 1997. The Movie Game, the Film Business in Britain, Europe and America. Cassell, London.

Danish Film Institute, 2008. Facts and Figures 2008. DFI, Copenhagen.

D'Astous, A., 1999. A study of individual factors explaining movie-goers' consultation of film critics. European Advances in Consumer Research 4, 201–207.

D'Astous, A., Touil, N., 1999. Consumer evaluations of movies on the basis of critics' judgments. Psychology and Marketing 16 (8), 677–694.

D'Astous, A., Colbert, F., 2002. Moviegoers' consultation of critical reviews: psychological antecedents and consequences. International Journal of Arts Management, Fall edition.

DeCordova, R., 1985. The emergence of the star system in America. Wide Angle 6 (4), 4–13.

Dellarocas, C., 2003. The digitization of word of mouth: promise and challenges of online feedback mechanisms. Management Science 49, 1407–1424.

Dellarocas, C.N., Neveen, F.A., Zhang, X., 2007. Exploring the value of online product reviews in forecasting sales: the case of motion pictures. Journal of Interactive Marketing 21 (4), 23–45.

De Silva, I., 1998. Consumer selection of motion pictures. In: Litman, B.R. (Ed.), The Motion Picture Mega-Industry. Allyn and Bacon, Needham Heights, MA.

Deuchert, E., Adjamah, K., Pauly, F., 2005. For Oscar glory or Oscar money? Journal of Cultural Economics 29, 159–176.

De Vany, A.S., Walls, W.D., 1996. Bose–Einstein dynamics and adaptive contracting in the motion picture industry. The Economic Journal 106 (439), 1493–1514.

De Vany, A.S., Walls, W.D., 1999. Uncertainty in the movie industry: does star power reduce the terror of the box office? Journal of Cultural Economics 23 (4), 285–318.

De Vany, A.S., Walls, W.D., 2004. Motion picture profit, the stable Paretian hypothesis, and the curse of the superstar. Journal of Economic Dynamics & Control 28, 1035–1057.

De Vany, A.S., Walls, W.D., 2007. Estimating the effects of movie piracy on box-office revenue. Review of Industrial Organization 30, 291–301.

Dickinson, M., Street, S., 1985. Cinema and State. British Film Institute, London.

DiMaggio, P.J., Powell, W.W., 1983. The iron cage revisited: institutional isomorphism and collective rationality in organizational fields. American Sociological Review 48, 147–160.

DCMS/BBER, 2009. Digital Britain, the Interim Report. Department for Culture, Media and Sport and Department for Business. Enterprise and Regulatory Reform, London.

Dobele, A., Toelman, D., Beverland, M., 2005. Controlled infection! Spreading the brand message through viral marketing. Business Horizons 48, 143–149.

Dodds, J.C., Holbrook, M.B., 1988. What's an Oscar worth? An empirical estimation of the effects of nominations and awards on movie distribution and revenues. In: Austin, B.A. (Ed.), Current Research in film: Audiences, Economics and Law, Vol. 4. Ablex, New Jersey, pp. 72–88.

Drucker, P.F., 1954. The Practice of Management. Harper & Row, New York.

Drummond, S.J., 2000. Tainted by Experience. Faber and Faber, London.

du Gay, P., Hall, S., James, L., Mackay, H., 2000. Doing Cultural Studies: the Story of the Sony Walkman. Sage, London.

Durie, J. (Ed.), 1993. The Film Marketing Handbook: a Practical Guide to Marketing Strategies for Independent Films. MEDIA Business School, Madrid.

Durie, J., Pham, A., Watson, N., 2000. Marketing and Selling Your Film around the World. Silman-James Press, Los Angeles.

Dyer McCann, R., 1987. The First Tycoons. The Scarecrow Press, Inc., New York.

Dyer, R., 2007. Stars. British Film Institute, London.

Eberts, J., Illott, T., 1990. My Indecision is Final, the Rise and Fall of Goldcrest Films. Faber and Faber, St. Ives.

Ebewo, P.J., 2007. The emerging video film industry in Nigeria: challenges and prospects. Journal of Film and Video 59 (3), 46–47.

Elberse, A., 1999. International marketing of motion pictures: an analysis of adoption patterns in the US and the UK. Working Paper, Centre for Marketing, London Business School.

Elberse, A., Anand, B., 2007. The effectiveness of pre-release advertising for motion pictures: an empirical investigation using a simulated market. Information Economics and Policy 19 (3-4), 319–343. 2007.

Elberse, A., Eliashberg, J., 2003. Demand and supply dynamics for sequentially released products in international markets: the case of motion pictures. Marketing Science 22 (3), 329–354.

Eliashberg, J., Jonker, J.J., Sawhney, M.S., Wierenga, B., 2000. MOVIEMOD: an implementable decision support system for pre-release market evaluation of motion pictures. Marketing Science 19 (3), 226–243.

Eliashberg, J., Sawhney, M.B., 1994. Modelling goes to Hollywood: predicting individual differences in movie enjoyment. Management Science 40 (9), 1151–1173.

Eliashberg, J., Shugan, S.M., 1997. Film critics: influencers or predictors? Journal of Marketing 61, 68–78.

Elliott, R., Hamilton, E., 1991. Consumer choice tactics and leisure activities. International Journal of Advertising 10, 325–332.

Ellis, J.C., 1995. A History of Film, fourth ed. Allyn and Bacon, Boston.

Esan, O., 2008. Appreciating Nollywood: audiences and Nigerian 'Films, Particpations, 5 (1), found at http://www.participations.org/Volume%205/Issue%201%20-%20special/5_01_esan.htm accessed, 11/04/2009.

Esparza, N., Rossman, G., 2006. I'd like to thank the Academy, complementary productivity and social networks. California Center for Population Research On-Line Working Paper Series, UCLA.

European Audiovisual Observatory (EAO). http://www.obs.coe.int/about/oea/pr/mif2008_cinema.html accessed 14/10/2008.

Evans, R., 2003. The Kid Stays in the Picture, second ed. Faber and Faber, London.

Fellman, D.R., 2006. Theatrical distribution. In: Squire, J.E. (Ed.), The Movie Business Book, (International third ed.). McGraw-Hill, Maidenhead, pp. 362–374.

Felton, A.P., 1959. Making the marketing concept work. Harvard Business Review 37, 55–65. July/August.

Film Council, 2000. Towards a Sustainable UK Film Industry. London, May.

Finney, A., 1996. The State of European Cinema, a New Dose of Reality. Cassell, London.

Finney, A., 1998. The Egos have Landed, the rise and fall of Palace Pictures. Arrow, London.

Fill, C., 2009. Marketing Communications, Interactivity, Communities and Content, fifth ed. Pearson Education Limited, Harlow.

Fillis, I., 2004. Visual arts marketing. In: Kerrigan, F., Fraser, P., Özbilgin, M.F. (Eds.), Arts Marketing. Elsevier, Oxford.

Fillis, I., 2006. Art for art's sake or art for business sake: an exploration of artistic product orientation. The Marketing Review 6 (1), 29–40.

Fishbein, M., Ajzen, I., 1975. Attitude, Intention and Behavior. Addison-Wesley, Reading.

Fishoff, S., 1998. Favorite film choices: influences of the beholder and the beheld. Journal of Media Psychology 3 (4).

Fournier, S., 1998. Consumers and their brands: developing relationship theory in consumer research. Journal of Consumer Research 24 (March), 343–374.

Friedman, M., 1962. Capitalism and Freedom. University of Chicago Press, Chicago.

Friedman, R.G., 2006. Motion picture marketing. In: Squire, J.E. (Ed.), The Movie Business Book, International third ed. McGraw-Hill, Maidenhead, pp. 282–299.

Freeman, E., 1984. Strategic Management: a Stakeholder Approach. Pitman, Boston.

Fullerton, R.A., 1998. How modern is modern marketing? Marketing's evolution and the myth of the production era. Journal of Marketing 52, 108–125.

Garbarino, Johnson, 1999. The different roles of satisfaction, trust and commitment in customer relationships. Journal of Marketing 63, 70–94.

Garver, M.S., Min, S., 2001. The dynamic role of the sales function in supply chain management. In: Mentzer, J.T. (Ed.), Supply Chain Management. Sage Publications, Thousand Oaks, CA.

Goldberg, F., 1991. Motion Picture Marketing and Distribution. Focal Press, Boston/London.

Goodridge, M., 1995. A dead cert? Marketing Business Journal, November.

Gomery, D., 1991. Movie History: a Survey. Wadsworth, Belmont, CA.

Gore, C., 2004. The Ultimate Film Festival Survival Guide, third ed. Lone Eagle, Los Angeles.

Graham, G., Hill, J. The British newspaper industry supply chain in the digital age. Promotheus, 27 (2), 117–124.

Graham, G., Hill, J. The British newspaper industry value chain and the internet. OR Insight, in press.

Graham, G., Smart, A. The British newspaper supply chain influence model. SCM: an International Journal, in press.

Grönroos, C., 1994. Quo vadis, marketing? Toward a relationship marketing paradigm. Journal of Marketing Management 10, 347–360.

Grönroos, C., 1997. From marketing mix to relationship marketing – towards a paradigm shift in marketing. Management Decision 35 (3–4), 322–340.

Grönroos, C., 1999. Relationship marketing: challenges for the organization. Journal of Business Research 46, 327–335.

Grönroos, C., 1995. Relationship marketing: the strategy continuum. Journal of the Academy of Marketing Science 23 (Fall), 252–254.

Gubbins, M., 2008. 2008 Review of the year – crunch time. Screendaily.com (available at http://www.screendaily.com/2008-review-of-the-year-crunch-time/4042436.article) accessed on 04/05/2009.

Gummesson, E., 1997. Relationship marketing as a paradigm shift: some conclusions from the 30R approach. Management Decision 35 (3–4), 267–273.

Gwinner, K., Gremler, D., Bitner, M., 1998. Relational benefits in service industries: the customer's perspective. Journal of the Academy of Marketing Science 26, 101–114.

Hall, T., 1991. Bringing New Product to Market. Amacon, New York, NY.

Harbord, J., 2002. Film Cultures. Sage Publications, London.

Hargreaves, D.J., North, A.C. (Eds.), 1997. The Social Psychology of Music. Oxford University Press, Oxford.

Hart, H., 2008. YouTube streams free feature-length film, *Princess of Nebraska*. October 17th available at (http://www.wired.com/underwire/2008/10/youtube-streams/) accessed on 05/05/2009.

Haynes, J., Okome, O., 1998. Evolving popular media: Nigerian video films. Research in African literatures 29 (33), 106–128.

Heeler, R.M., Chung, E.K., 2000. The economics basis of marketing. In: Baker, M.J. (Ed.), Marketing Theory. Thomson Learning, London.

Henderson, D., 2001. IEA (Occasional paper series no. 115), London.

Hennig-Thurau, T., Walsh, G., Wruck, O., 2001. An investigation into the factors determining the success of service innovations: the case of motion pictures. Academy of Marketing Science Review, 2001(06), online at http://www.amsreview.org/articles/hennig06-2001.pdf.

Hennig-Thurau, T., Gwinner, K., Walsh, G., Gremler, D.D., 2004. Electronic word-of-mouth via consumer-opinion platforms: what motivates consumers to articulate themselves on the internet. Journal of Interactive Marketing 18 (1), 38–52.

Hennig-Thurau, T., Houston, M.B., Walsh, G., 2006. The differing roles of success drivers across sequential channels: an application to the motion-picture industry. Journal of the Academy of Marketing Science 34 (Fall), 559–575.

Herman, G., Leyens, J-P., 1977. Rating Films on TV. Journal of Communication 27 (4), 48–53.

Hesmondhalgh, D., 2007. The Cultural Industries, second ed. Sage, London, Los Angeles and New Delhi.

Higgins, C., 2005. The producers. The Guardian, 16th April.

Higson, A., Maltby, R., 1999. Film Europe and Film America: Cinema, Commerce and Cultural Exchange 1920–1939. Exeter University Press, Exeter.

Hirschman, Elizabeth C, 1991. Secular morality and the dark side of consumer behavior: or how semiotics saved my life. In: Holman, Rebecca H., Solomon, Michael R. (Eds.), Advances in Consumer Research Vol. 18. Association for Consumer Research, Provo, UT, pp. 1–6.

Holbrook, M.B., Addis, M., 2008. Art versus commerce in the movie industry: a two-path model of motion-picture success. Journal of Cultural Economics 32, 87–107.

Holbrook, M.B., Hirschman, E.C., 1982. The experiential aspects of consumption: consumer fantasies, feelings, and fun. The Journal of Consumer Research 9 (2), 132–140.

Holbrook, M.B., 1999. Popular appeal versus expert judgements of motion pictures. Journal of Consumer Research 26 (2), 144–155.

Holden, A., 1993. The Oscars. The Secret History of Hollywood's Academy Awards. Little Brown and Company, London.

Holmes, John H., Lett, John D., 1977. Product sampling and word of mouth. Journal of Advertising Research 17 (October), 35–40.

Howe, C., 2008. Crowdsourcing, Why the Power of the Crowd is Driving the Future of Business. Crown Business.

Hsu, Greta, 2006. Jacks of all trades and masters of none: audiences' reactions to spanning genres in feature film production. Administrative Science Quarterly 51, 420–450.

Huettig, M.D., 1944. Economic Control of the Motion Picture Industry. University of Pennsylvania Press, Philadelphia.

Hunt, T., 2009. The whuffie factor. Using the Power of Social Networks to Build Your Business. Crown Business.

Iansiti, M., MacCormack, A., 1997. Developing product on Internet time. Harvard Business Review 75 (September/October), ,108–117.

Ilott, T., 1996. Budgets and Markets, a Study of the Budgeting of European Film. Routledge, London.

Jäckel, A., 2003. European Film Industries. BFI Publishing, London.

Jacobs, L., 1968. The Rise of the American Film. Teachers College, New York.

Jedidi, K., Krider, R.E., Weinberg, C.B., 1998. Clustering at the movies. Marketing Letters 9 (4), 393–405.

Jenkins, H., 2004. The cultural logics of media convergence. International Journal of Cultural Studies 7 (1), 33–43.

Jenkins, H., 2006. Convergence Culture, Where Old and New Media Collide. New York University Press, New York and London.

Jin, D.Y., 2006. Cultural politics in Korea's contemporary films under neoliberal globalization. Media. Culture and Society 28 (1), 5–23.

Johnston, K.M., 2008. Convergence: the international journal of research into new media technologies. Convergence 14 (2), 145–160.

Jobber, D., 1998. Principles and Practice of Marketing. McGraw Hill, London.

Joeckel, S., 2003. Contemporary Austrian and Irish Cinema. Edition 451, Stuttgart.

Johnston, K.M., 2008. The coolest way to watch movie trailers in the world', trailers in the digital age. Convergence 14 (2), 145–160.

Jones, H.E., Conrad, H.S., 1930. Rural preferences in motion pictures. Journal of Social Psychology 1, 419–423.

Jones, C., DeFillippi, R.J., 1993. Back to the future in film: combining industry and self-knowledge to meet the career challenges of the 21st century. Academy of Management Executive 10 (4), 89–103.

Jones, K., 1998. Whats the Story: British Film, London Film Festival.

Jones, J.M., Ritz, C.J., 1991. Incorporating distribution into new product diffusion models. International Journal of Research in Marketing 8, 91–112.

Jordon, N., 1997. Public Interview at Galway Arts Festival, Galway.

Jowett, G.S., 1985. Giving them what they want: movie audience research before 1950. Current Research in film, Audiences. Economics and Law 1, 19–35.

Kagan, N., 2000. The Cinema of Stanley Kubrick, third ed. Continuum International Publishing Group, New York.

Katz, E., Lazarsfeld, P.E., 1955. Personal Influence: the Part Played by People in the Flow of Mass Communication. Free Press, Glencoe, IL.

Kay, J., 2008. What Jimmy Greaves can teach us about the Toronto film festival. The Guardian, 16th September.

Kay, J., 2009. What will cinema-going look like in 10 years. Screendaily.com.

Kenney, R.W., Klein, B., 1983. The economics of block booking. Journal of Law and Economics 26, 497–540.

Kermode, M., 2009. Review of The Boat that Rocked, BBC Radio 5, http://www.bbc.co.uk/blogs/markkermode/2009/04/5_live_review_the_boat_that_ro.html (accessed April 24th 2009).

Kernan, L., 2004. Coming Attractions: Reading American Movie Trailers. University of Texas Press.

Kerrigan, F., 2001. The good, the bad and the ugly: the role of trust in marketing films. Academy of Marketing Annual Conference, Cardiff Business School.

Kerrigan, F, 2002. Does structure matter? An analysis of the interplay between company structure and the marketing process in the film industry. Academy of Marketing Conference. University of Nottingham Business School.

Kerrigan, F., Culkin, N., 1999, A reflection on the American domination of the film industry: an historical and industrial perspective. University of Hertfordshire Business School Working Paper's Series: 15.

Kerrigan, F., O'Reilly, D.T., 2008. Branding in film, branding of film. Academy of Marketing Conference, Aberdeen.

Kerrigan, F., Özbilgin, M., 2002. Art for the masses or art for the few? Ethical issues in film marketing in the UK. Journal of Non-profit and Voluntary Sector Marketing 7 (3), 195–203.

Kerrigan, F., Özbilgin, M.F., 2003. Film marketing in Europe – policy and practice. AIMAC Conference. Boconni University, Milan.

Kerrigan, F., Özbilgin, M.F., 2004. Film marketing in Europe – bridging the gap between policy and practice. International Journal of Non-profit and Voluntary Sector Marketing 9 (3), 229–237.

Kerrigan, F., 2004. Film marketing. In: Kerrigan, F., Fraser, P., Özbilgin, M.F. (Eds.), Arts Marketing. Elsevier, Oxford.

Kerrigan, F., Fraser, P., Özbilgin, M.F. (Eds.), 2004. Arts Marketing. Elsevier, Oxford.

Kerrigan, F., 2005. Evaluating the impact of an integrated supply chain on the process of marketing European feature films. Unpublished PhD thesis. University of Hertfordshire Business School.

Kerrigan, F., Yalkin, C., 2009. Revisiting the role of critical reviews in film marketing. In: Hemmungs Wirtén, E., Ryman, M. (Eds.), Mashing-up Culture: The Rise of User-generated Content, Proceedings from the COUNTER workshop Mashing-up Culture. Uppsala University, pp. 162–179. May 13–14, 2009.

King, B., 1985. Articulating stardom. Screen 26 (5), 27–50.

Kim, E.M., 2004. Market competition and cultural intentions between Hollywood and the Korean film industry. The International Journal on Media Management 6 (3–4), 207–216.

Kim, S., 1998. Cine-mania or Cinephilia: film festivals and the identity question. UTS Review (now Cultural Studies review) 4 (2), 174–187.

Kindem, G., 1982. Hollywood's movie star system: a historical overview. In: Kindem, F. (Ed.), The American Movie Industry: the Business of Motion Pictures. Southern Illinois University Press, Carbondale and Edwardsville, pp. 79–93.

Kindem, G. (Ed.), 2000. The International Movie Industry. Southern Illinois University Press, Carbondale and Edwardsville.

Kirsner, S., 2008. Inventing the Movies: Hollywood's Epic Battle between Innovation and the Status Quo, from Thomas Edison to Steve Jobs. Createspace, New York.

Kiss, J., 2009. The pirate bay trial: guilty verdict. The Guardian, 17th April 2009 available at: http://www.guardian.co.uk/technology/2009/apr/17/the-pirate-bay-trial-guilty-verdict, downloaded on 05/05/2009.

Kohli, A.K., Jaworsk, B.J., 1990. Market orientation: the construct, research propositions, and managerial implications. Journal of Marketing 54 (2), 1–18.

Kotler, P., 2002. Marketing Management: Analysis, Planning, Implementation, and Control. Prentice Hall, London.

Kozinets, R.V., 1999. E-tribalised marketing? The strategic implications of virtual communicates of consumption. European Management Journal 17, 252–264.

Kozinets, R.V., 2002. The field behind the screen: using netnography for marketing research in online communities. Journal of Marketing Research 39, 61–72.

Kuhn, M., 2003. One Hundred Weddings and a Funeral. Thorogood, London.

Kula, S., 2004. Appraisal of audiovisual records in the documentation of popular culture, collective memory and national identity. 15th International Congress on Archives, Vienna. http://www.wien2004.ica.org/imagesUpload/pres_354_KULA_Z-AMIA01.pdf (accessed 1/3/2009).

Lau, G., Lee, S., 2000. Consumers' trust in a brand and the link to brand loyalty. Journal of Market Focused Management 4, 341–370.

Lazersfeld, P.F., 1947. Audience research in the movie field. Annals of the American Academy of Political and Social Sciences 254, 160–168.

Lazarsfeld, P.F., Merton, R.K., 1948. Mass communication, popular taste, and organized social action. In: Schramm, W., Roberts, D.F. (Eds.), Process and Effect of Mass Communication. University of Illinois Press, Urbana, pp. 554–578.

Leadbetter, C., 2009. Keynote presentation. In: Innovative Media for the Digital Economy Springboard Event. The Commonwealth Club, London.

Leenders, M.A.A.M., Gemser, G., Wijnberg, N.M., 2004. Effects of award competitions on market competition in the motion picture industry. In: 6th World media Economics Conference. Cenre d'études sur les media Montreal, Canada.

Lehu, J.M., 2007. Branded Entertainment: Product Placement and Brand Strategy in the Entertainment Business. Kogan Page, London/Philadelphia.

Levitt, T., 1960. Marketing myopia. Harvard Business Review, July–August.

Levy, E., 2001. Oscar Fever, the History and Politics of the Academy Award. Continuum, New York.

Lewis, J.D., Weigert, A., 1985. Trust as a social reality. Social Forces 63 (4), 967–985.

Lim, D., 2008. Bridging generations and hemispheres. New York Times, 12th September, available at (http://www.nytimes.com/2008/09/14/movies/14lim.html?_r=1) accessed on 05/05/2009.

Litman, B.R., 1983. Predicting success of theatrical movies: an empirical study. Journal of Popular Culture 16 (4), 159–175.

Litman, B.R., 1998. The Motion Picture Mega Industry. Allyn and Bacon, Boston.

Litman, B.R., Ahn, H., 1998. Predicting financial success of motion pictures. In: Litman, B.R. (Ed.), The Motion Picture Mega Industry. Allyn and Bacon, Needham Heights, MA.

Litman, B.R., Kohl, L., 1989. Predicting financial success of motion pictures: the 80s experience. Journal of Media Economics 2, 35–49.

Lorenzen, M., Täube, F.A., 2008. Breakout from Bollywood? The roles of social networks and regulation in the evolution of Indian film industry. Journal of International Management 14, 286–299.

López-Sintas, J., García-Álvarez, E., 2006. Patterns of audio-visual consumption: the reflection of objective divisions in class structure. European Sociological Review 22 (4), 397–411.

MacNab, G., 1993. J. Arthur Rank and the British Film Industry. Routledge, London.

Madichie, N., Ibeh, K., 2006. A commentary on the internationalisation of the Nigerian movie industry. Institute for Small Business and Entrepreneurship (ISBE) Conference, Cardiff, UK.

Mahajan, V., Muller, E., Wind, J., 2000. New-product Diffusion Models. Kluwer Academic Publishers, Boston, MA.

Manyin, M.E., 2006. South Korea–U.S. Economic Relations: Cooperation, Friction, and Prospects for a Free Trade Agreement (FTA). The Library of Congress, Congressional Research Service, Washington D.C. http://fpc.state.gov/documents/organization/61526.pdf accessed 03/03/2009.

Manyin, M.E., Cooper, W.H., 2006. The Proposed South Korea–U.S. Free Trade Agreement (KORUS FTA). The Library of Congress, Congressional Research Service, Washington D.C. http://www.sice.oas.org/TPD/USA_KOR/Studies/CRSREPORT_e.pdf accessed 03/03/2009.

Mayer, R.C., Davis, J.H., Schoorman, F.D., 1995. An integrative model of organizational trust. Academy of Management Review 20 (3), 709–734.

Marich, R., 2005. Marketing to Moviegoers. Elsevier, Oxford.

Mathieu, C., Standvad, S.M., 2008. Is this what we should be comparing when comparing film production regimes? A systematic typological scheme and application. Creative Industries Journal 1 (2), 171–192.

McKnight, H., Cummings, L., Chervany, N., 1998. Initial trust formation in new organizational relationships. Academy of Management Review 23 (3), 473–491.

Mentzer, J.T., DeWitt, W., Keebler, J.S., Min, S., Nix, N.W., Smith, C.D., Zacharia, Z.G., 2000a What is supply chain management. In: Mentzer, J.T. (Ed.), Supply Chain Management. Sage Publications, Thousand Oaks, CA.

Mentzer, J.T., Foggin, J.H., Golicic, S.L., 2000b. The enablers, impediments, and benefits. Supply Chain Management Review, September/October.

Mentzer, J.T., Soonhong, M., Zacharia, Z.G., 2000c. The nature of interfirm partnering in supply chain management. Journal of Retailing 76 (Winter), 549–568.

Meyers, P.W., Tucker, F.G., 1989. Defining the roles for logistics during routine and radical technological innovation. Journal of Academy of Marketing Science 17 (1), 73–82.

Mezias, J., Mezias, S., 2000. Resources partitioning and the founding of specialist firms: the American feature film industry, 1912–1929. Organization Science 11, 306–322.

M dot Strange, 2008. The indie filmmaker's guide to building audiences online. Power to the Pixel, the Digital Distribution and Film Innovation Forum, London.

Miller, T., 1996. The crime of Monsieur Lang: GATT, the screen, and the new international division of cultural labour. In: Moran, A. (Ed.), Film Policy: Film Policy. International, National and Regional Perspectives. Routledge, London and New York, pp. 72–85.

Min, S., 2000. The role of marketing in supply chain management. In: Mentzer, J.T. (Ed.), Supply Chain Management. Sage Publications, Thousand Oaks, CA.

Min, S., 2001. The role of marketing in supply chain management. In: Mentzer, J.T. (Ed.), Supply Chain Management. Sage Publications, Thousand Oaks, CA.

Montal, S., 2006. Film festivals and markets. In: Squire, J.E. (Ed.), The Movie Business Book, (International third ed.). McGraw-Hill, Maidenhead, pp. 315–330.

Montgomery, L., 2009. Space to grow: copyright, cultural policy and commercially-focused music in China. Chinese Journal of Cultural Communication, 1 (March), 36–49.

Montgomery, L., Fitzgerald, B., 2006. Copyright and the creative industries in China. International Journal of Cultural Studies 9 (3), 407–418.

Moorman, C., Deshpande, R., Zaltman, G., 1993. Relationships between providers and users of market research: the role of personal trust. Working Paper No. 93-111, Marketing Science Institute, Cambridge, MA.

Moran, A. (Ed.), 1996. Film Policy. International, National and Regional Perspectives. Routledge, London and New York.

Moreau, F., Peltier, S., 2004. Cultural diversity in the movie industry: a cross-national study. Journal of Media Economics 17 (2), 123–143.

Moul, C.C., 2007. Measuring word-of-mouth's impact on theatrical movie admissions. Journal of Economics and Management Strategy 16 (4), 859–892.

Moul, C.C., Shugan, S.M., 2005. Theatrical release and the launching of motion pictures. In: Moul, C.C. (Ed.), A Concise Handbook of Movie Industry Economics. Cambridge University Press, New York, pp. 80–137.

Mullally, F., 1946. Films, An Alternative to Rank: an Analysis of Power and Policy in the British Film Industry. Socialist Book Centre, London.

Mulvey, L., 1975. Visual pleasure and narrative cinema. Screen 16 (3), 6–18.

Muniz, A.M., O'Guinn, T.C., 2001. Brand community. Journal of Consumer Research 27 (4), 412–432.

Nayar, P.K., 2009. Seeing Stars, Spectacle, Society and Celebrity Culture. Sage, New Delhi.

Navaie, N.S., 2004. Societal arts marketing: a multi-sectoral, inter-disciplinary and international perspective. In: Kerrigan, F., Fraser, P., Özbilgin, M.F. (Eds.), Arts Marketing. Elsevier, Oxford.

Narver, J.C., Slater, S.F., 1990. The effect of a market orientation on business profitability. Journal of Marketing 54, 20–35.

Neelamegham, R., Chintagunta, P., 1999. A Bayesian model to forecast new product performance in domestic and international markets. Marketing Science 18 (2), 115–136.

Nelson, R., Donihue, M., Waldman, D., Wheaton, C., 2001. What's an Oscar worth? Economic Inquiry 39, 1–16.

Nelson, R.A., Reid, C., Gilmore, O., 2007. An analysis of the out-of-market gap for DVDs in the U.S. Review of Industrial Organization 30 (4), 303–323.

Nichols, B., 1994. Discovering form, inferring meaning: new cinemas and the film festival circuit. Film Quarterly 47 (3), 16–30.

Nikolychuk, L., Kerrigan, F., Abbott, P., 2009. UK Independent Television & Film Production Sectors: Exploring New Collaborative (Business) Models. School of Humanities, King's College London, ISBN-978-1-897747-22-5. Available at: http://www.kcl.ac.uk/content/1/c6/04/29/17/UKIndependentTelevisionFilm ProductionSectors.pdf.

Nikunen, K., 2007. The intermedial practices of fandom. Convergence 28 (2), 111–128.

Noh, J., 2009. Korean Film Council unveils five-year funding plan. Screen-daily.com, available at (http://www.screendaily.com/korean-film-council-unveils-five-year-funding-plan/5000888.article) accessed online 08/05/09.

Nowell-Smith, G., 1981. Six authors in Pursuit of *The Searchers'*. In: Caughie, J. (Ed.), Theories of Authorship. Routledge and Keegan Paul/British Film Institute, London.

Okome, O., 2007a. Introducing the special issue on West African cinema: Africa at the movies. Postcolonial Test 3 (2), 1–17.

Okome, O., 2007b. Nollywood: spectatorship, audience and the sites of consumption. Postcolonial Test 3 (2), available at http://journals.sfu.ca/pocol/index.php/pct/article/view/763/425, accessed on 12/03/2009.

Olorunyomi, Sola, 1995. Glendora review. African Quarterly on the Arts 1 (2), 54–56.

Olsberg, SPI, TBR Economics, 2006. UK Film Sales Sector Study. UK Film Council, London.

O'Reilly, D., 2004. The marketing of popular music. In: Kerrigan, F., Fraser, P., Özbilgin, M.F. (Eds.), Arts Marketing. Elsevier, Oxford.

Özbilgin, M., Kerrigan, F., 2002. Educating Rita or freeing Willy? Academy of Marketing Conference, Nottingham.

PACT/MMC, 1994. Factors Influencing the Production, Supply and Exhibition of Independent Films in the UK Market. Bridge Media, London.

Park, S.H., 2002. Film censorship and political legitimation in South Korea, 1987. Cinema Journal 42 (1), 120–138.

Park, S.H., 2007. Korean cinema after liberation, production, industry and regulatory trends. In: Gateward, F.K. (Ed.), Seoul Searching: Culture and Identity in Contemporary Korean Cinema. Suny Press, New York, pp. 15–36.

Paquet, D., 2005. The Korean film industry, 1992 to the Present. In: Shin, C.Y., Stringer, J. (Eds.), New Korean Cinema. Edinburgh University Press, Edinburgh, pp. 54–55.

Perren, A., 2001. Sex, Lies and Marketing: Miramax and the development of the quality indie blockbuster. Film Quarterly, Winter.

Petrie, D.J., 1991. Creativity and Constraint in the British Film Industry. Macmillan Press Ltd., London.

Phillips, J., 1991. You'll Never Eat Lunch in this Town Again. Faber and Faber, London.

Puttnam, D., 1997. The Undeclared War, the Struggle for Control for the World's Film Industry. Harper Collins Publishers, London.

Radbourne, J., 2002. Social intervention or market intervention? A problem for governments in promoting the value of the arts. International Journal of Arts Management 5 (1), 50–61.

Ravid, S.A., 1999. Information, blockbusters, and stars: a study of the film industry. The Journal of Business 72 (4), 463–492.

Reingen, P.H., Foster, B.L., Brown, J.J., Seidman, S.B., 1984. Brand congruence in interpersonal relations: a social network analysis. Journal of Consumer Research 11 (3), 771–783.

Rentschler, R., 1999. Innovative Arts Marketing. Allen & Unwin, Leonards.

Rentschler, R., 2004. Museum marketing: understanding different types of audiences. In: Kerrigan, F., Fraser, P., Özbilgin, M.F. (Eds.), Arts Marketing. Elsevier, Oxford.

Robertson, T., 2003. Advertising Effectiveness in UK Film Distribution. UK Film Council, London.

Rogers, E.M., 1962. Diffusion of Innovations. The Free Press, New York.

Rosar, W.H., 2002. Film music – what's in a name? The Journal of Film Music 1 (1), 1–18.

Said, E.W., 1994. Culture and Imperialism. Vintage Books, US.

Sawheny, M.S., Eliashberg, J., 1996. A parsimoinious model for forecasting gross box-office revenues of motion pictures. Marketing Science 15 (2), 113–131.

Schaefer, A., Kerrigan, F., 2008. Trade Associations and Corporate Social responsibility: evidence from the UK water and film industries. Business Ethics, A European Review 17 (2), 171–195.

Schlesinger, L., Heskett, J., 1991. Breaking the cycle of failure in services. Sloan Management Review 32 (Spring), 17–28.

Shouten, J.W., McAlexander, J., 1995. Subcultures of consumption: an ethnography of the new bikers. Journal of Consumer Research 22 (June), 43–61.

Schroder, J.E., 2002. Visual Consumption. Routledge, London.

Scott, A.J., 2005. On Hollywood, the Place, the Industry. Princeton University Press, Princeton and Oxford.

Scott, A.O., 2008. Movie Review: the Princess of Nebraska. New York Times, October 20th, available at: http://movies.nytimes.com/2008/10/20/movies/20wang.html, accessed online 05/05/2009.

Sheth, J.N., Parvatiyar, A., 1995. Relationship marketing in consumer markets: antecedents and consequences. Journal of the Academy of Marketing Science 23 (Fall), 255–271.

Shim, D., 2006. Hybridity and the rise of Korean popular culture in Asia. Media. Culture and Society 28 (1), 25–44.

Shin, C.J., Stringer, J., 2007. Storming the big screen, the *Shiri* syndrome. In: Gateward, F.K. (Ed.), Seoul Searching: Culture and Identity in Contemporary Korean Cinema. Suny Press, New York, pp. 55–72.

Shin, J., 2005. Globalisation and New Korean cinema. In: Shin, C.J., Stringer, J. (Eds.), New Korean Cinema. Edinburgh University Press, Edinburgh, pp. 54–55.

Simonton, D.K., 2002. Collaborative aesthetics in the feature film: cinematic components predicting the differential impact of 2,323 Oscar-nominated movies. Empirical Studies of the Arts 20, 115–125.

Simonton, D.K., 2004. Film awards as indicators of cinematic creativity and achievement: a quantitative comparison of the Oscars and six alternatives. Creativity Research Journal 16 (2–3), 163–172.

Smith, A., 1776. The wealth of nations. In: Skinner, A. (Ed.), The Wealth of Nations. Pelican, Harmondsworth.

Smith, C.N., Quelch, J.A., 1993. Ethics in Marketing. Richard D. Irwin, Inc, Boston, MA.

Sniezek, J.A., Van Swol, L.M., 2001. Trust, confidence and expertise in a judge-advisor system. Organizational Behavior and Human Decision Processes 84 (2), 288–307.

Srinivas, L., 2002. The active audience: spectatorship, social relations and the experience of cinema in India. Media,. Culture and Society 24, 155–173.

Staiger, J., 2005. Media Reception Studies. New York University Press, New York.

Stiles, P., 1997. Corporate governance and ethics. In: Davies, P.W.F. (Ed.), Current Issues in Business Ethics. Routledge, London, pp. 39–48.

Storper, M., 1989. The transition to flexible specialization: the division of labour, external economies, and the crossing of industrial divides. Cambridge Journal of Economics 13, 273–305.

Storper, M., Christopherson, S., 1987. Flexible specialization and regional industrial agglomerations: the case of the US motion-picture industry. Annals of the Association of American Geographers 77, 260–282.

Stringer, J., 2005. Putting Korean Cinema in its place: genre classifications and the contexts of reception.

Sochay, S., 1994. Predicting the performance of motion pictures. Journal of Media Economics 7 (4), 1–20.

Swami, S., Eliashberg, J., Weinberg, C.B., 1999. Silverscreener: a modeling approach to movie screens management. Marketing Science 18 (3), 352–372.

Robinson, D., 1996. From Peep Show to Palace, the Birth of American Film. Columbia University Press, New York.

Tshang, F.T., 2007. Balancing the tensions between rationalization and creativity in the video games industry. Organization Science 18 (6), 989–1005.

Travis, R., 1990. The routinization of film criticism. Journal of Popular Culture 23 (4), 51–65.

Economist, The, 2007. Endless summer. April 28th, 73–74.

Thompson, D.N., 2003. AOL Time Warner, Terra Lycos, Vivendi, and the transformation of marketing. Journal of Business Research 56 (11), 861–866.

Thompson, K., Bordwell, D., 2003. Film History, an Introduction, second ed. McGraw-Hill, New York.

Thompson, C.J., Rindfleisch, A., Arsel, Z., 2006. Emotional branding and the strategic value of the Doppelgänger brand image. Journal of Marketing 70 (January), 50–64.

Till, S., 2009. Film industry faces its own epic adventure. Screendaily.com, May 7th (available at http://www.screendaily.com/news/opinion/film-industry-faces-its-own-epic-adventure/5000875.article) accessed online 07/05/2009.

Turan, K., 2002. Sundance to Sarajevo: Film Festivals and the World they Made. University of California Press, Los Angeles.

Trumpbour, J., 2002. In: Selling Hollywood to the World: U.S. and European Struggles for Mastery of the Global Film Industry, 1920–1950. Cambridge University Press, Cambridge, UK.

Tzokas, N., Saren, M., 1999. Value transformation in relationship marketing. Australasian Marketing Journal 7 (1), 52–62.

Ulff-Møller, J., 2001. Hollywood's Film Wars with France, Film-trade Diplomacy and the Emergence of the French Film Quota Policy. University of Rochester Press, Rochester, NY.

Unwin, E., Kerrigan, F., Waite, K., Grant, D., 2007. Getting the picture: programme awareness amongst film festival customers. International Journal of Nonprofit and Voluntary Sector Marketing 12 (3), 231–245.

Ukadike, N.F., 2002. Questioning African Cinema: Conversations with Film-makers. University of Minnesota Press, Minneapolis.

UK Film Council/Stimulating World Research, 2007. A Qualitative Study of Avid Cinema-goers. UK Film Council, London.

Vargo, S.L., Lusch, L.S., 2004. Evolving to a new dominant logic for marketing. Journal of Marketing 68 (1), 1–17.

Vargo, S.L., Lusch, L.S., 2006. Service-dominant logic: what it is, what it is not, what it might be. In: Lusch, L.S., Vargo, S.L. (Eds.), The Service-dominant Logic of Marketing: Dialog, Debate, and Directions. ME Sharpe, New York, pp. 43–56.

van Eijck, K., van Rees, K., 2000. Media orientation and media use: television viewing behaviour of specific reader types from 1975 to 1995. Communication Research 27, 574–616.

Verdaasdonk, D., 2005. The impact of festival showing and awards on the programming of movies at the box office in The Netherlands. AIMAC, Québec.

Vincendeau, G., 2005. Stars and stardom in French cinema. Continuum International Publishing Group, London.

Vogel, H.L., 2001. Entertainment Industry Economics: a Guide for Financial Analysis, fifth ed. Cambridge University Press, Cambridge.

Vogel, H.L., 2006. Entertainment Industry Economics: a Guide for Financial Analysis, sixth ed. Cambridge University Press, Cambridge.

Wallace, W.T., Seigerman, A., Holbrook, M.B., 1993. The role of actors and actresses in the success of films: how much is a movie star worth? Journal of Cultural Economics 17 (1), 1–24.

Ward, A., 2009. UK Film Council search engine for audiences in the digital age. Screendaily.com, 28th January (Available at http://www.screendaily.com/uk-film-council-search-engine-for-audiences-in-the-digital-age/4042883.article, accessed on 05/05/2009).

Wasko, J., 1994. Hollywood in the information age: beyond the silver screen. Polity Press, Oxford.

Waterman, D., 1987. Electronic media and the economics of the first sale doctrine. In: Thorne, R., Vierra, J.D. (Eds.), Handbook of entertainment, publishing and the arts. Clark Boardman and Co. Ltd, New York, pp. 3–13.

Waterman, D., Lee, S.C., 2003. Time consistency and the distribution of theatrical films: An empirical study of the video window. Working Paper, Indiana University Department of Telecommunications.

Wayne, M., 2002. The Politics of Contemporary European Cinema, Histories, Borders, Diasporas. Intellect Books, Bristol.

Webb, J., 2009. Understanding Representation. Sage, London.

Westbrook, R.A., 1987. Product/consumption-based effective response and post-purchase processes. Journal of Marketing Research 24 (3), 258–270.

Whysall, P., 2000. Addressing ethical issues in retailing: a stakeholder perspective. International Review of Retail Distribution and Consumer Research 10 (3), 305–318.

Wisner, J.D., Tan, K.C., 2000. Supply chain management and its impact on purchasing. Journal of Supply Chain Management 36 (4), 33–42.

Wohlfeil, M., Whelan, S., 2008. Confessions of a Movie-Fan: Introspection into the Experiential Consumption of "Pride & Prejudice". European Advances in Consumer Research 8, 137–143.

Wyatt, J., 1994. High Concept, Movies and Marketing in Hollywood. University of Texas Press, Austin.

Yim, H., 2002. Cultural identity and cultural policy in South Korea. International Journal of Cultural Policy 8 (1), 37–48.

Zacharia, Z.G., 2000. Research and development in supply chain management. In: Mentzer, J.T. (Ed.), Supply Chain Management. Sage, Thousand Oakes, CA.

Zufryden, D.S., 1996. Linking advertising to box office performance of new film releases: a marketing planning model. Journal of Advertising Research 36 (4), 29–41.

Zukor, A., 1954. The Public is Never Wrong. Cassell and Co., London.

WEBSITES

http://www.obs.coe.int/about/oea/pr/mif2008_cinema.html, accessed 14/10/2008

http://www.bbfc.co.uk/policy/policy-thecategories.php accessed 01/02/2009

http://www.dfi.dk/english/about/aboutdfi.htm accessed 20/02/2009

http://www.mpaa.org/FlmRat_Ratings.asp accessed 01/02/2009

www.hollywoodreporter.com, accessed 11/03/2008

http://koreanfilm.org/history.html accessed 01/01/2009

http://www.skillset.org/film/jobs/distribution/article_4156_1.asp (accessed 18/04/09)

http://www.coe.int/t/dg4/eurimages/default_en.asp/)

http://www.kum.dk/sw3076.asp

http://www.dfi.dk/english/about/aboutdfi.htm

http://www.martweiss.com/film/dogma95-thevow.shtml

http://www.variety.com/index.asp?layout=festivals&jump=story&id=2470&articleid=VR1117998976&cs=1 (accessed 19/04/2009)

www.summits.co.uk (accessed 19/04/2009)

http://www.variety.com/index.asp?layout=festivals&jump=story&id=2470&articleid=VR1117998976&cs=1 (accessed 19/04/2009)

http://www.screenonline.org.uk/film/distribution/distribution2.html (accessed 18/04/2009)

www.impawards.com/2002/crossroads.html

http://media.movieweb.com/teasers/k/g/h/PGduUkfkZg5kgh_d.jpg

http://www.impawards.com/2004/bride_and_prejudice.html

http://www.movieposterdb.com/poster/51747a6

http://www.movieposterdb.com/poster/e4e82431

http://www.impawards.com/2004/sideways.html

http://bp3.blogger.com/_WkKZJVG5wTk/RfJsE4yow_I/AAAAAAAAMd8/N7j-
4cfLgH0/s1600-h/dirty_pretty_things.jpg

http://www.joblo.com/newsimages1/2046-poster.jpg

http://www.movieposterdb.com/poster/e6b483d3

http://www.moviegoods.com/Assets/product_images/1000/478528.1000.A.jpg

http://www.consuminglouisville.com/images/Kill_bill_vol_one_ver.jpg

http://www.filmcatcher.com/uploads/img/product/kill_bill_vol_two_ver6.jpg

http://www.imdb.com/title/tt0127536/posters

http://www.strategicfilmmarketing.com/home.html

http://news.bbc.co.uk/1/hi/entertainment/7595352.stm accessed 02/05/2009

http://news.bbc.co.uk/1/hi/entertainment/7595352.stm

http://www.youtube.com/watch?v=F7zypg6UJ1g&NR=1

http://www.imdb.com/video/screenplay/vi2175533337/

FILM FESTIVALS

AFI Fest (2009) http://www.afi.com/, accessed 25/04/2009

American Film Market (2009) http://www.ifta-online.org/afm/home.asp, accessed
25/04/2009

Berlin Film Festival (2009) http://www.berlinale.de/en/das_festival/festivalprofil/
profil_der_berlinale/index.html, accessed 25/04/2009

Cannes Film Festival (2009) http://www.festival-cannes.com/en.html, accessed
25/04/2009

Festival Panafrican du Cinéma et de la Télévision de Ouagadougou (2009) http://
www.fespaco.bf/, accessed 25/04/2009

Hong Kong International Film Festival (2009) http://www.hkiff.org.hk/eng/main.
html, accessed 25/04/2009

International Documentary Film Festival Amsterdam (2009) http://www.idfa.nl/,
accessed 25/04/2009

MIFED http://www.mifed.com/default_e.asp, accessed 25/04/2009

Pusan International Film Festival (2009) http://www.piff.org/intro/default.asp,
accessed 02/05/2009

Sundance Film Festival (2009) http://festival.sundance.org/2009/, accessed 25/04/
2009

ShoWest (2009) http://www.showest.com/filmexpo/index.jsp, accessed 25/04/
2009

Slamdance (2009) http://www.slamdance.com/, accessed 25/04/2009

Telluride Film Festival (2009) http://telluridefilmfestival.org/, accessed 05/05/2009

Tokyo festivals *(2009) http://www.tiff-jp.net/en/*, accessed 25/04/2009

Toronto International Film Festival (2009) http://www.tiff09.ca/default.aspx, accessed 25/04/2009

Venice Film Festival (2009) http://www.labiennale.org/en/cinema/ accessed 01/05/2009

AWARDS

The British Academy of Film and Television Awards http://www.bafta.org/, accessed 25/04/2009

Critics' Choice Awards http://www.vh1.com/shows/events/critics_choice_awards/_2009/, accessed 25/04/2009

Director's Guild of America's http://www.dga.org/index2.php3?chg=, accessed 25/04/2009

European Film Academy's annual awards http://www.europeanfilmacademy.org/, accessed 25/04/2009

Independent Spirit Awards http://www.spiritawards.com/, accessed 25/04/2009

Los Angeles Film Critics Association http://www.lafca.net/awards.html, accessed 25/04/2009

New York Film Critics Circle http://www.nyfcc.com/awards.php, accessed 25/04/2009

Oscar awards http://www.oscar.com/, accessed 25/04/2009

Producers Guild of America's Golden Laurel Awards http://www.producersguild.org/pg/awards_a/, accessed 25/04/2009

Screen Actors Guild (SAG) Awards http://www.sagawards.org/, accessed 25/04/2009

Golden Globes http://www.goldenglobes.org/, accessed 25/04/2009

LIST OF THE FILM IN ALPHABETICAL ORDER

2046 (2004)

About Schmidt (2002)

A Life Less Ordinary (1997)

About a Boy (2002)

Adaptation (2002)

All About My Mother (1999)

Amelie (2001)

American Pie (1999)

An Inconvenient Truth (2006)

Año uña (2007)

Babette's Feast (1987)

Battleship Potemkin (1925)

Bend It Like Beckham (2002)

Best in Show (2000)

Billy Elliot (2000)

Birth of a Nation (1915)

Black Gold (2006)

Blood Diamond (2006)

Bloody Sunday (2002)

Blue Velvet (1986)

Bowling for Columbine (2002)

Bread and Roses (2000)

Bride and Prejudice (2004)

Bridget Jones Diary (2001)

Captain Corelli's Mandolin (2001)

Caramel (2007)

City of God (2003)

Cloverfield (2008)

Crash (1996)

Crossroads (2002)

Dirty Pretty Things (2002)

Easy Rider (1969)

Elizabeth (1998)

Eraserhead (1977)

Erin Brockovich (2000)

Farenheit 9/11 (2004)

Forrest Gump (1994)

Four Weddings and a Funeral (1994)

Gangster No. 1 (2000)

Gegen Die Wand (2004)

Gosford Park (2001)

Gregory's Girl (1981)

Halloween (1978)

Harry Potter (2001)

Harry Potter and the Philosopher's Stone (2001)

Hellboy (2004)

High Fidelity (2000)

Honest (2000)

Injustice (2001)

Interview (with a Vampire)(1994)
In the Mood For Love (2000)
In this World (2002)
Intolerance (1916)
Its a Wonderful Life (1946)
Ironman (2008)
Jaws (1975)
Jenin, Jenin: A One-Sided Movie (2002)
Jenin: Massacring the Truth (2004)
Judith of Bethulia (1914)
Kill Bill (2003)
Kill Bill, Volume 2 (2004)
La Strategia del Ragno (1970)
Linha de Passe (2008)
Living in Bondage (1992)
Living in Bondage 2 (1993)
Lock, Stock and Two Smoking Barrels (1998)
Lost Highway (1997)
Love Actually (2003)
Mamma Mia (2008)
Marriage Story (1992)
Michael Clayton (2007)
Mrs Brown (1997)
Natural Born Killers (1994)
Notting Hill (1999)
Oceans 12 (2004)
Once (2006)
Osuofia In London (2003)
Osuofia In London 2 (2004)
Pearl Harbour (2001)
Pelle the Conqueror (1988)
Persepolis (2007)
Pink Panther Two (2009)
Plunkett and MacLeane (1999)
Pokemon (1998)
Pokemon: The First Movie (1999)
Pretty Woman (1990)
Resident Evil (2002)

Resident Evil: Extinction (2007)
Revolutionary Road (2008)
Rocky (1976)
Saturday Night and Sunday Morning (1960)
Sex, lies and videotape (1989)
Shallow Grave (1994)
Shiri (1999)
Sideways (2004)
Slumdog Millionaire (2008)
Snakes on a Plane (2006)
Sopyonje (1993)
Tell No One (2006)
The Avengers (1998)
The Beach (2000)
The Blair Witch Project (1999)
The Boat that Rocked (2009)
The Bourne Supremacy (2004)
The Bourne Ultimatum (2007)
The Princess of Nebraska (2007)
In the Company of Wolves (1984)
The Crying Game (1992)
The Curious Case of Benjamin Button (2008)
The Duchess (2008)
The Elephant Man (1980)
The Full Monty (1997)
The Gift (2008)
The Godfather (1972)
The Good Girl (2002)
The Graduate (1967)
The Idiots (1998)
The Last Broadcast (1998)
The Last Temptation of Christ (1988)
The Lord of the Rings (2001)
The Object of My Affection (1998)
The Reader (2008)
The Secret Laughter of Women (1999)
The Straight Story (1999)
The Third Man (1946)

The Young Victoria (2009)

Trainspotting (1996)

V for Vendetta (2005)

Waking Ned (1998)

Watchmen (2009)

We Are the Strange (2007)

We're No Angels (1989)

LIST OF THE FILM WITH LINKS

2046 (2004) http://www.imdb.com/title/tt0212712/ accessed 10/03/2009

About Schmidt (2002) http://www.imdb.com/title/tt0257360/ accessed 06/05/2009

A Life Less Ordinary (1997) http://www.imdb.com/title/tt0119535/ accessed 10/03/2009

About a Boy (2002) http://www.imdb.com/title/tt0276751/ accessed 26/02/2009

Adaptation (2002) http://www.imdb.com/title/tt0268126/ accessed 10/03/2009

All About My Mother (1999) http://www.imdb.com/title/tt0185125/ accessed 26/02/2009

Amelie (2001) http://uk.rottentomatoes.com/m/amelie/ accessed 26/02/2009

American Pie (1999) http://www.imdb.com/title/tt0163651/ accessed 01/04/2009

An Inconvenient Truth (2006) http://www.imdb.com/title/tt0497116/ accessed 01/04/2009

Año uña (2007) http://www.imdb.com/title/tt0984969/ accessed 26/02/2009

Babette's Feast (1987) http://www.imdb.com/title/tt0092603/ accessed 06/04/2009

Battleship Potemkin (1925) http://www.imdb.com/title/tt0015648/ accessed 01/04/2009

Bend It Like Beckham (2002) http://www.imdb.com/title/tt0286499/ accessed 06/05/2009

Best in Show (2000 http://www.imdb.com/title/tt0218839/ accessed 25/04/2009

Billy Elliot (2000) http://www.imdb.com/title/tt0249462/ accessed 26/02/2009

Birth of a Nation (1915) http://www.imdb.com/title/tt0004972/ accessed 26/02/2009

Black Gold (2006) http://www.imdb.com/title/tt0492447/ accessed 01/04/2009

Blood Diamond (2006) http://www.imdb.com/title/tt0450259/ accessed 01/04/2009

Bloody Sunday (2002) http://www.imdb.com/title/tt0280491/ accessed 01/04/2009

Blue Velvet (1986) http://www.imdb.com/title/tt0090756/ accessed 27/02/2009

Bonfire of the Vanities (1990) http://www.imdb.com/title/tt0099165/ accessed 11/03/2009

Bowling for Columbine (2002) http://www.imdb.com/title/tt0310793/ accessed 01/04/2009

Bread and Roses (2000) http://www.imdb.com/title/tt0212826/ accessed 01/04/2009

Bride and Prejudice (2004) http://www.imdb.com/title/tt0361411/ accessed 10/03/2009

Bridget Jones Diary (2001) http://www.imdb.com/title/tt0243155/ accessed 26/02/2009

Captain Corelli's Mandolin (2001) http://www.imdb.com/title/tt0238112/ accessed 10/03/2009

Caramel (2007) http://www.imdb.com/title/tt0825236/ accessed 01/04/2009

City of God (2003) http://uk.rottentomatoes.com/m/city_of_god/ accessed 26/02/2009

Cloverfield (2008) http://www.cloverfieldmovie.com/

Crash (1996) http://www.imdb.com/title/tt0115964/ accessed 10/03/2009

Crossroads (2002) http://www.imdb.com/title/tt0275022/ accessed 06/05/2009

Dirty Pretty Things (2002) http://www.imdb.com/title/tt0301199/ accessed 06/05/2009

Easy Rider (1969) http://www.imdb.com/title/tt0064276/ accessed 11/03/2009

Elizabeth (1998) http://www.imdb.com/title/tt0127536/ accessed 27/02/2009

Eraserhead (1977) http://www.imdb.com/title/tt0074486/ accessed 27/02/2009

Erin Brockovich (2000) http://www.imdb.com/title/tt0195685/ accessed 01/04/2009

Farenheit 9/11 (2004) http://www.imdb.com/title/tt0361596/ accessed 01/04/2009

Forrest Gump (1994) http://www.imdb.com/title/tt0109830/ accessed 01/04/2009

Four Weddings and a Funeral (1994) http://www.imdb.com/title/tt0109831/ accessed 26/02/2009

Gangster No. 1 (2000) http://www.imdb.com/title/tt0210065/ accessed 01/04/2009

Gegen Die Wand (2004) http://www.imdb.com/title/tt0347048/ accessed 06/05/2009

Gregory's Girl (1981) http://www.imdb.com/title/tt0082477/ accessed 06/04/2009

Gosford Park (2001) http://www.imdb.com/title/tt0280707/ accessed 11/03/2009

Halloween (1978) http://www.imdb.com/title/tt0077651 accessed 11/03/2009

Harry Potter (2001) http://www.imdb.com/title/tt0241527/ accessed 26/02/2009

Harry Potter and the Philosopher's Stone (2001) http://www.imdb.com/title/tt0241527/ accessed 25/04/2009

Hellboy (2004) http://www.imdb.com/title/tt0167190/ accessed 26/02/2009

High Fidelity (2000) http://www.imdb.com/title/tt0146882/ accessed 26/02/2009

Honest (2000) http://www.imdb.com/title/tt0192126/ accessed 01/04/2009

Injustice (2001) http://www.imdb.com/title/tt0297189/ accessed 01/04/2009

Its a Wonderful Life (1946) http://www.imdb.com/title/tt0038650/ accessed 25/05/2009

Interview (with a Vampire)(1994) http://www.imdb.com/title/tt0110148/ accessed 25/02/2009

In the Mood For Love (2000) http://www.lovehkfilm.com/reviews/in_the_mood_for_love.htm accessed 06/05/2009

In this World (2002) http://www.imdb.com/title/tt0310154/ accessed 06/05/2009

Intolerance (1916) http://www.imdb.com/title/tt0006864/ accessed 25/02/2009

Ironman (2008) http://www.imdb.com/title/tt0371746/ accessed 26/02/2009

Jaws (1975) http://www.imdb.com/title/tt0073195/ accessed 25/02/2009

Jenin, Jenin: A One-Sided Movie (200) http://www.imdb.com/title/tt0363720/ accessed 25/02/2009

Judith of Bethulia (1914) http://www.imdb.com/title/tt0004181/ accessed 25/02/2009

Kill Bill (2003) http://www.imdb.com/title/tt0266697/ accessed 06/05/2009

Kill Bill, Volume 2 (2004) http://www.imdb.com/title/tt0378194/ accessed 06/05/2009

La Strategia del Ragno (1970) http://www.imdb.com/title/tt0066413/maindetails accessed 11/03/2009

Linha de Passe (2008) http://www.imdb.com/title/tt0803029/ accessed 01/04/2009

Living in Bondage (1992) http://www.imdb.com/title/tt0489511/ accessed 06/04/2009

Living in Bondage 2 (1993) http://www.imdb.com/title/tt0765097/ accessed 06/04/2009

Lock, Stock and Two Smoking Barrels (1998) http://www.imdb.com/title/tt0120735/ accessed 26/02/2009

Lost Highway (1997) http://www.imdb.com/title/tt0116922/ accessed 27/02/2009

Love Actually (2003) http://www.imdb.com/title/tt0314331/ accessed 26/02/2009

Mamma Mia (2008) http://www.imdb.com/title/tt0795421/ accessed 26/02/2009

Marriage Story (1992) http://en.wikipedia.org/wiki/Marriage_Story accessed 06/04/2009

Michael Clayton (2007) http://www.imdb.com/title/tt0465538/ accessed 01/04/2009

Mrs Brown (1997) http://www.imdb.com/title/tt0119280/ accessed 01/04/2009

Natural Born Killers (1994) http://www.imdb.com/title/tt0110632/ accessed 11/03/2009

Notting Hill (1999) http://www.imdb.com/title/tt0125439/ accessed 25/02/2009

Oceans 12 (2004) http://www.imdb.com/title/tt0349903/ accessed 11/03/2009

Once (2006) http://www.imdb.com/title/tt0907657/ accessed 26/04/2009

Osuofia In London (2003) http://www.imdb.com/title/tt0493828/ 11/03/2009

Osuofia In London 2 (2004) http://www.imdb.com/title/tt0493829/ accessed 11/03/2009

Pearl Harbour (2001) http://www.imdb.com/title/tt0213149/ accessed 01/04/2009

Pelle the Conqueror (1988) http://www.amazon.co.uk/Pelle-Conqueror-DVD-Hvenegaard/dp/B0009S9LRQ accessed 06/04/2009

Persepolis (2007) http://www.imdb.com/title/tt0808417/ accessed 01/04/2009

Pink Panther Two (2009) http://www.imdb.com/title/tt0838232/ accessed 11/03/2009

Plunkett and MacLeane (1999) http://www.imdb.com/title/tt0134033/ accessed 11/03/2009

Pokemon (1998) http://www.imdb.com/title/tt0176385/ accessed 26/02/2009

Pokemon: The First Movie (1999) http://www.imdb.com/title/tt0190641/ accessed 01/04/2009

Pretty Woman (1990) http://www.imdb.com/title/tt0100405/ accessed 11/03/2009

Resident Evil (2002) http://www.imdb.com/title/tt0120804/ accessed 26/02/2009

Resident Evil: Extinction (2007) http://www.imdb.com/title/tt0432021/ accessed 06/05/09

Revolutionary Road (2008) http://www.imdb.com/title/tt0959337/ accessed 11/03/2009

Rocky (1976) http://www.imdb.com/title/tt0075148/ accessed 06/05/2009

Saturday Night and Sunday Morning (1960) http://www.imdb.com/title/tt0054269/ accessed 06/04/2009

Sex, lies and videotape (1989) http://www.imdb.com/title/tt0098724/ accessed 11/03/2009

Shallow Grave (1994) http://www.imdb.com/title/tt0111149/ accessed 11/03/2009

Shiri (1999) http://www.hancinema.net/korean_movie_Shiri.php accessed 06/04/2009

Sideways (2004) http://www.imdb.com/title/tt0375063/ accessed 26/02/2009

Slumdog Millionaire (2008) http://www.imdb.com/title/tt1010048/ accessed 26/02/2009

Snakes on a Plane (2006) http://www.imdb.com/title/tt0417148/ accessed 06/05/2009

Sopyonje (1993) http://www.imdb.com/title/tt0108192/ accessed 06/04/2009

Tears of the Sun (2003) http://www.imdb.com/title/tt0314353/ accessed 05/05/2009

Tell No One (2006) http://www.imdb.com/title/tt0362225/ accessed 06/04/2009

The Avengers (1998) http://www.imdb.com/title/tt0118661/ accessed 26/02/2009

The Beach (2000) http://www.imdb.com/title/tt0163978/ accessed 01/04/2009

The Boat that Rocked (2009) http://www.imdb.com/title/tt1131729/ accessed 30/04/2009

The Blair Witch Project (1999) http://www.blairwitch.com/ accessed 05/05/2009

The Bourne Supremacy(2004) http://www.imdb.com/title/tt0372183/ accessed 01/04/2009

In the Company of Wolves (1984) http://www.imdb.com/title/tt0087075/ accessed 25/05/2009

The Conformist (1970) http://www.imdb.com/title/tt0065571/ accessed 11/03/2009

The Crying Game (1992) http://www.imdb.com/title/tt0104036/ accessed 25/02/2009

The Curious Case of Benjamin Button (2008) http://www.imdb.com/title/tt0421715/ accessed 11/03/2009

The Duchess (2008) http://www.imdb.com/title/tt0864761/ accessed 11/03/2009

The Elephant Man (1980) http://www.imdb.com/title/tt0080678/ accessed 27/02/2009

The Full Monty (1997) http://www.imdb.com/title/tt0119164/ accessed 26/02/2009

The Godfather (1972) http://www.imdb.com/title/tt0068646/ accessed 11/03/2009

The Good Girl (2002) http://www.imdb.com/title/tt0279113/ accessed 05/05/2009

The Graduate (1967) http://www.imdb.com/title/tt0061722/ accessed 06/04/2009

The Idiots (1998) http://www.imdb.com/title/tt0154421/ accessed 01/04/2009

The Last Broadcast (1998) http://www.imdb.com/title/tt0122143/ accessed 05/05/2009

The Last Temptation of Christ (1988) http://www.imdb.com/title/tt0095497/ accessed 11/03/2009

The Lord of the Rings (2001) http://www.imdb.com/title/tt0120737/ accessed 26/02/2009

The Object of My Affection (1998) http://www.imdb.com/title/tt0120772/ accessed 06/06/2009

The Princess of Nebraska (2007) http://www.imdb.com/title/tt1092411/ releaseinfo accessed 05/05/2009

The Reader (2008) http://www.imdb.com/title/tt0976051/ accessed 11/03/2009

The Secret Laughter of Women (1999) http://www.imdb.com/title/tt0132502/ accessed 11/03/2009

The Straight Story (1999) http://www.imdb.com/title/tt0166896/ accessed 27/02/2009

The Third Man (1946) http://www.imdb.com/title/tt0041959/ accessed 06/04/2009

The Young Victoria (2009) http://www.imdb.com/title/tt0962736/ accessed 06/05/2009

Trainspotting (1996) http://www.imdb.com/title/tt0117951/ accessed 26/02/2009

V for Vendetta (2005) http://www.imdb.com/title/tt0434409/ accessed 11/03/2009

Waking Ned (1998) http://www.imdb.com/title/tt0166396/ accessed 26/02/2009

Watchmen (2009) http://www.imdb.com/title/tt0409459/ accessed 26/02/2009

We Are the Strange (2007) http://www.imdb.com/title/tt0923985/ accessed 26/02/2009

We're No Angels (1989) http://www.imdb.com/title/tt0098625/ accessed 26/02/2009

Subject Index

Author Index